Richard Sala

FANTAGRAPHICS BOOKS
Seattle, WA

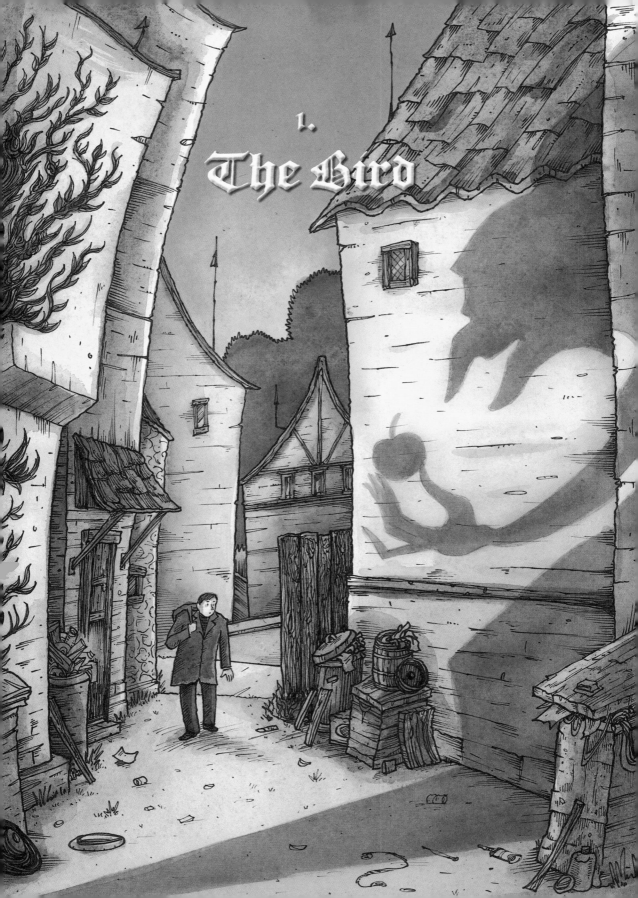

1.
The Bird

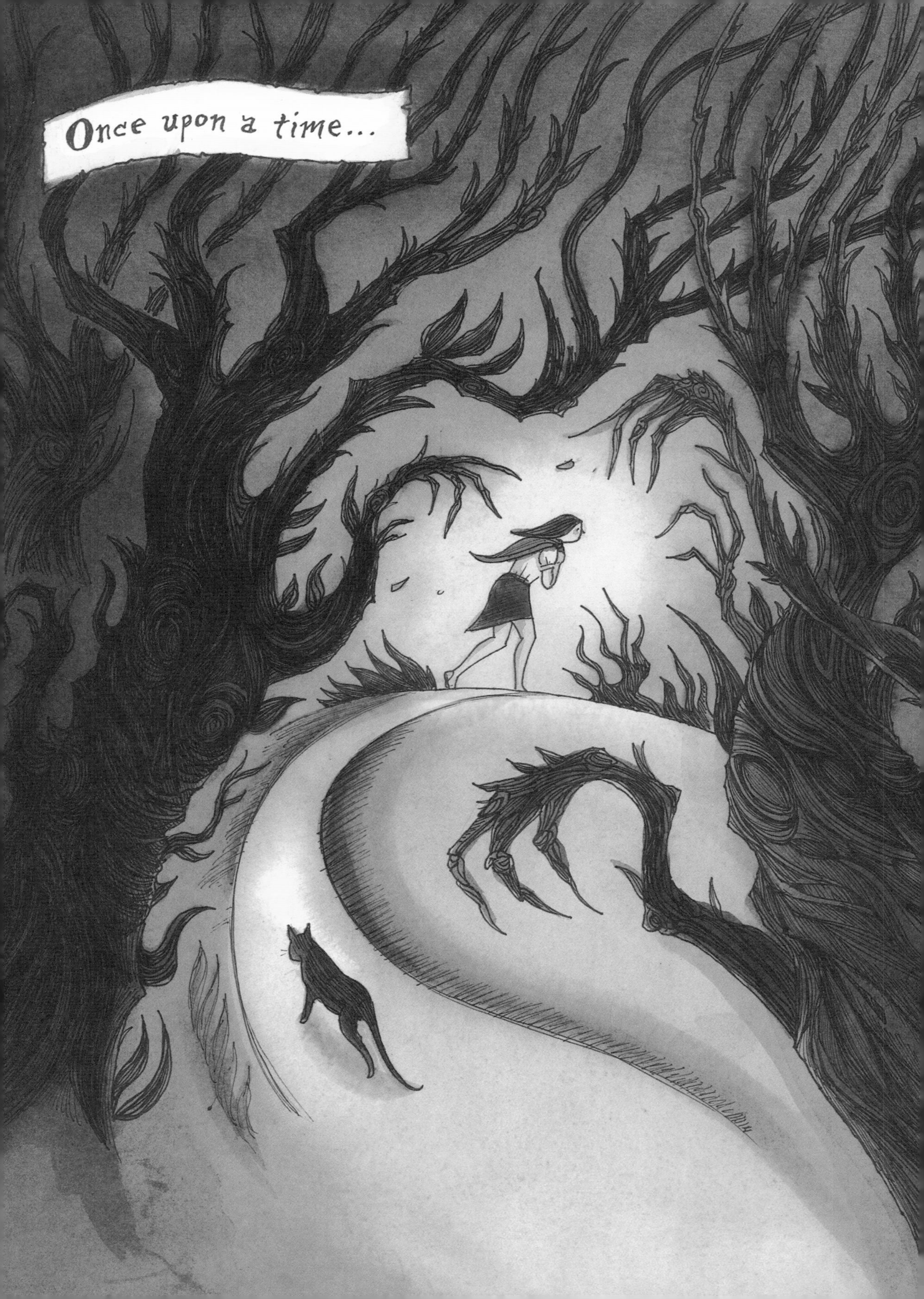
Once upon a time...

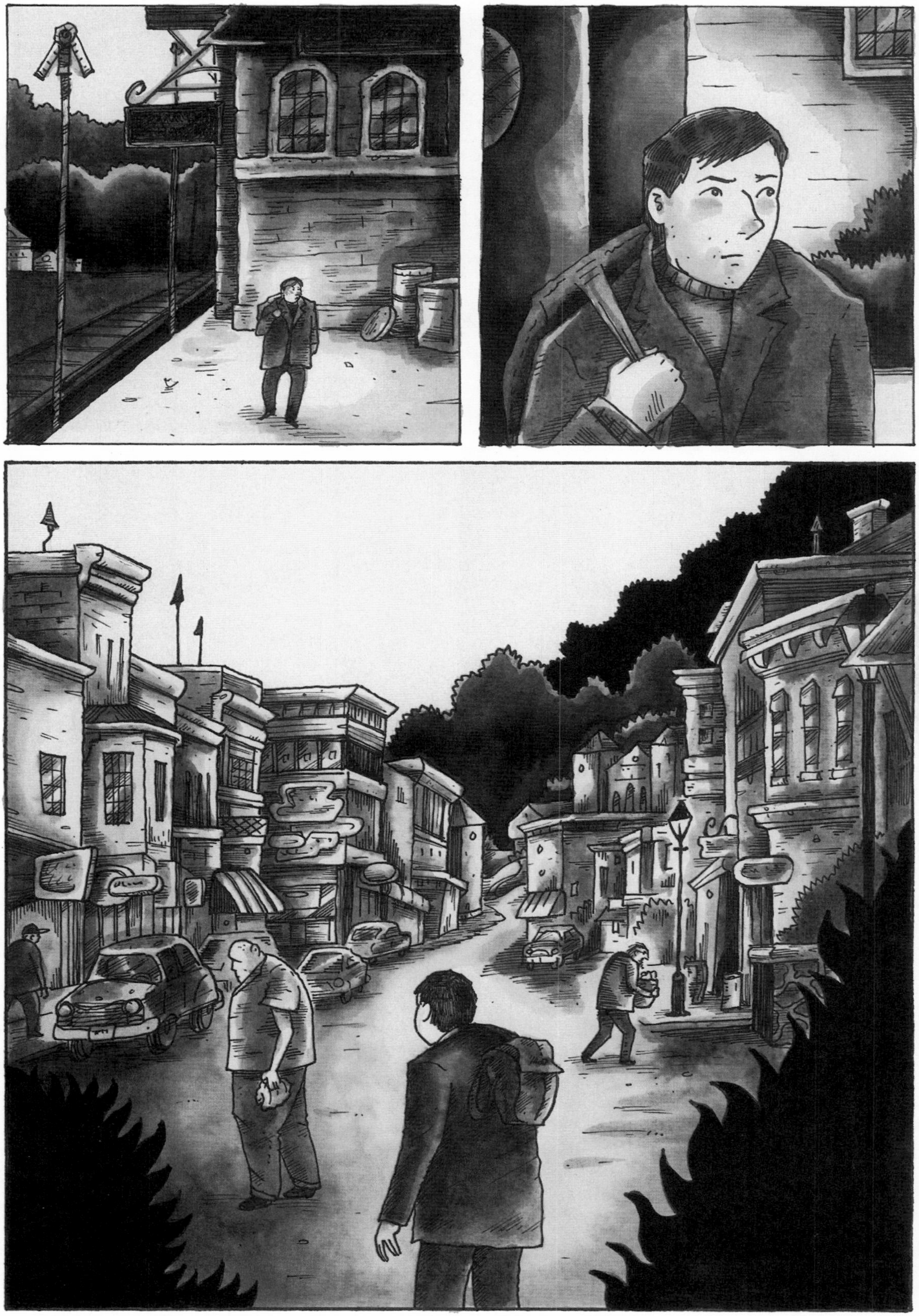

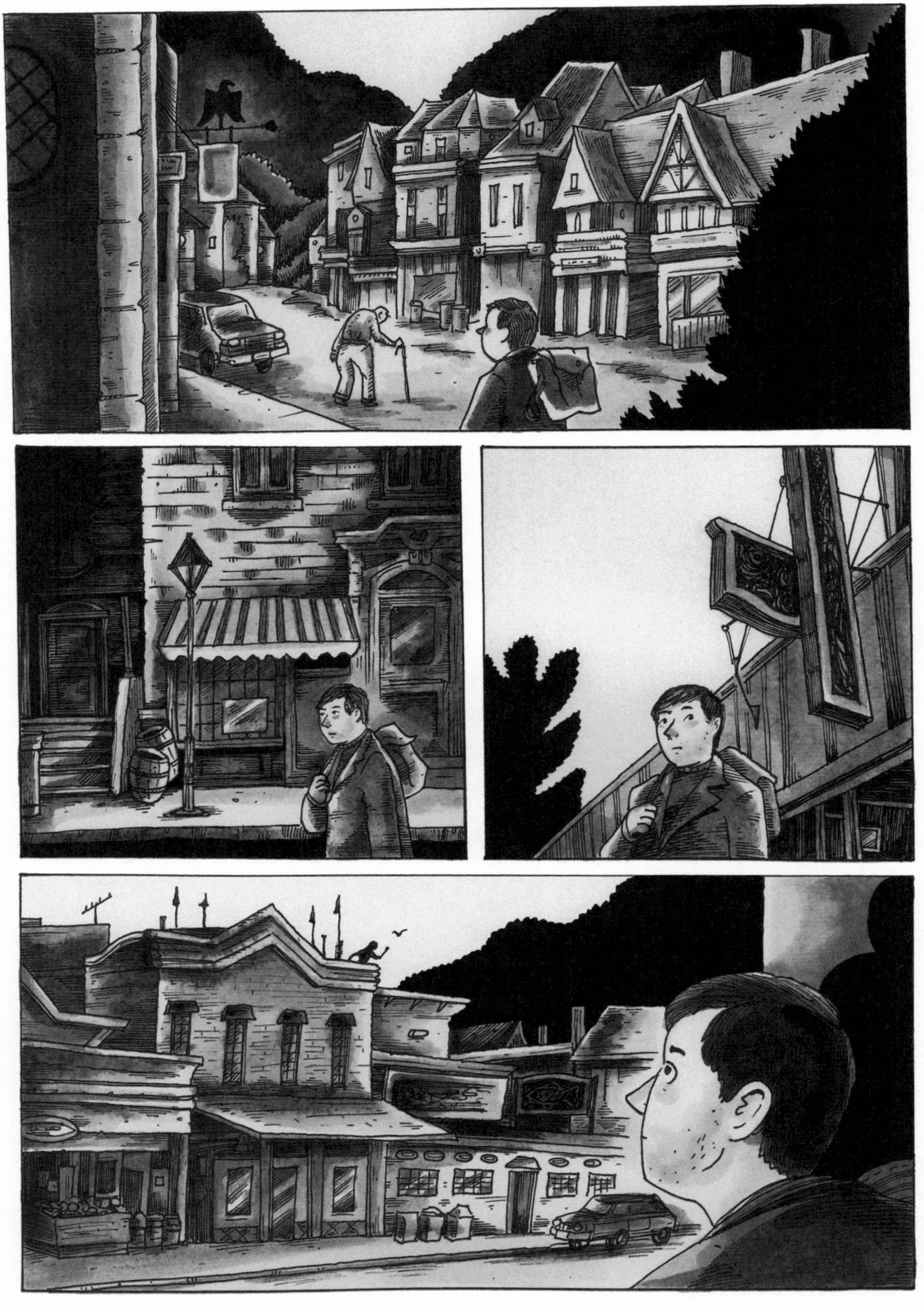

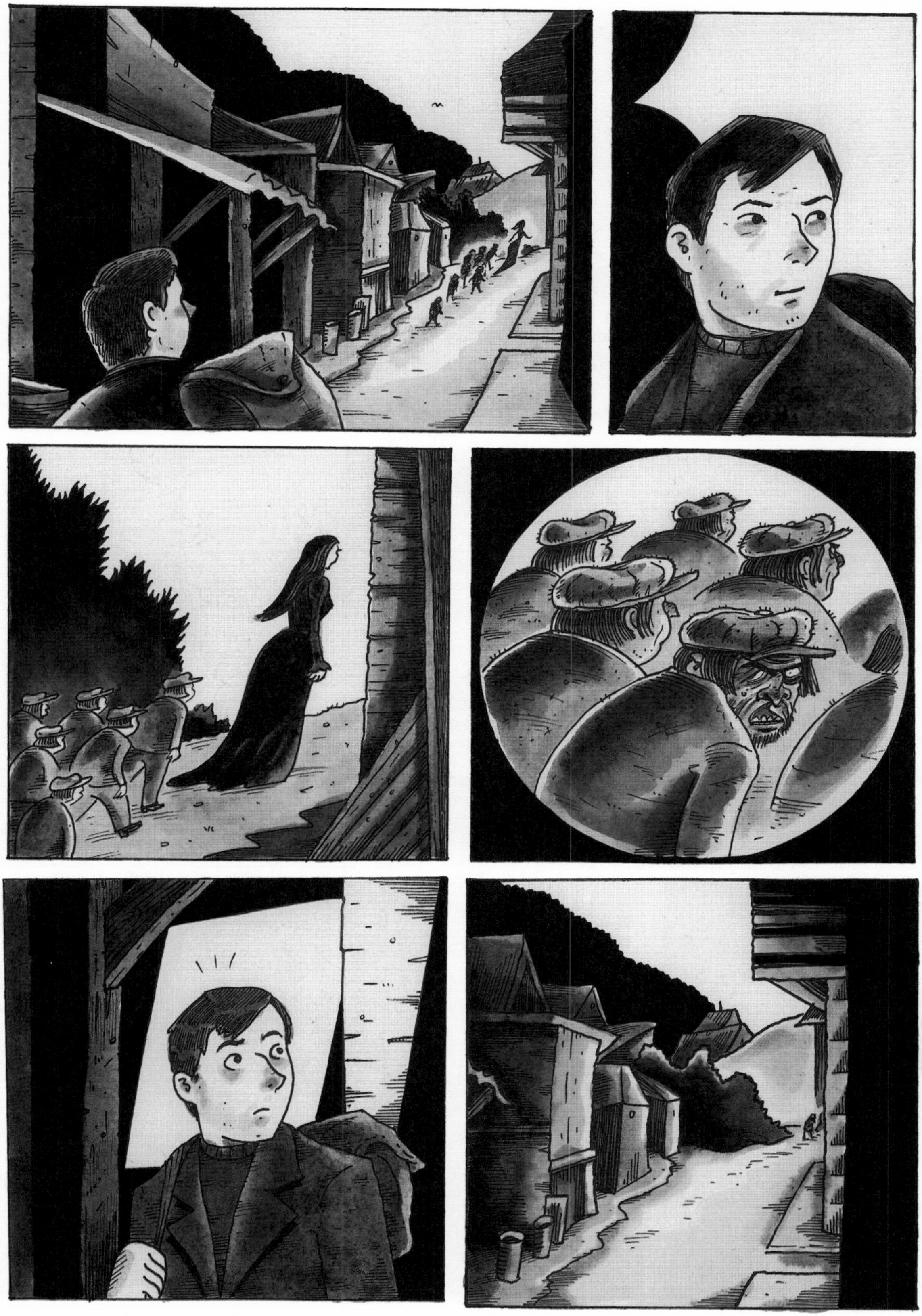

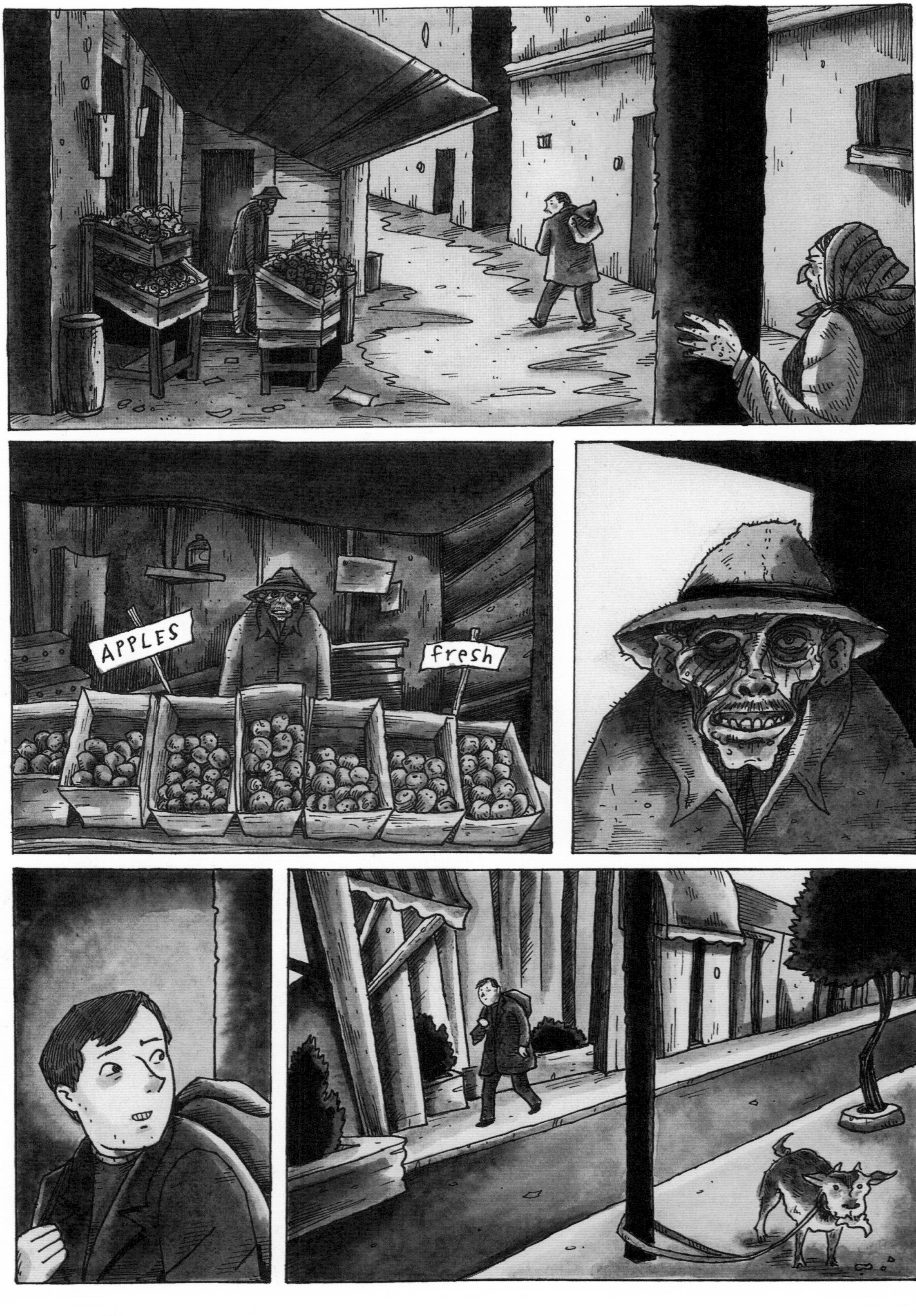
APPLES
fresh

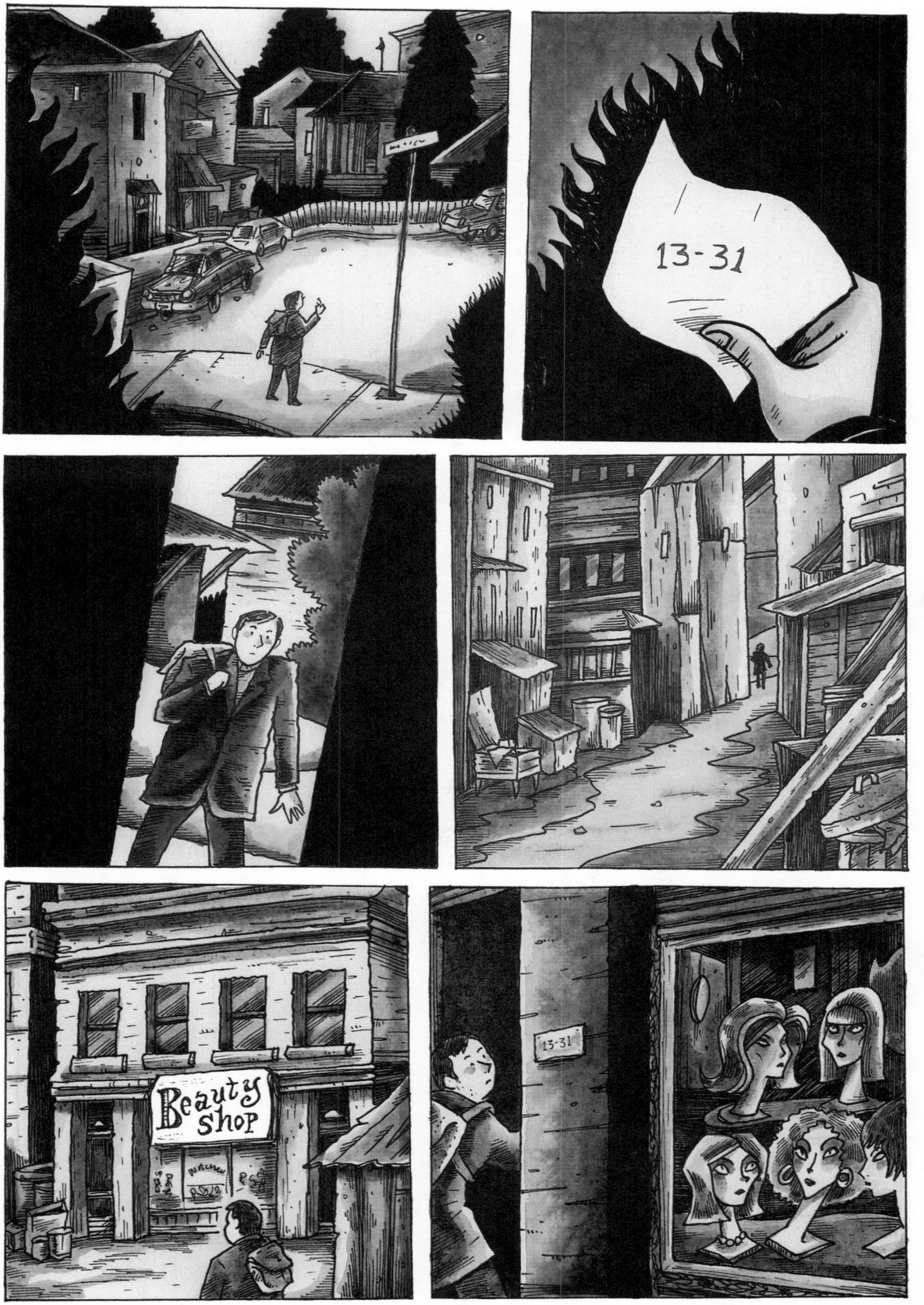
13-31
Beauty shop
13-31

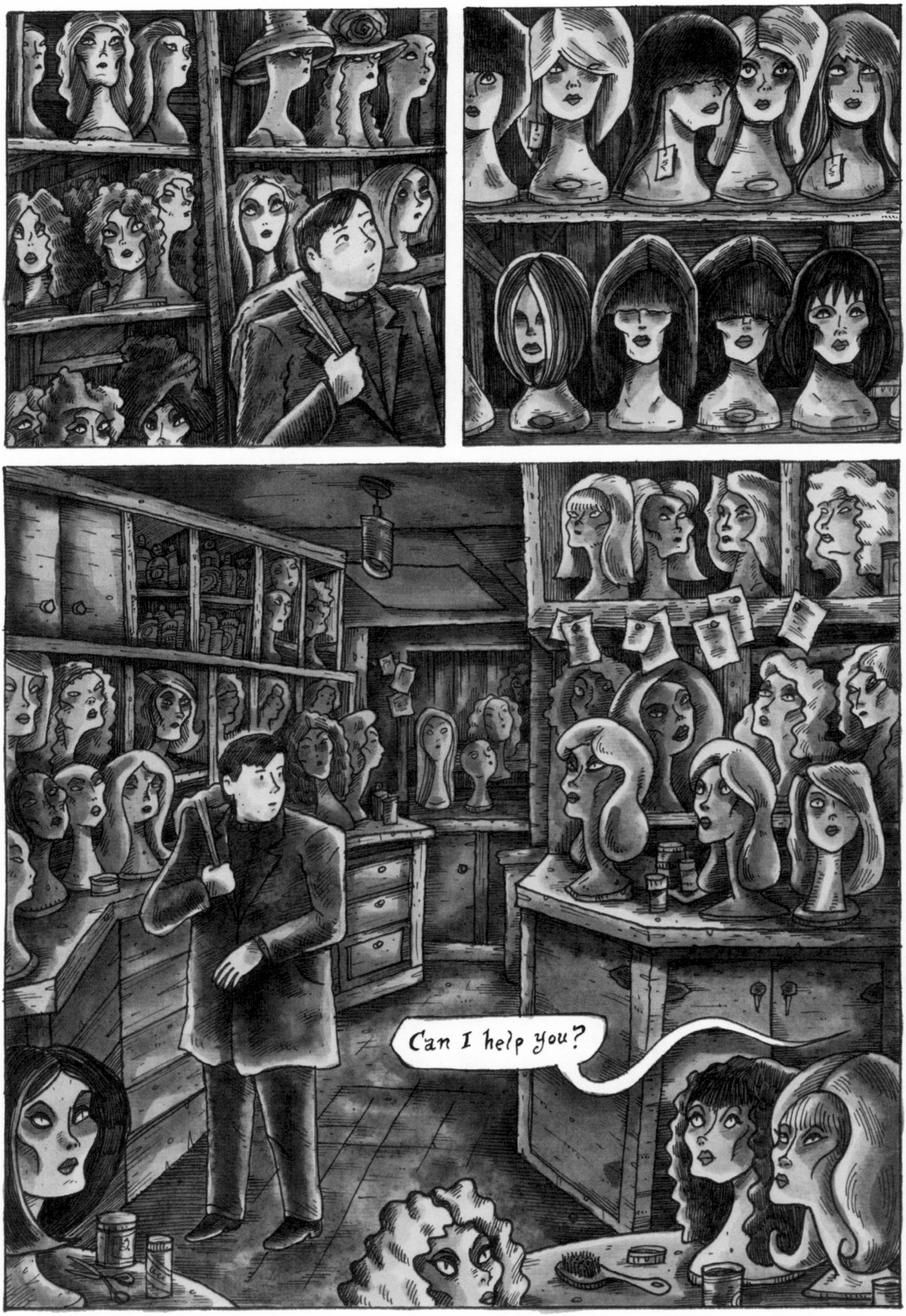
Can I help you?

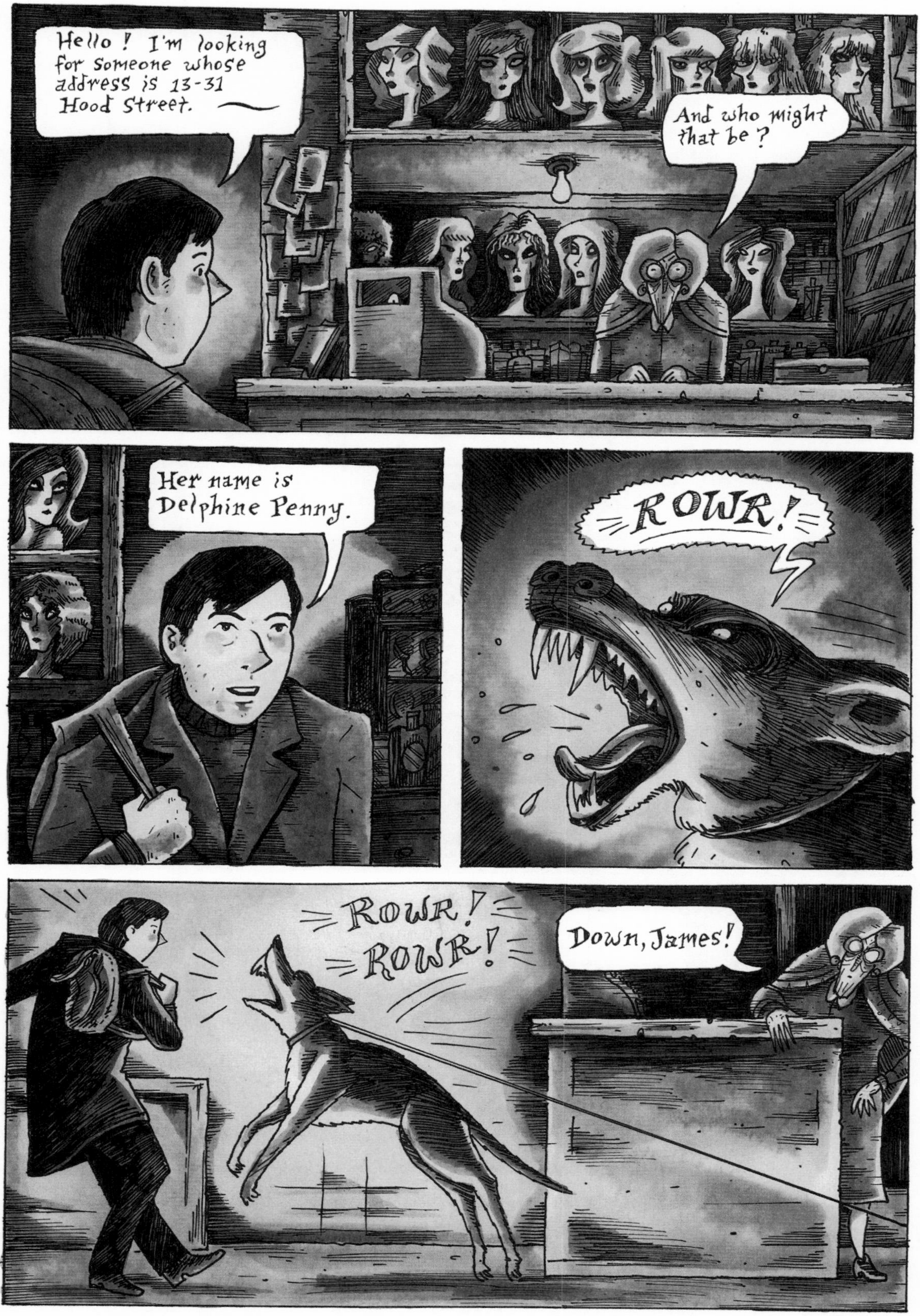
Hello! I'm looking for someone whose address is 13-31 Hood Street.
And who might that be?
Her name is Delphine Penny.
ROWR!
ROWR! ROWR!
Down, James!

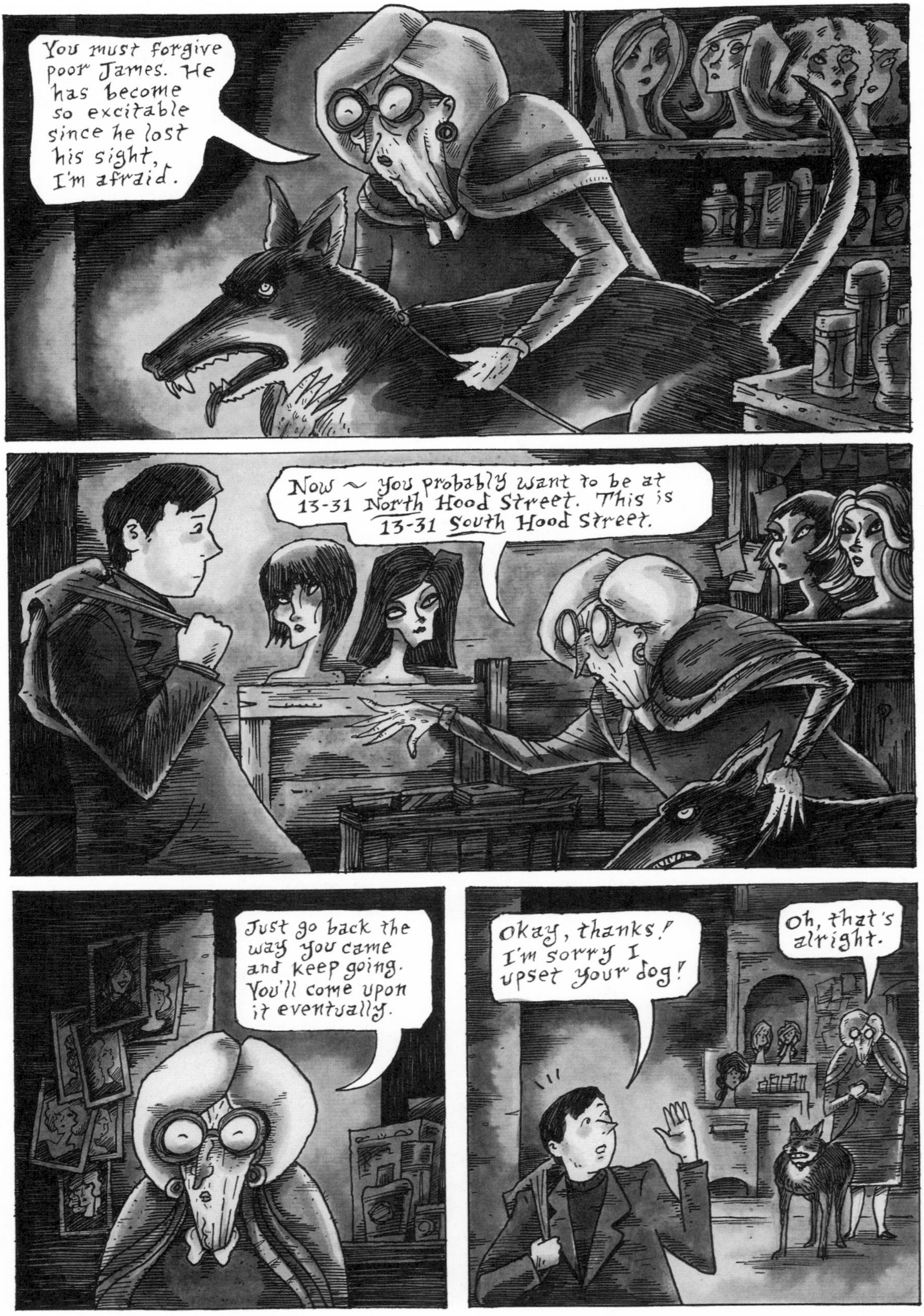
You must forgive poor James. He has become so excitable since he lost his sight, I'm afraid.
Now ~ You probably want to be at 13-31 North Hood Street. This is 13-31 South Hood Street.
Just go back the way you came and keep going. You'll come upon it eventually.
Okay, thanks! I'm sorry I upset your dog!
Oh, that's alright.

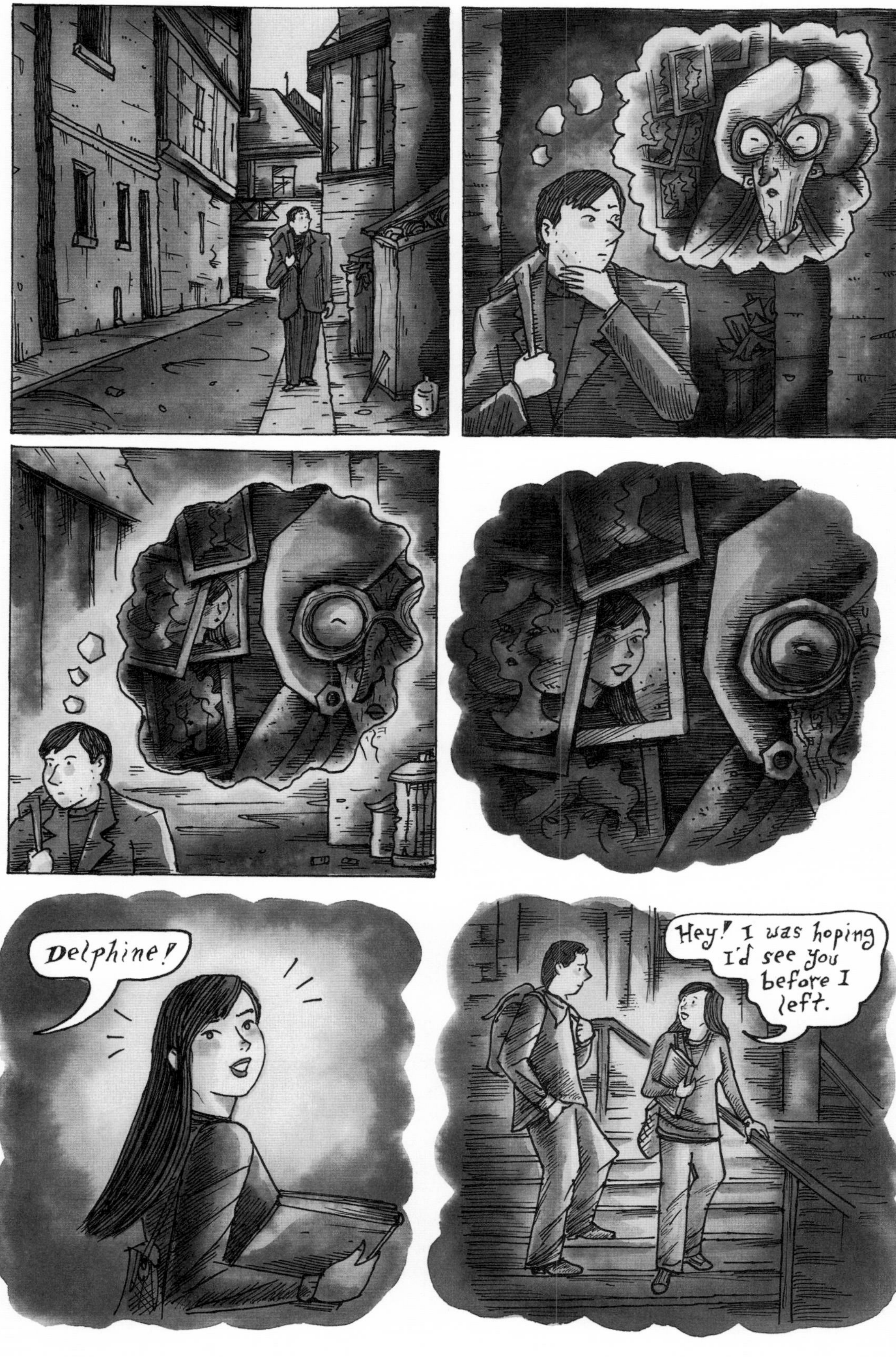
Delphine!
Hey! I was hoping I'd see you before I left.

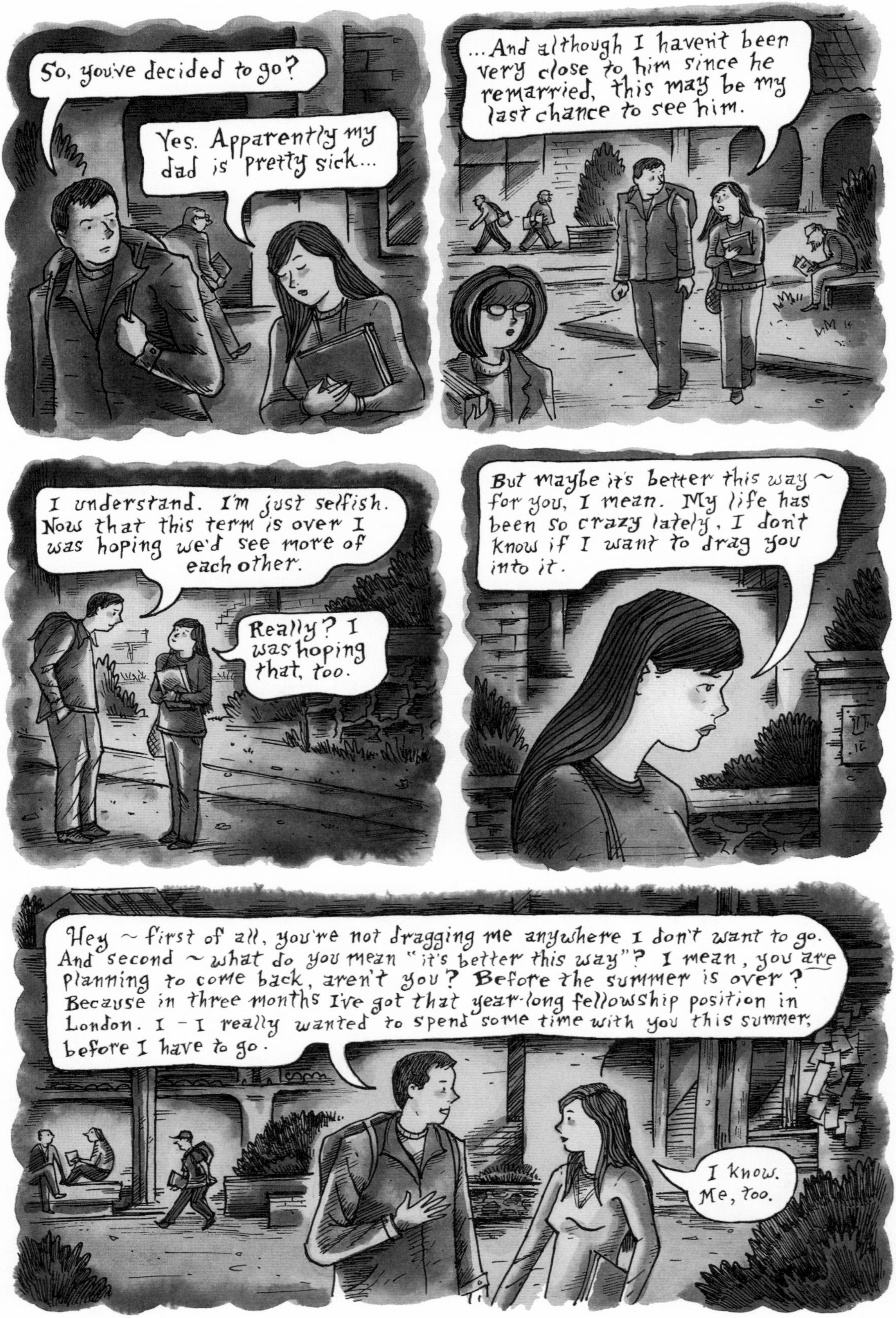

So, you've decided to go?
Yes. Apparently my dad is pretty sick...
...And although I haven't been very close to him since he remarried, this may be my last chance to see him.
I understand. I'm just selfish. Now that this term is over I was hoping we'd see more of each other.
Really? I was hoping that, too.
But maybe it's better this way ~ for you, I mean. My life has been so crazy lately, I don't know if I want to drag you into it.
Hey ~ first of all, you're not dragging me anywhere I don't want to go. And second ~ what do you mean "it's better this way"? I mean, you are planning to come back, aren't you? Before the summer is over? Because in three months I've got that year-long fellowship position in London. I - I really wanted to spend some time with you this summer, before I have to go.
I know. Me, too.

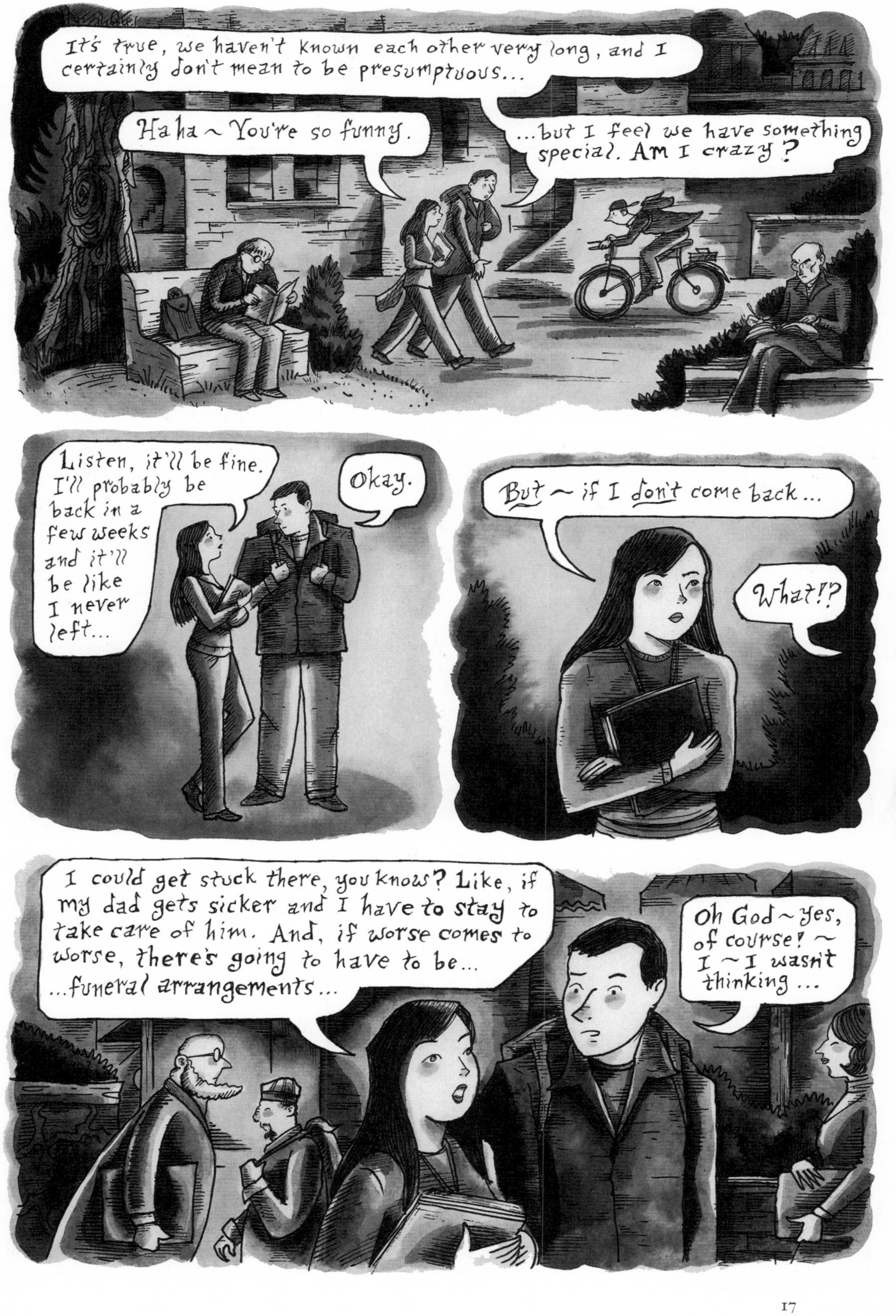
It's true, we haven't known each other very long, and I certainly don't mean to be presumptuous...
Ha ha ~ You're so funny.
...but I feel we have something special. Am I crazy?
Listen, it'll be fine. I'll probably be back in a few weeks and it'll be like I never left...
Okay.
But ~ if I don't come back...
What!?
I could get stuck there, you know? Like, if my dad gets sicker and I have to stay to take care of him. And, if worse comes to worse, there's going to have to be... ...funeral arrangements...
Oh God ~ yes, of course! ~ I ~ I wasn't thinking...

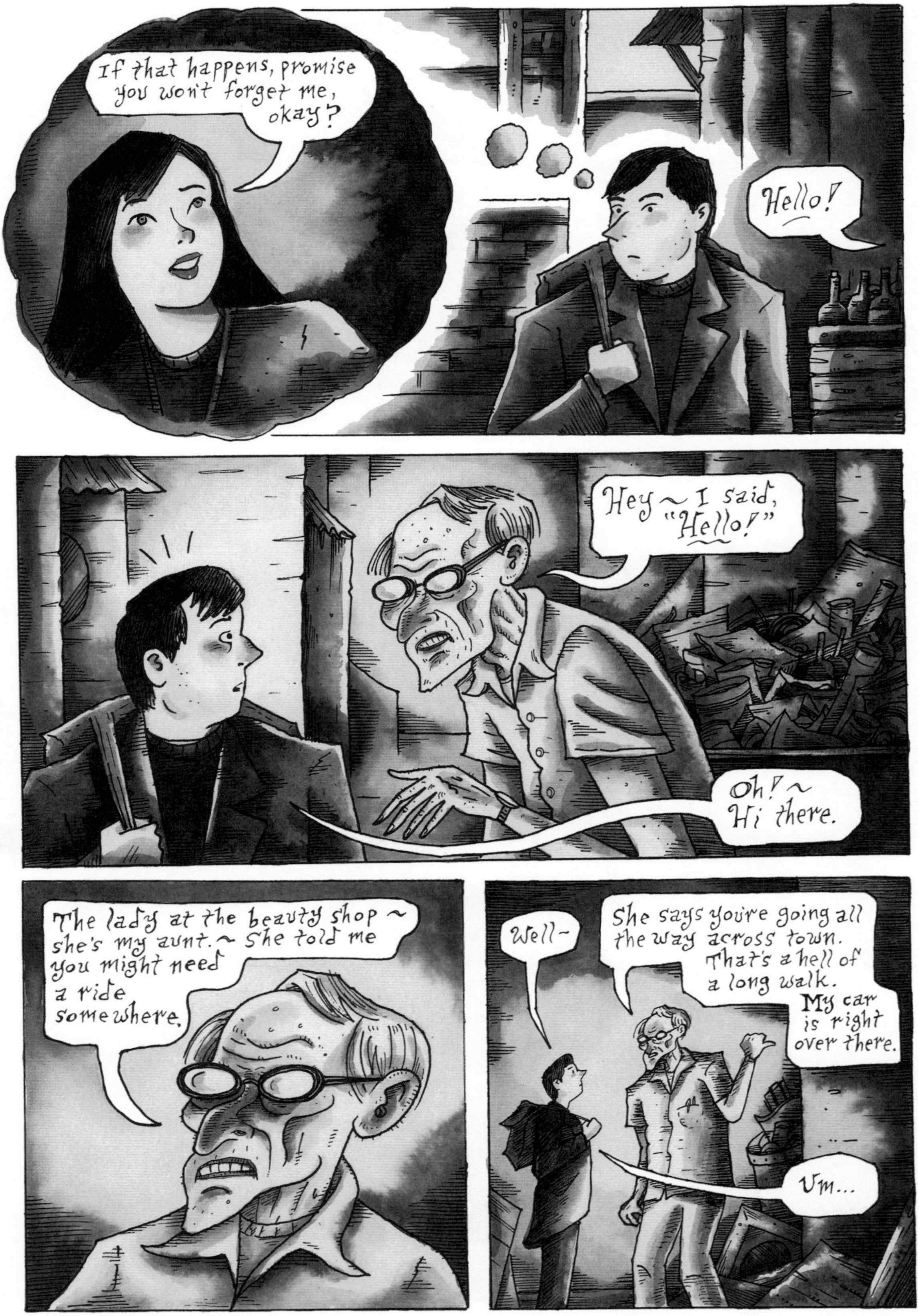
If that happens, promise you won't forget me, okay?
Hello!
Hey ~ I said, "Hello!"
Oh! ~ Hi there.
The lady at the beauty shop ~ she's my aunt. ~ She told me you might need a ride somewhere.
Well ~
She says you're going all the way across town. That's a hell of a long walk.
My car is right over there.
Um...

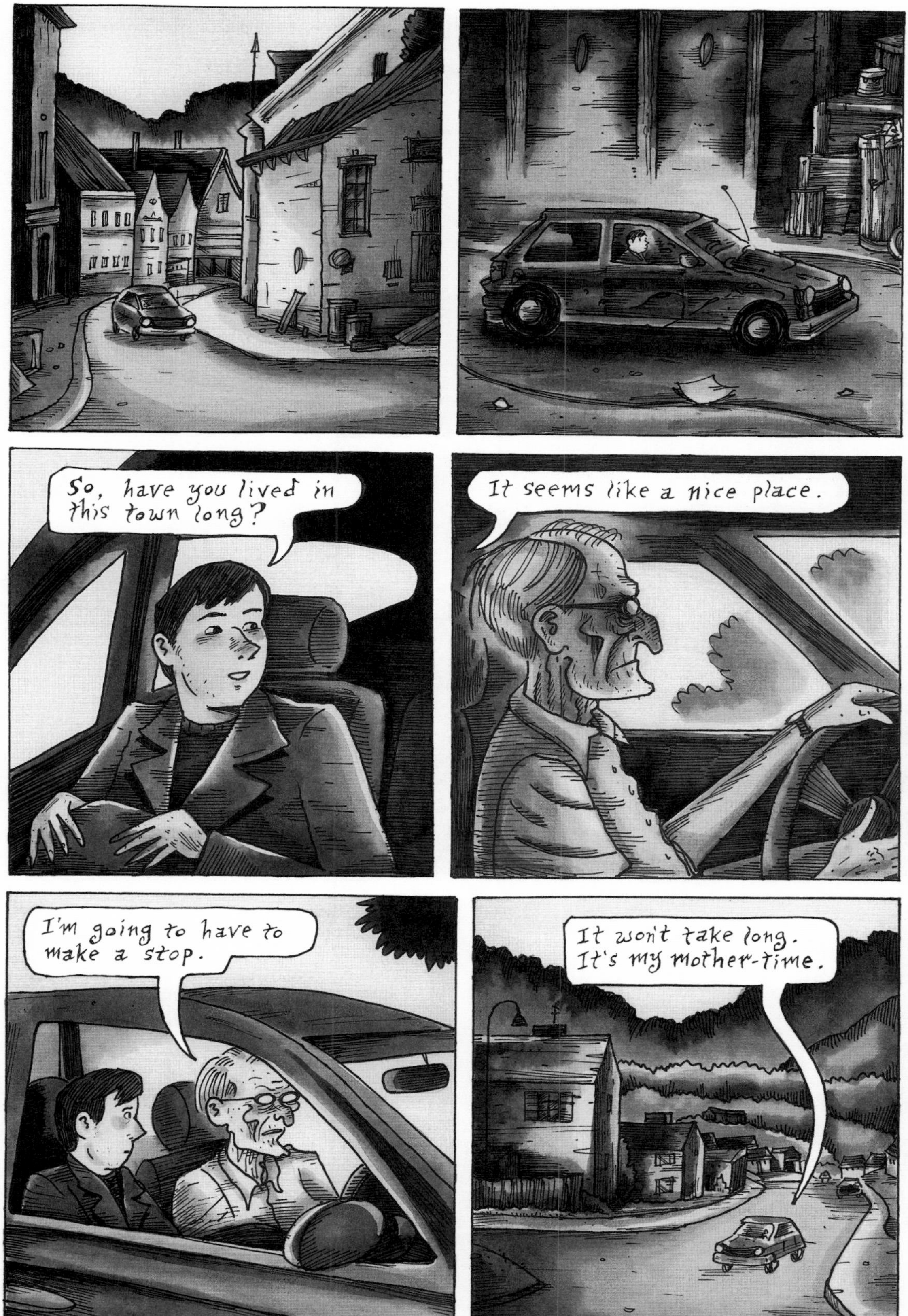
So, have you lived in this town long?
It seems like a nice place.
I'm going to have to make a stop.
It won't take long. It's my mother-time.

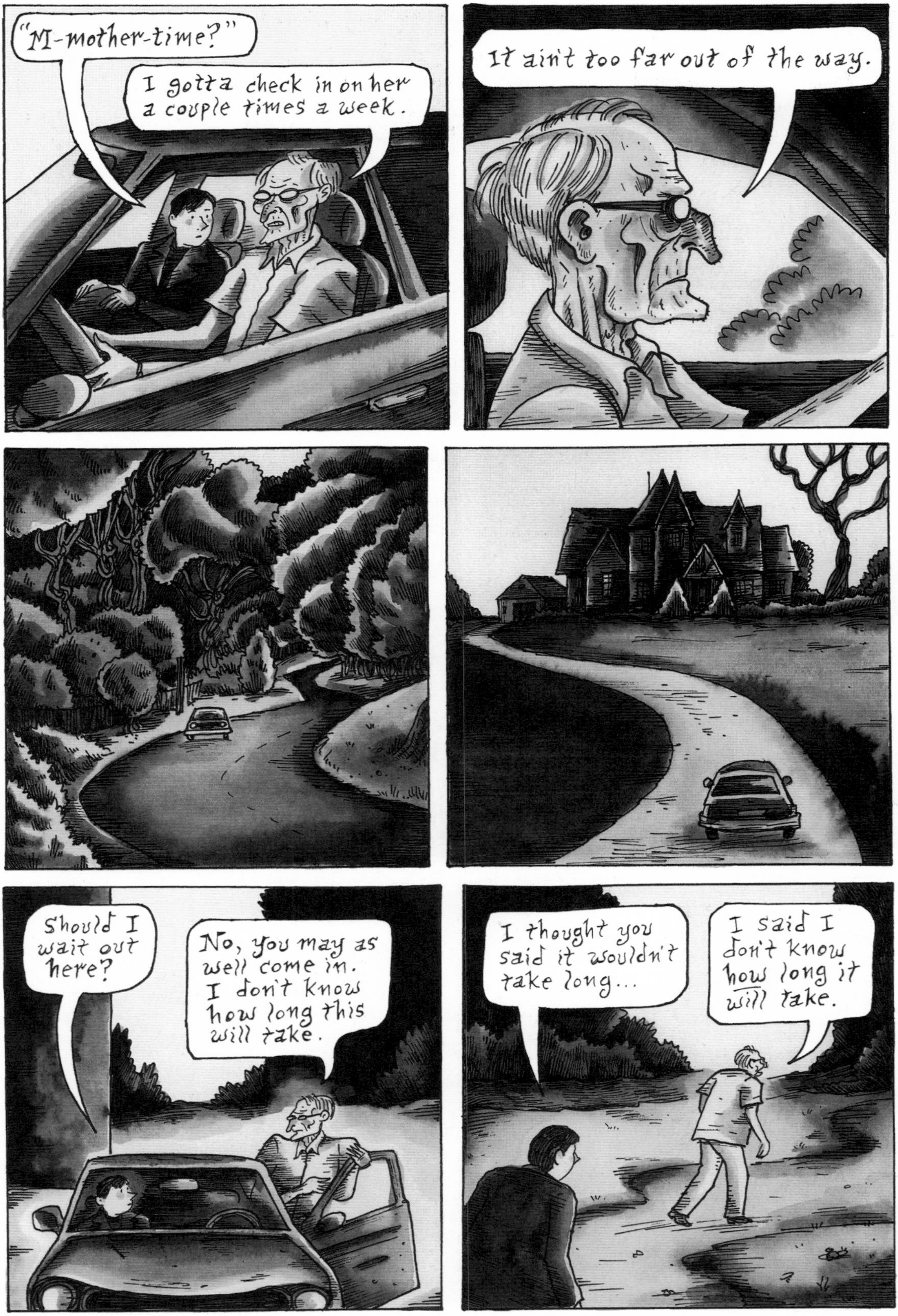
"M-mother-time?"
I gotta check in on her a couple times a week.
It ain't too far out of the way.
Should I wait out here?
No, you may as well come in. I don't know how long this will take.
I thought you said it wouldn't take long...
I said I don't know how long it will take.

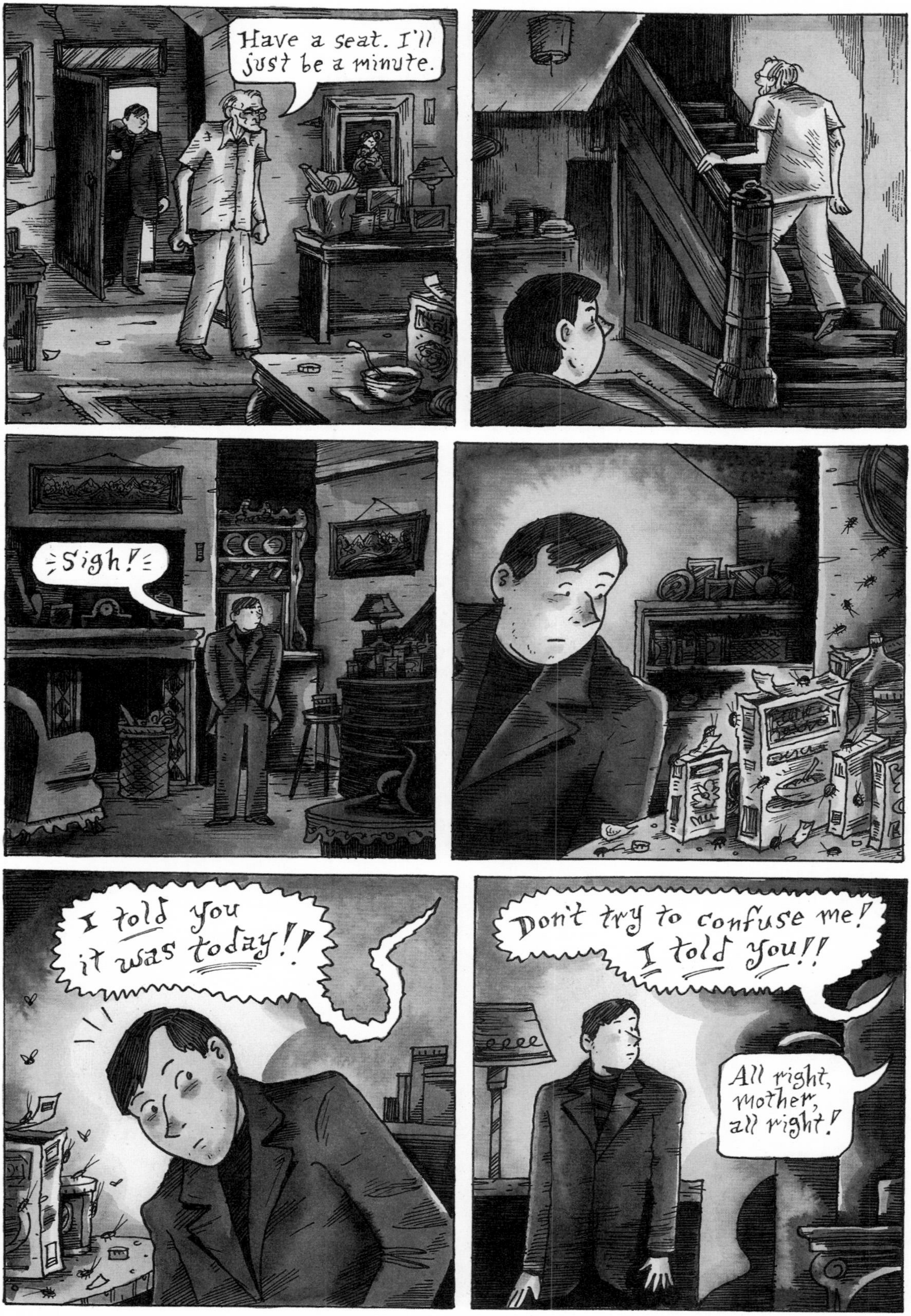
Have a seat. I'll just be a minute.
Sigh!
I told you it was today!!
Don't try to confuse me! I told you!!
All right, mother, all right!

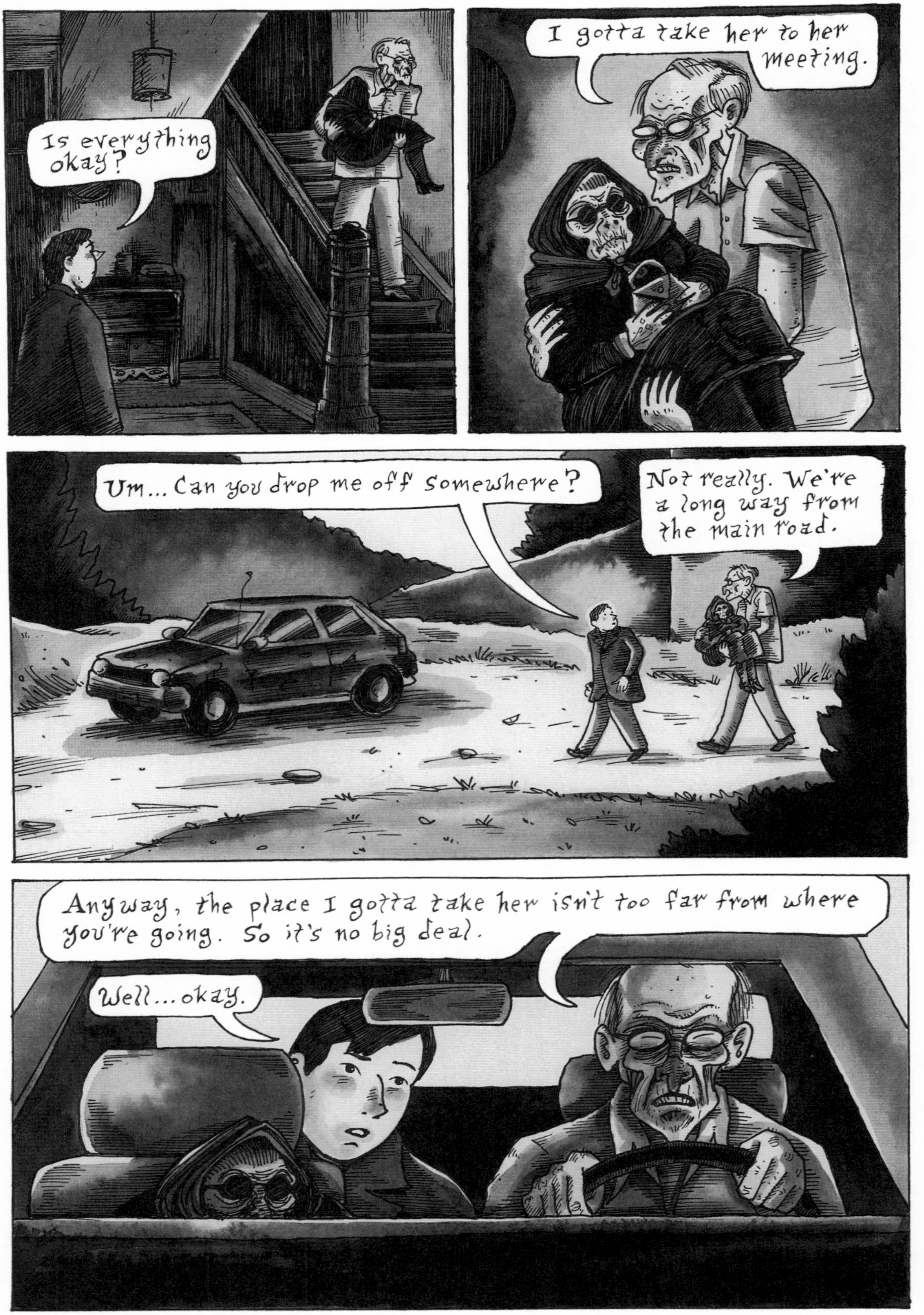

Is everything okay?
I gotta take her to her meeting.
Um... Can you drop me off somewhere?
Not really. We're a long way from the main road.
Anyway, the place I gotta take her isn't too far from where you're going. So it's no big deal.
Well... okay.

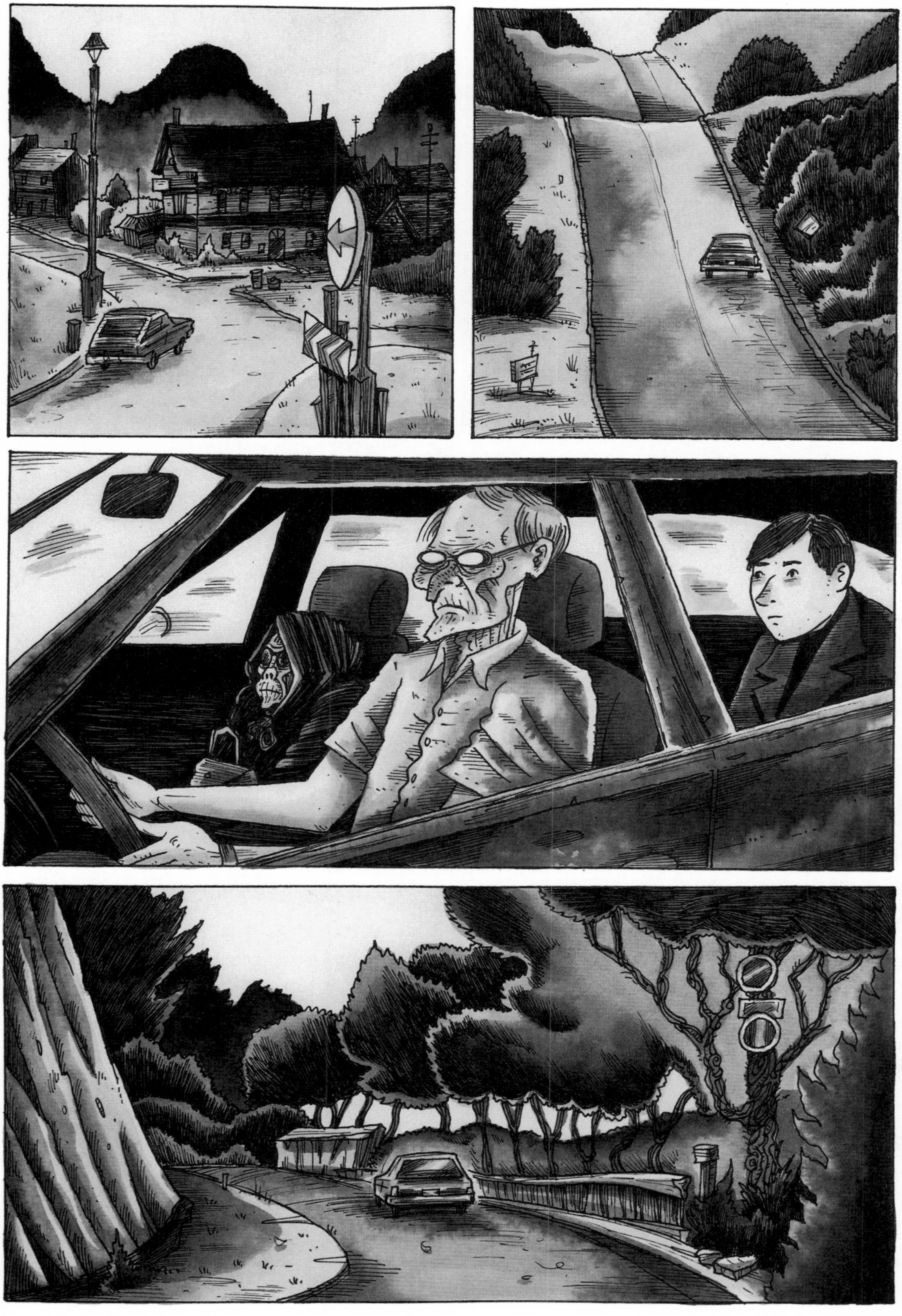

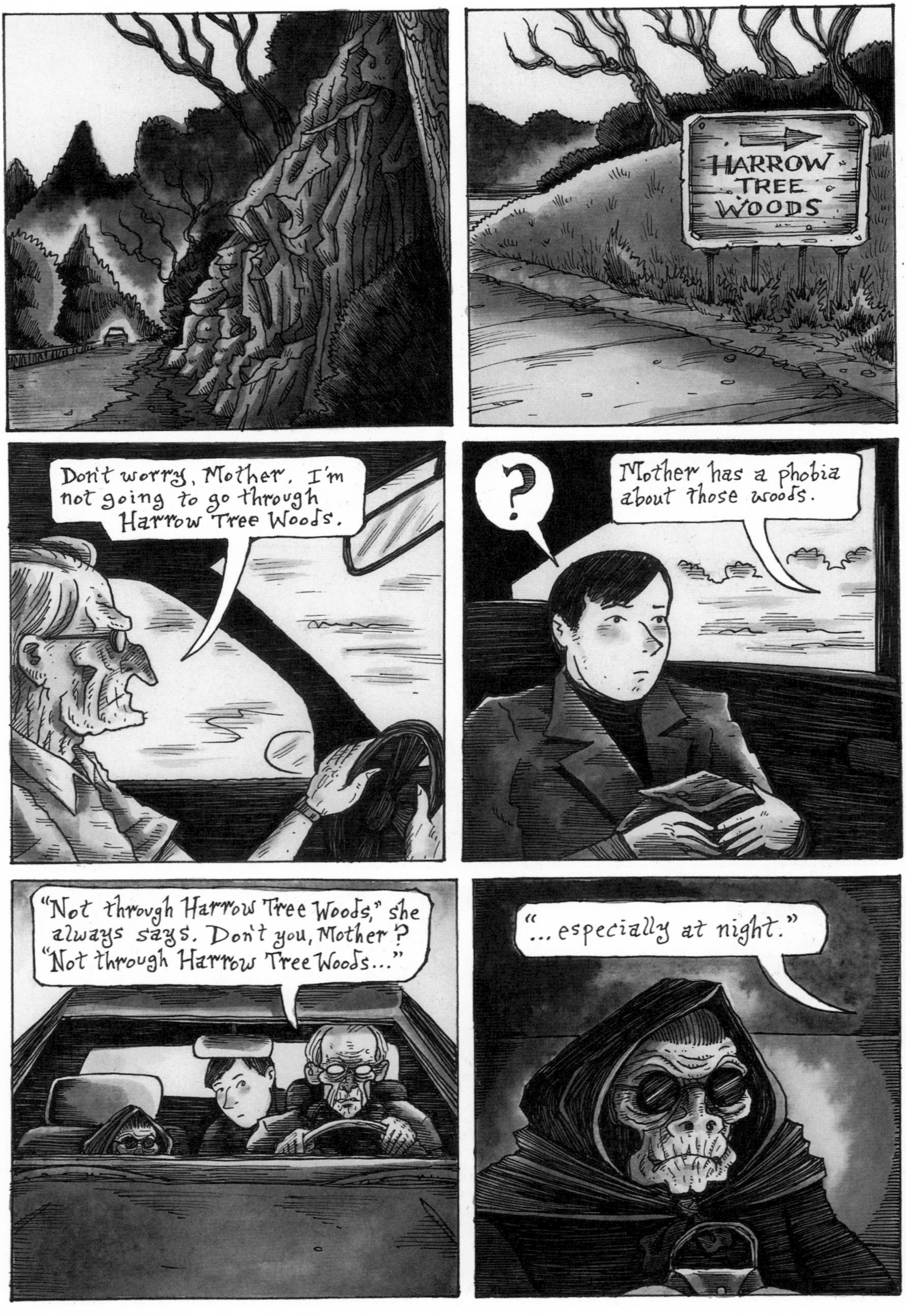
HARROW TREE WOODS
Don't worry, Mother. I'm not going to go through Harrow Tree Woods.
?
Mother has a phobia about those woods.
"Not through Harrow Tree Woods," she always says. Don't you, Mother? "Not through Harrow Tree Woods..."
"...especially at night."

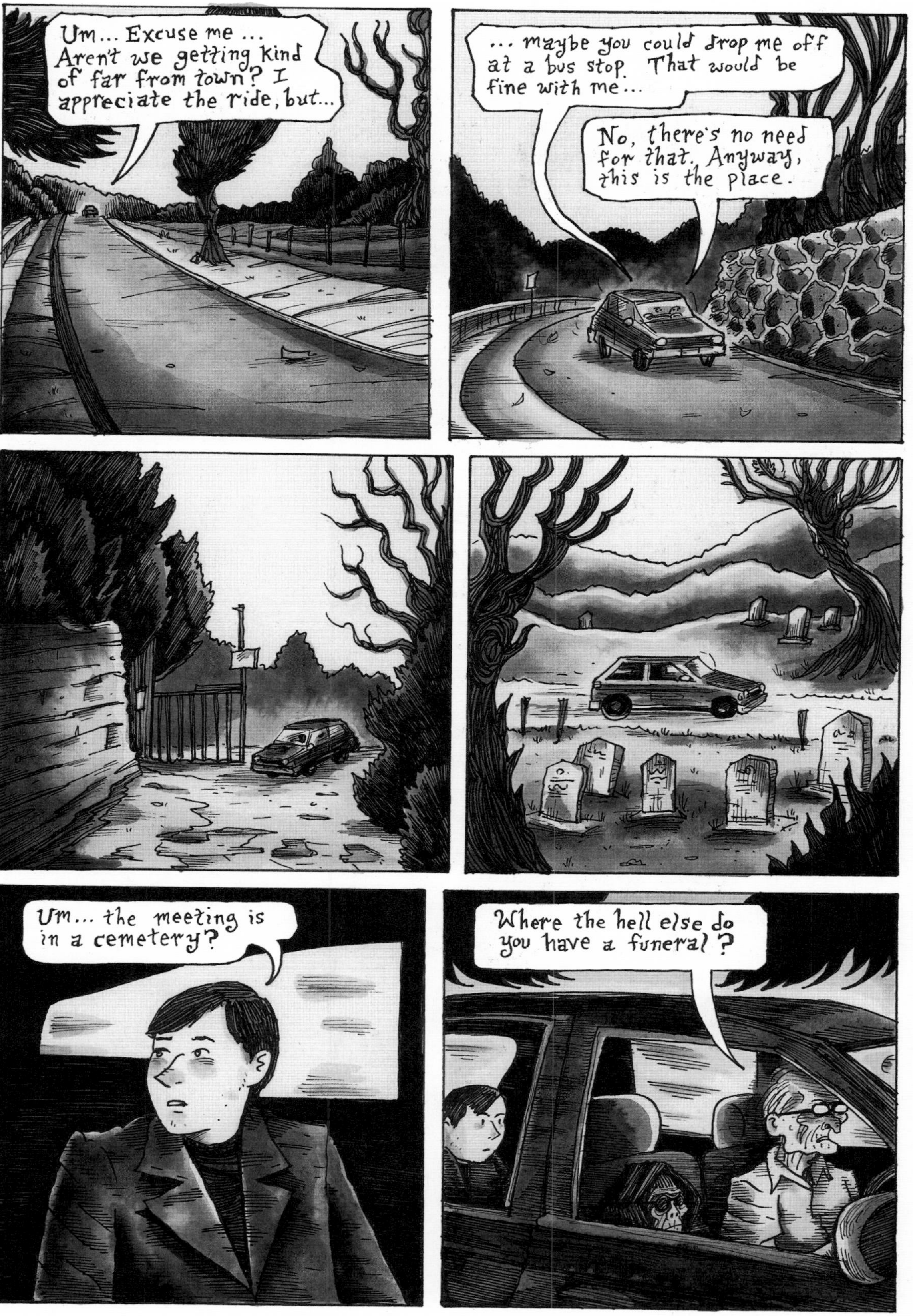
Um... Excuse me ... Aren't we getting kind of far from town? I appreciate the ride, but...
... maybe you could drop me off at a bus stop. That would be fine with me...
No, there's no need for that. Anyway, this is the place.
Um... the meeting is in a cemetery?
Where the hell else do you have a funeral?

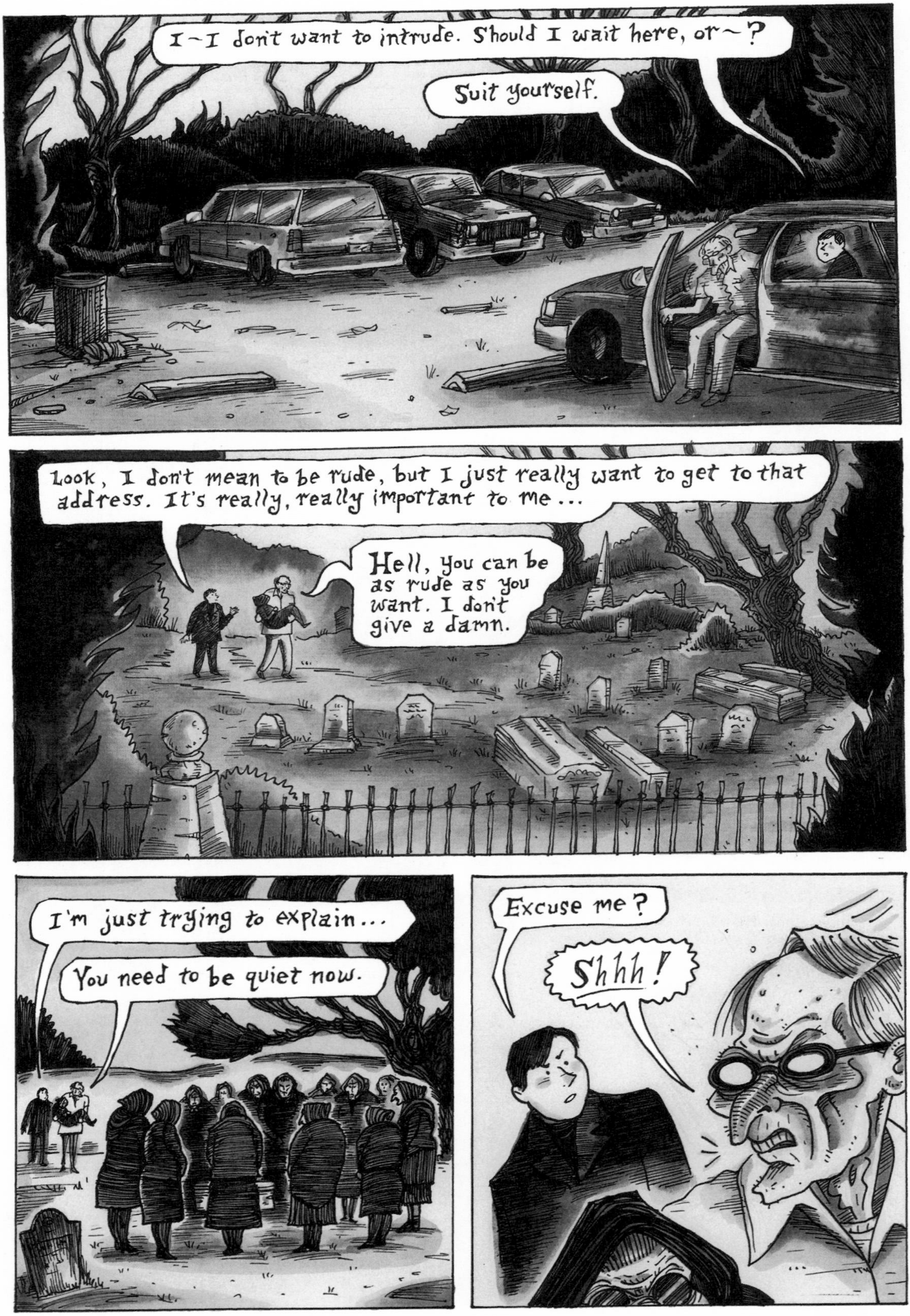
I~I don't want to intrude. Should I wait here, or~?
Suit yourself.
Look, I don't mean to be rude, but I just really want to get to that address. It's really, really important to me...
Hell, you can be as rude as you want. I don't give a damn.
I'm just trying to explain...
You need to be quiet now.
Excuse me?
Shhh!

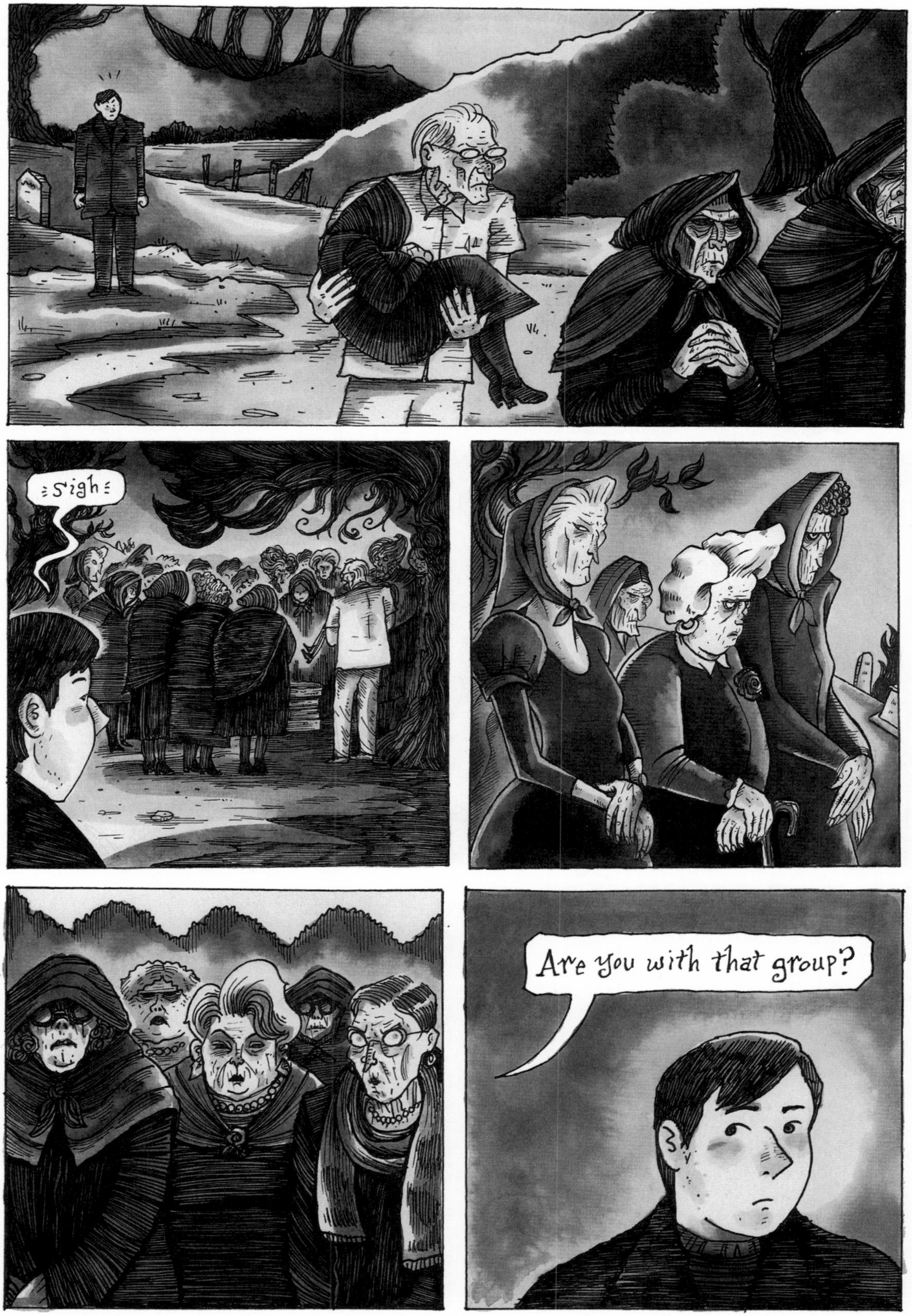
Sigh
Are you with that group?

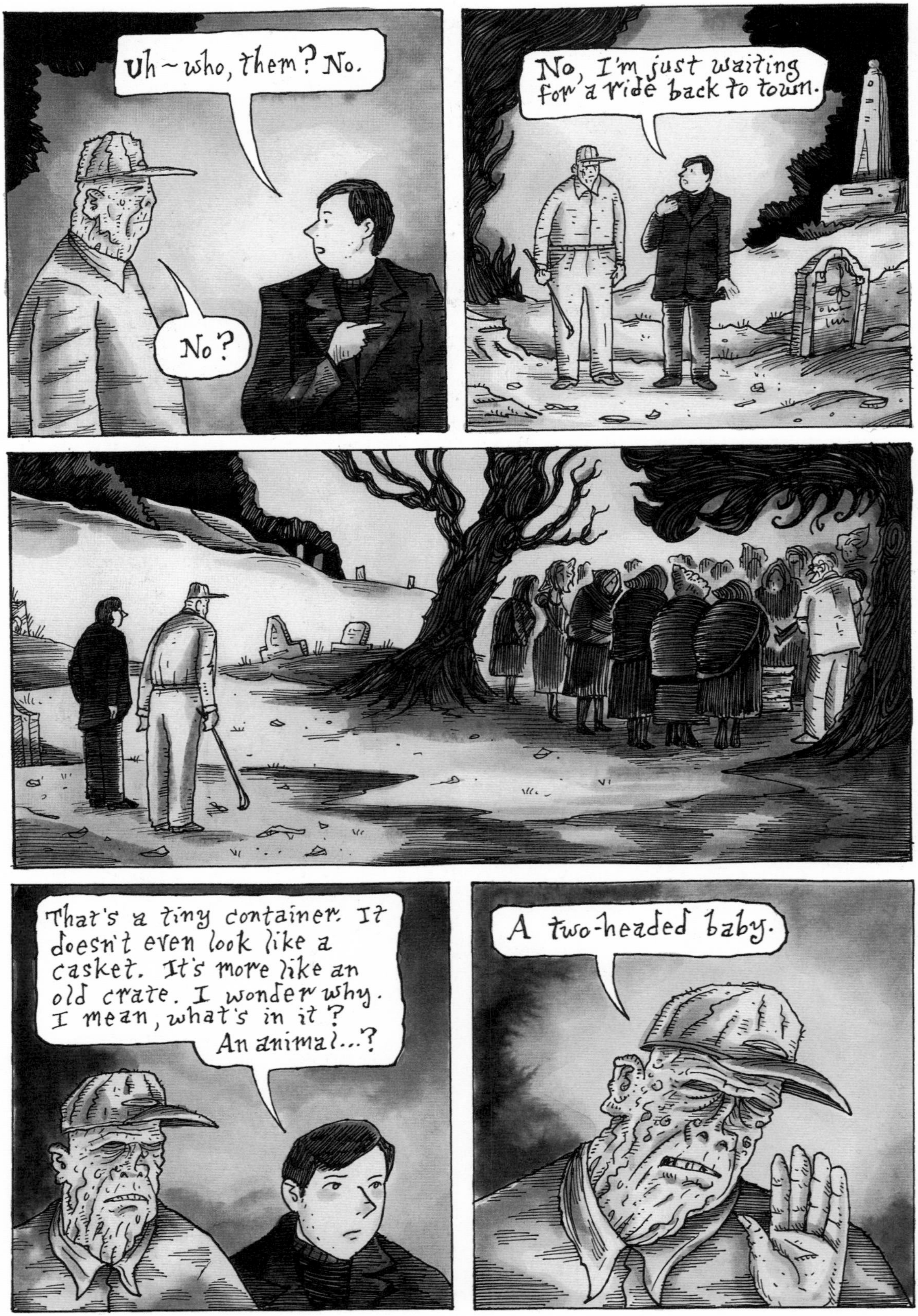

Uh~who, them? No.
No?
No, I'm just waiting for a ride back to town.
That's a tiny container. It doesn't even look like a casket. It's more like an old crate. I wonder why. I mean, what's in it? An animal...?
A two-headed baby.

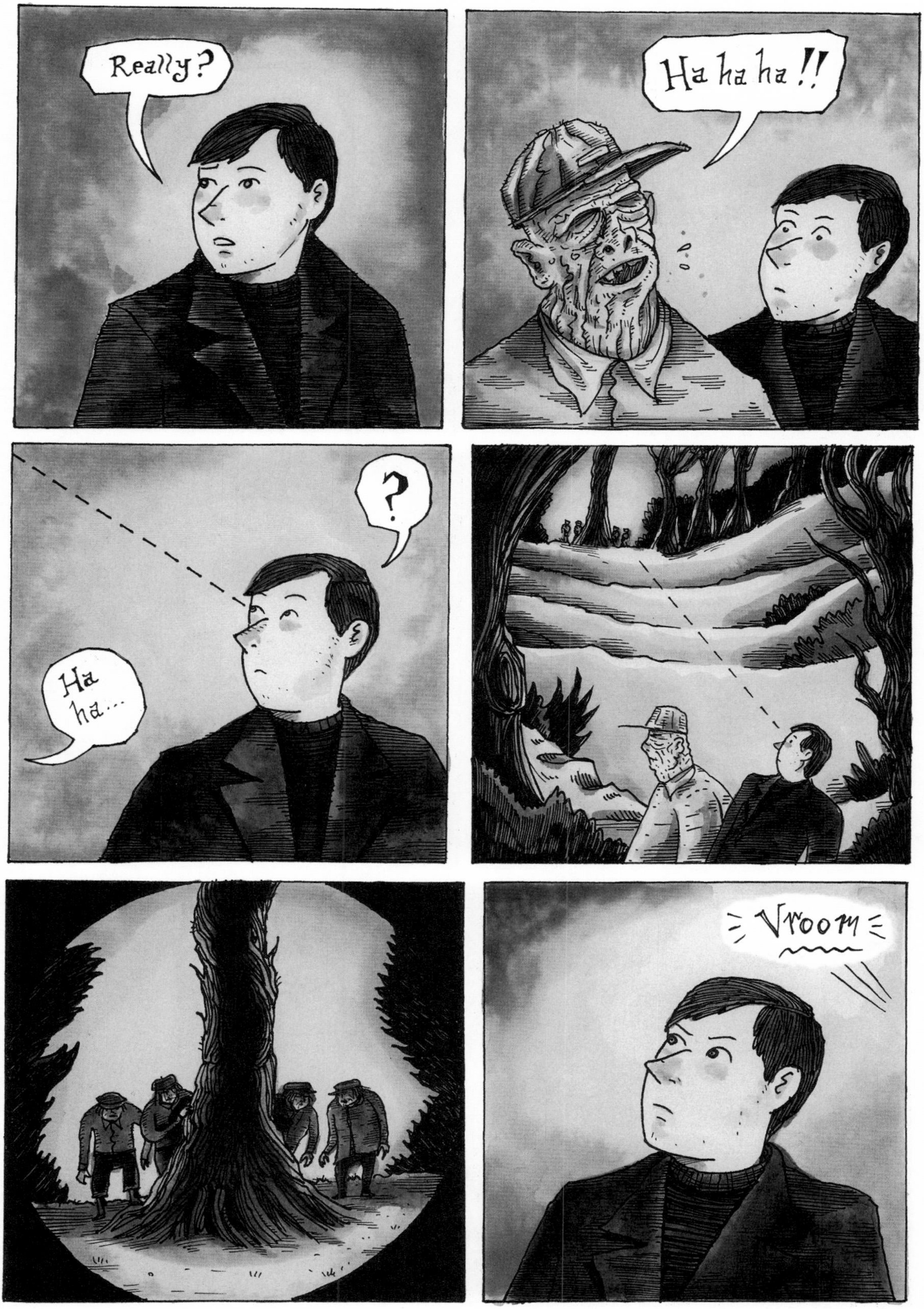
Really?
Ha ha ha!!
?
Ha ha...
Vroom

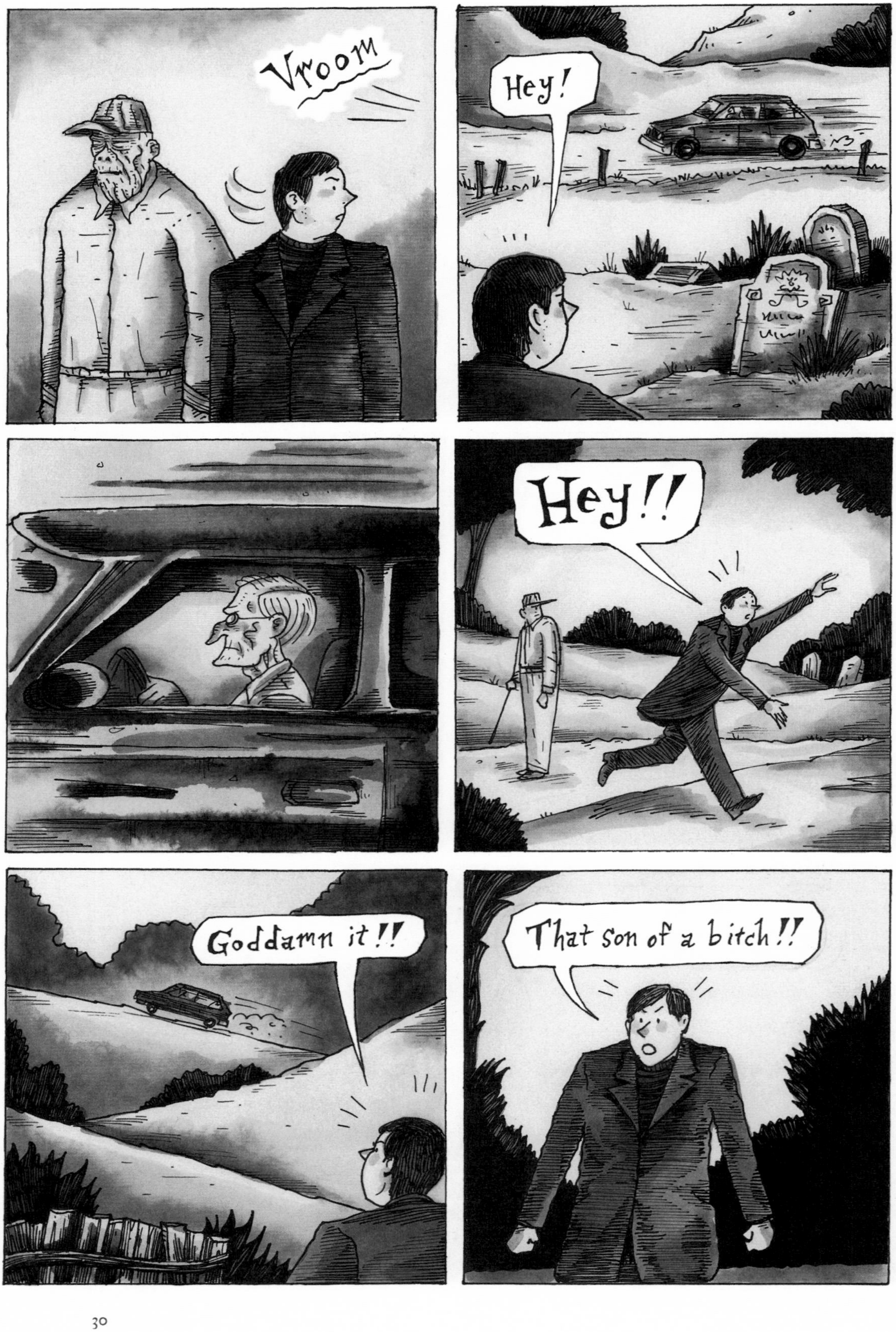
Vroom
Hey!
Hey!!
Goddamn it!!
That son of a bitch!!

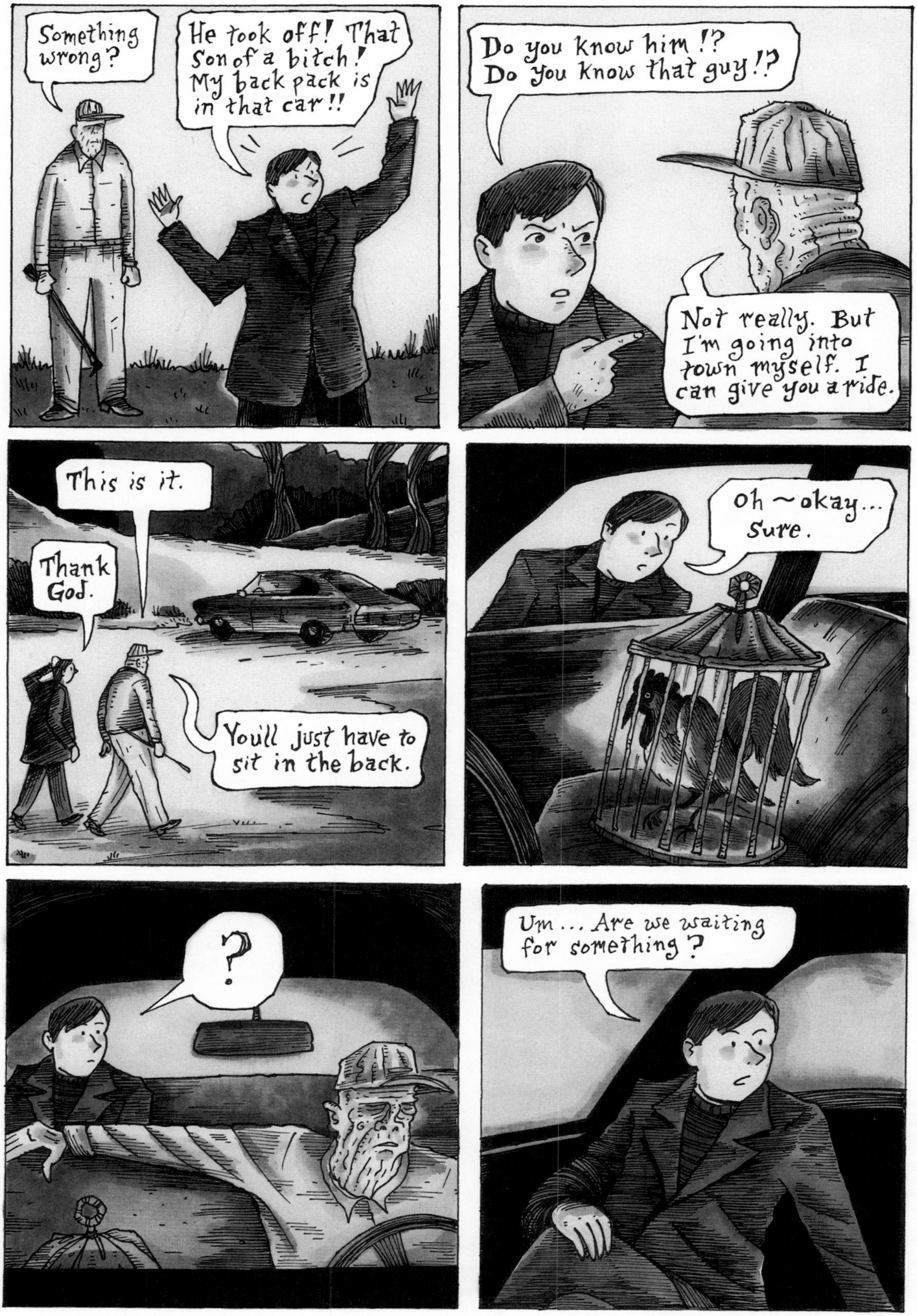

Something wrong?
He took off! That Son of a bitch! My back pack is in that car!!
Do you know him!? Do you know that guy!?
Not really. But I'm going into town myself. I can give you a ride.
This is it.
Thank God.
You'll just have to sit in the back.
Oh ~ okay... sure.
?
Um... Are we waiting for something?

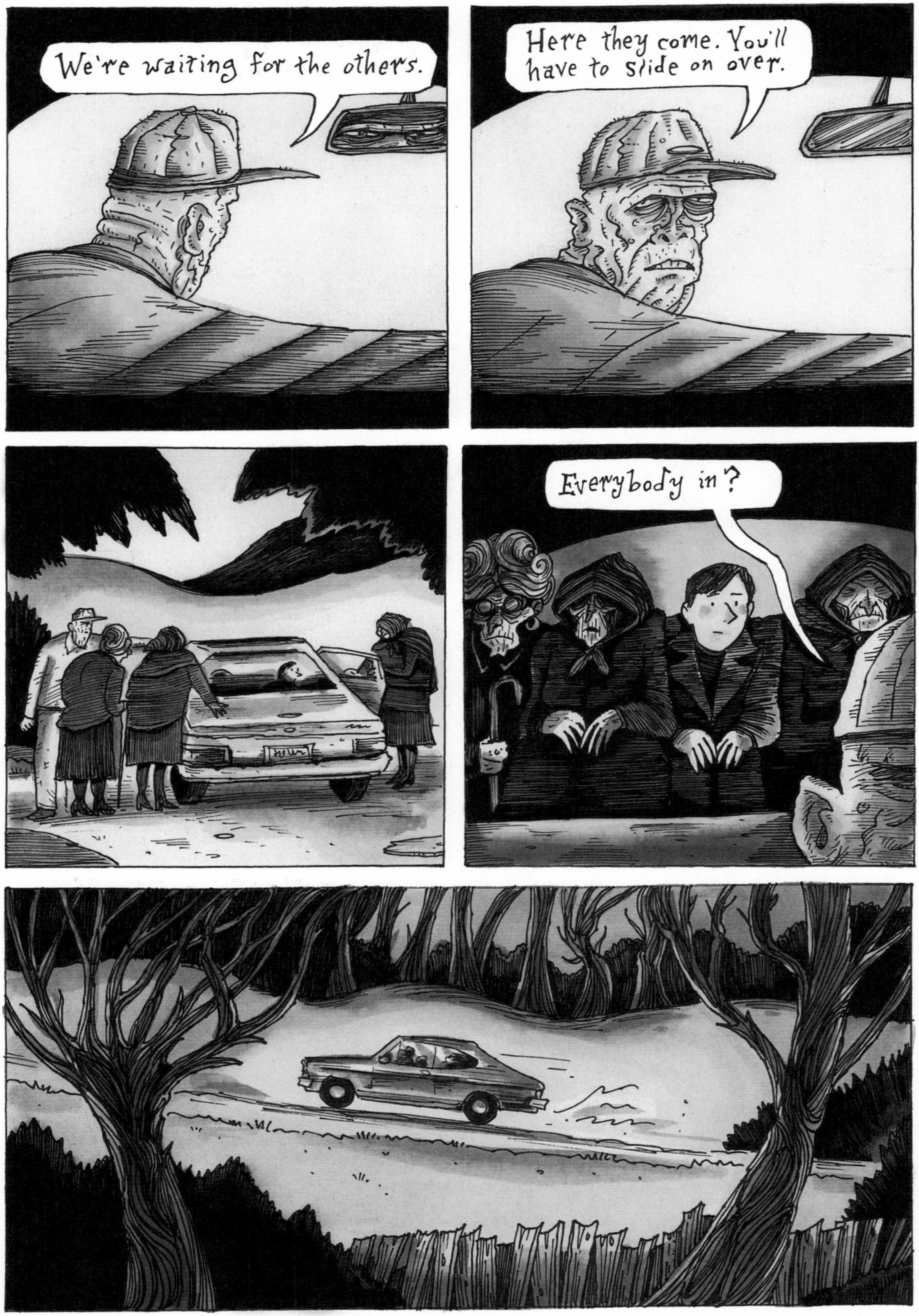
We're waiting for the others.
Here they come. You'll have to slide on over.
Everybody in?

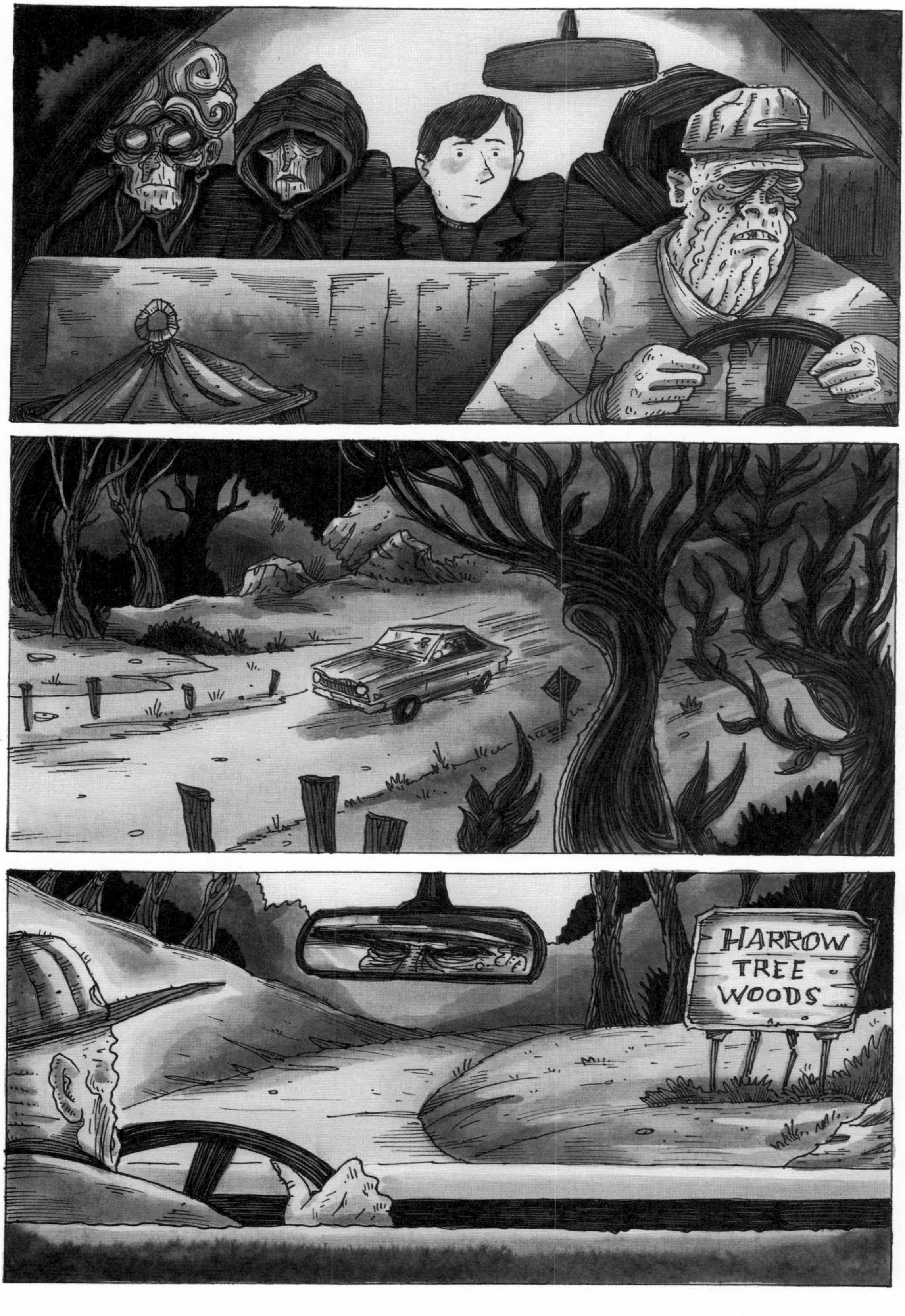
HARROW
TREE
WOODS

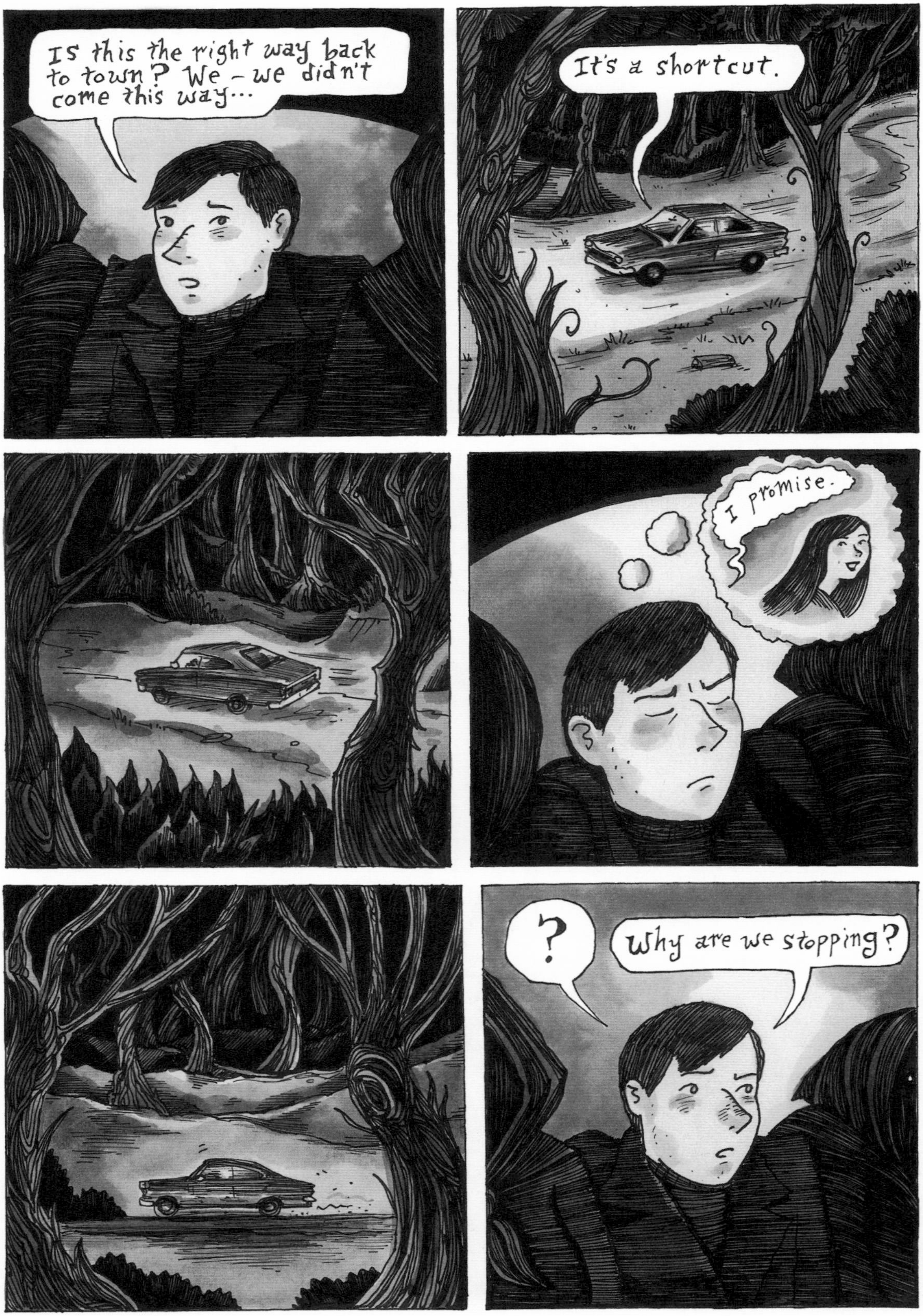
Is this the right way back to town? We - we didn't come this way...
It's a shortcut.
I promise.
?
Why are we stopping?

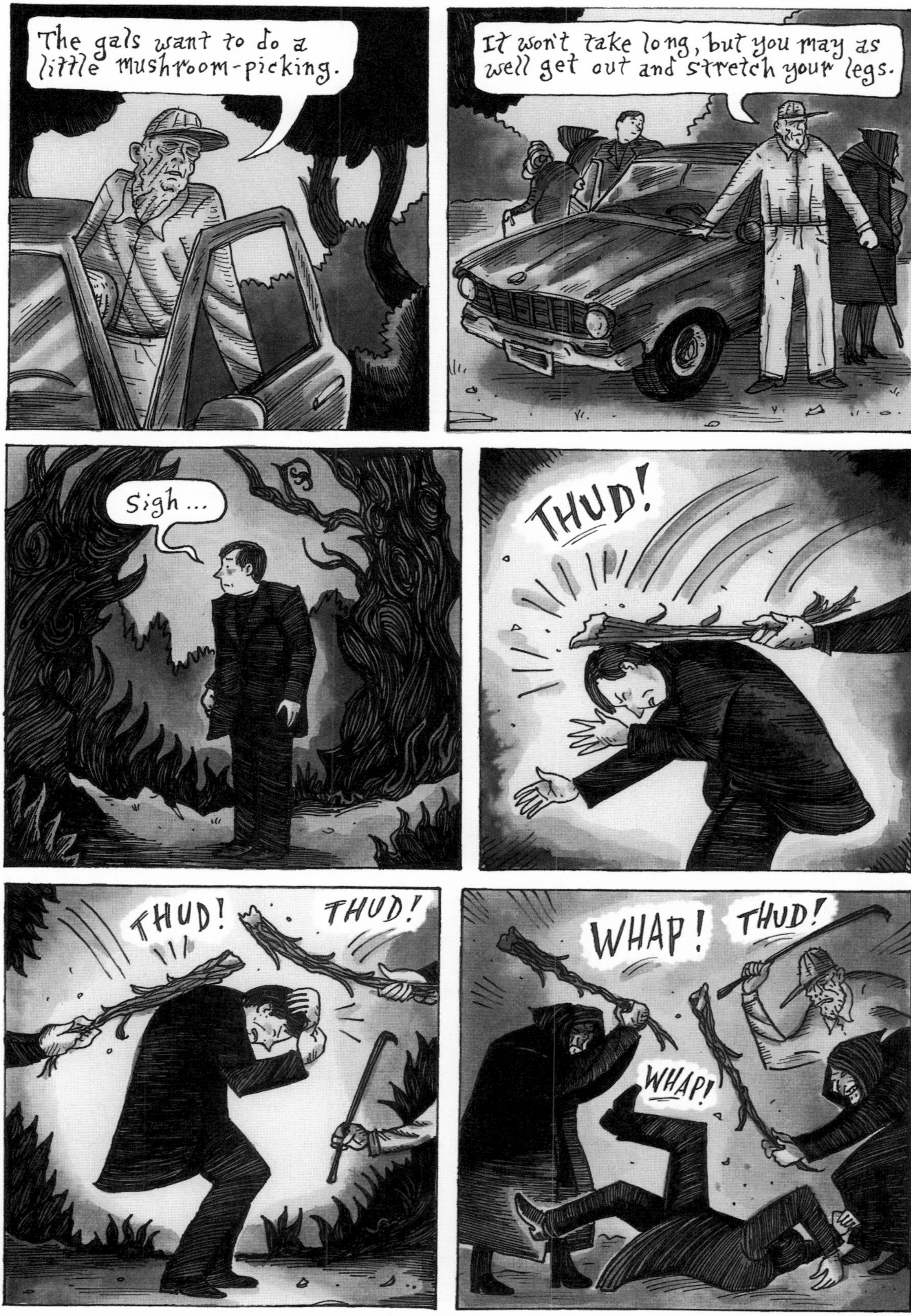
The gals want to do a little mushroom-picking.
It won't take long, but you may as well get out and stretch your legs.
Sigh...
THUD!
THUD!
THUD!
WHAP!
THUD!
WHAP!

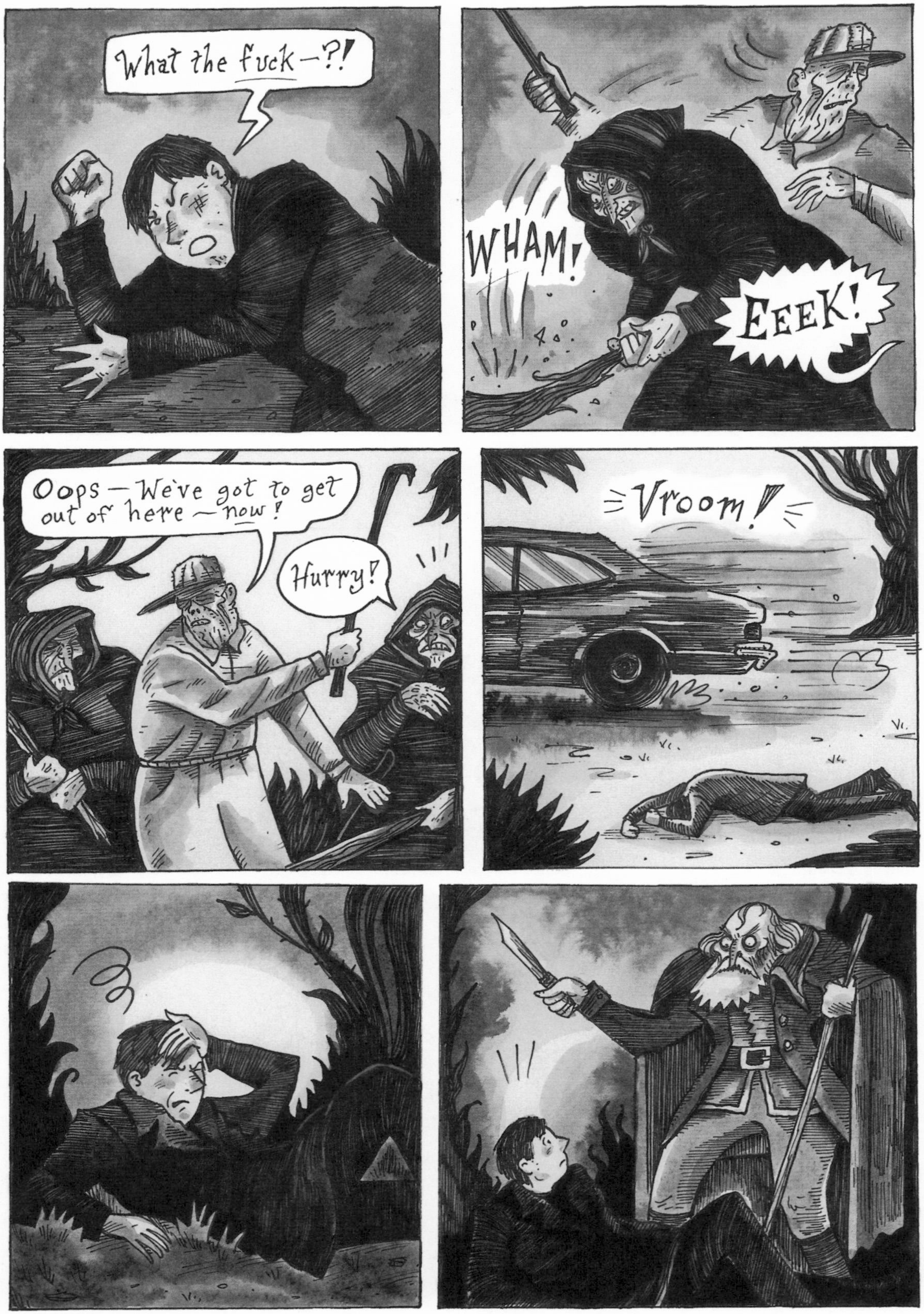
What the fuck—?!
WHAM!
EEEK!
Oops — We've got to get out of here — now!
Hurry!
Vroom!

2.

The Frog

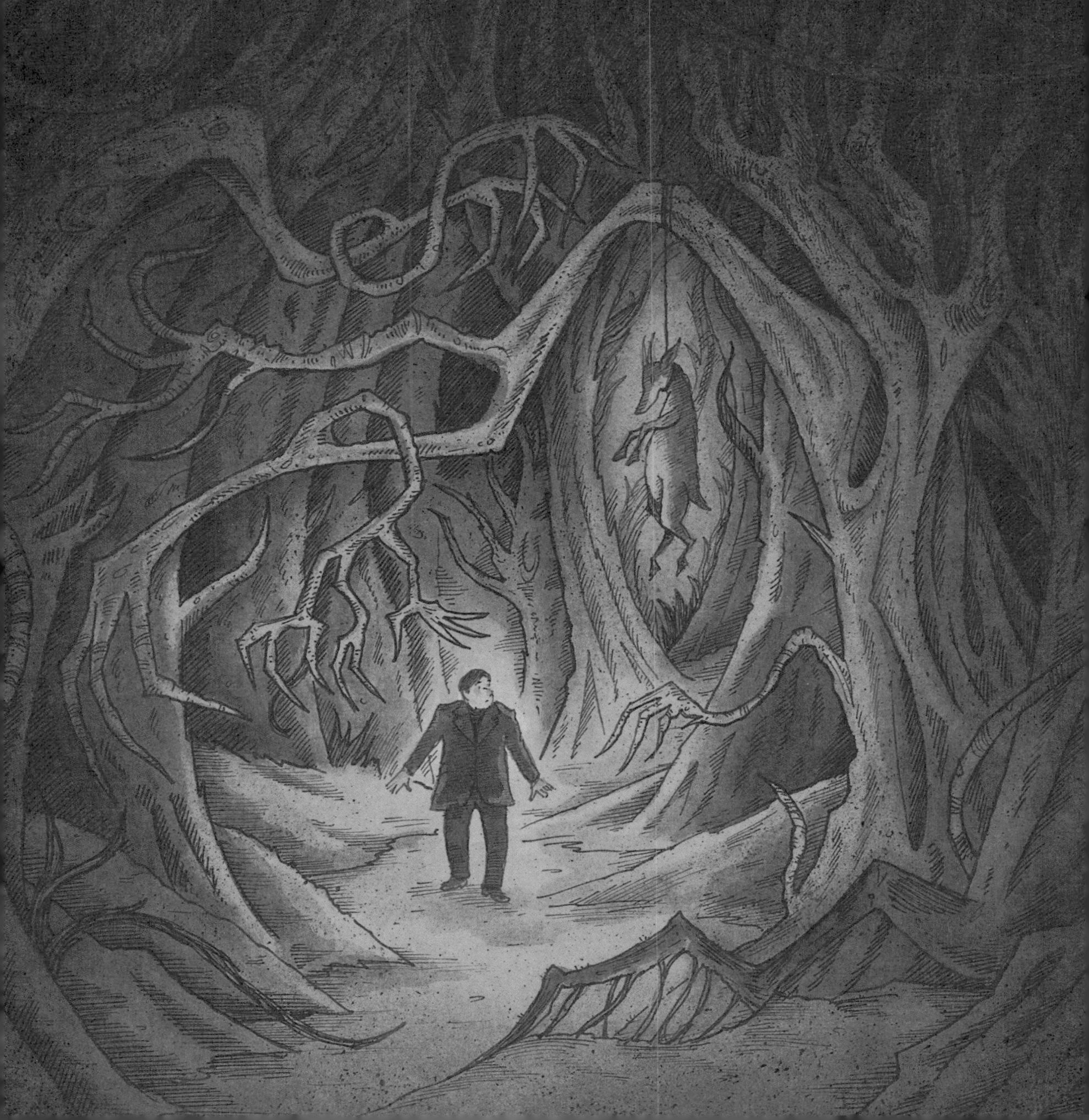

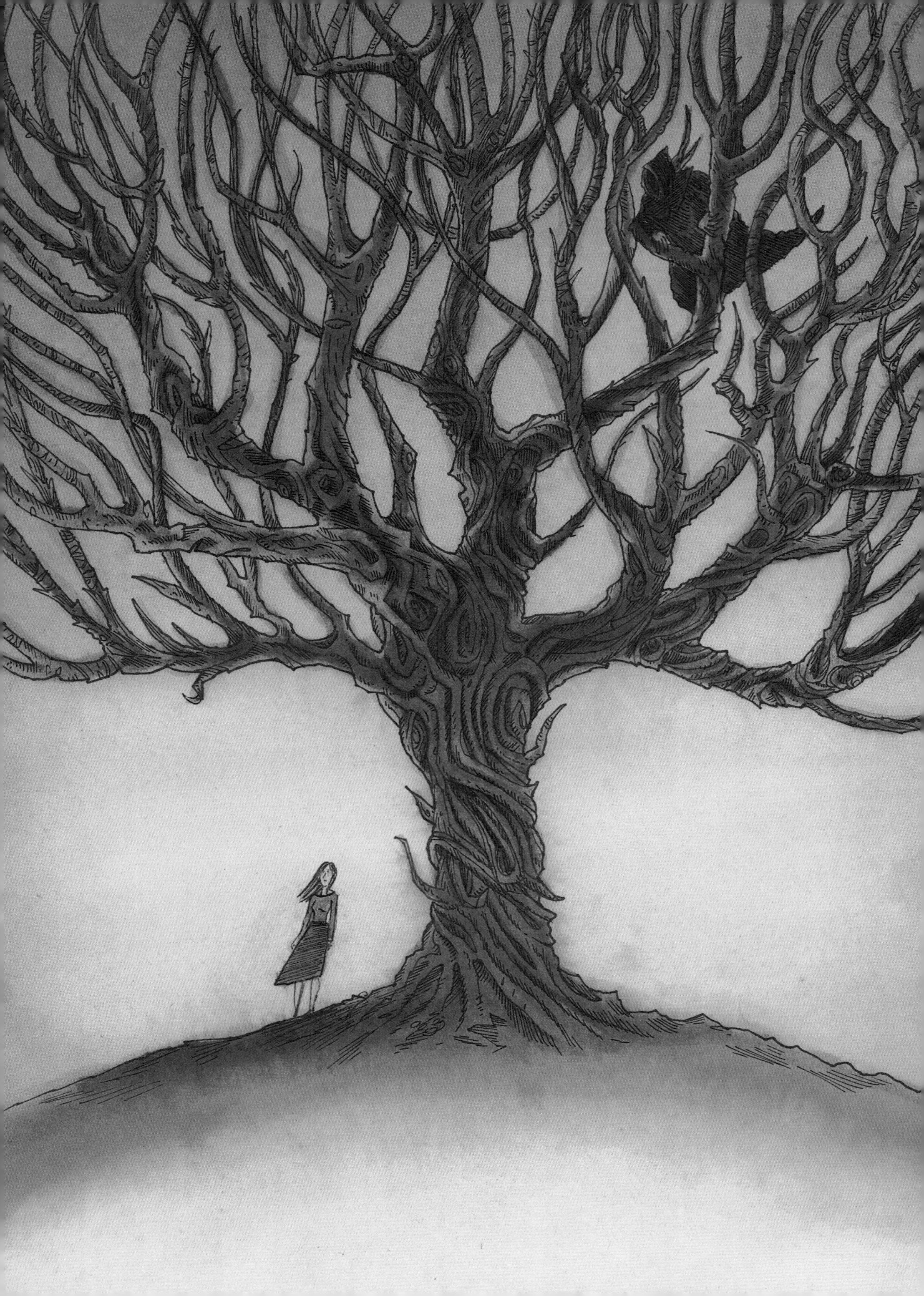

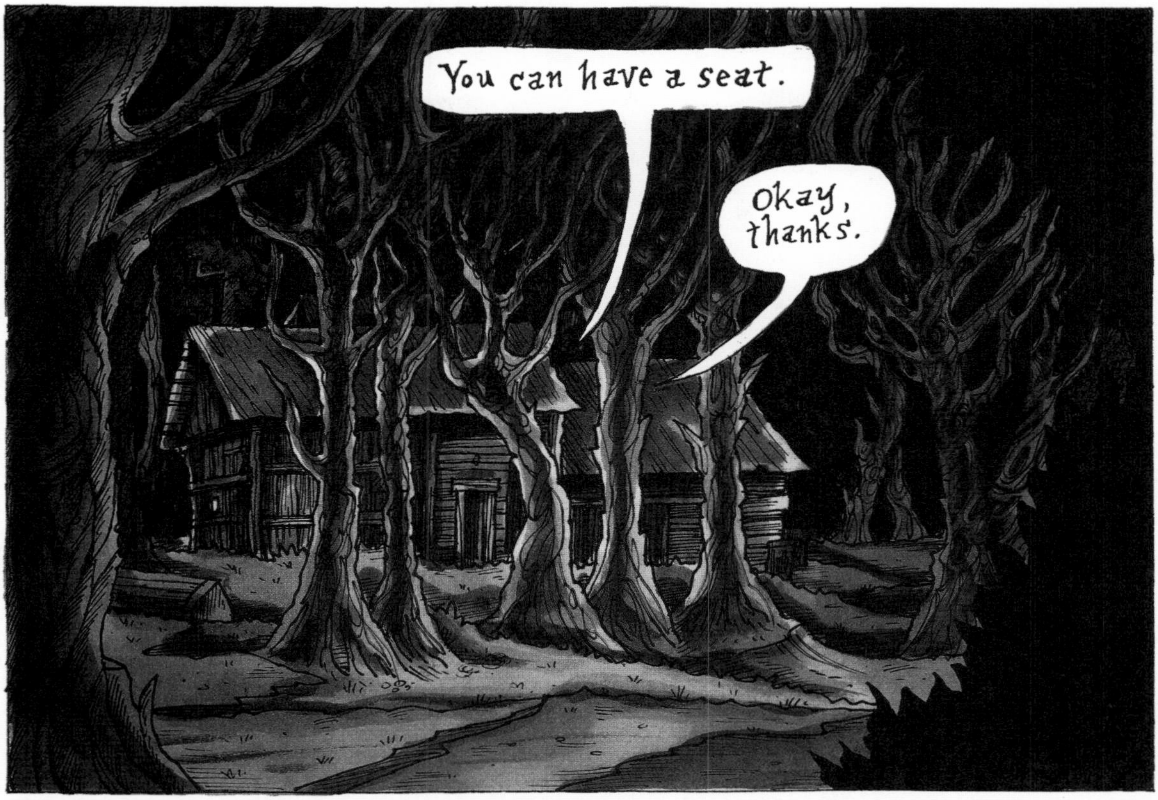
You can have a seat.
Okay, thanks.

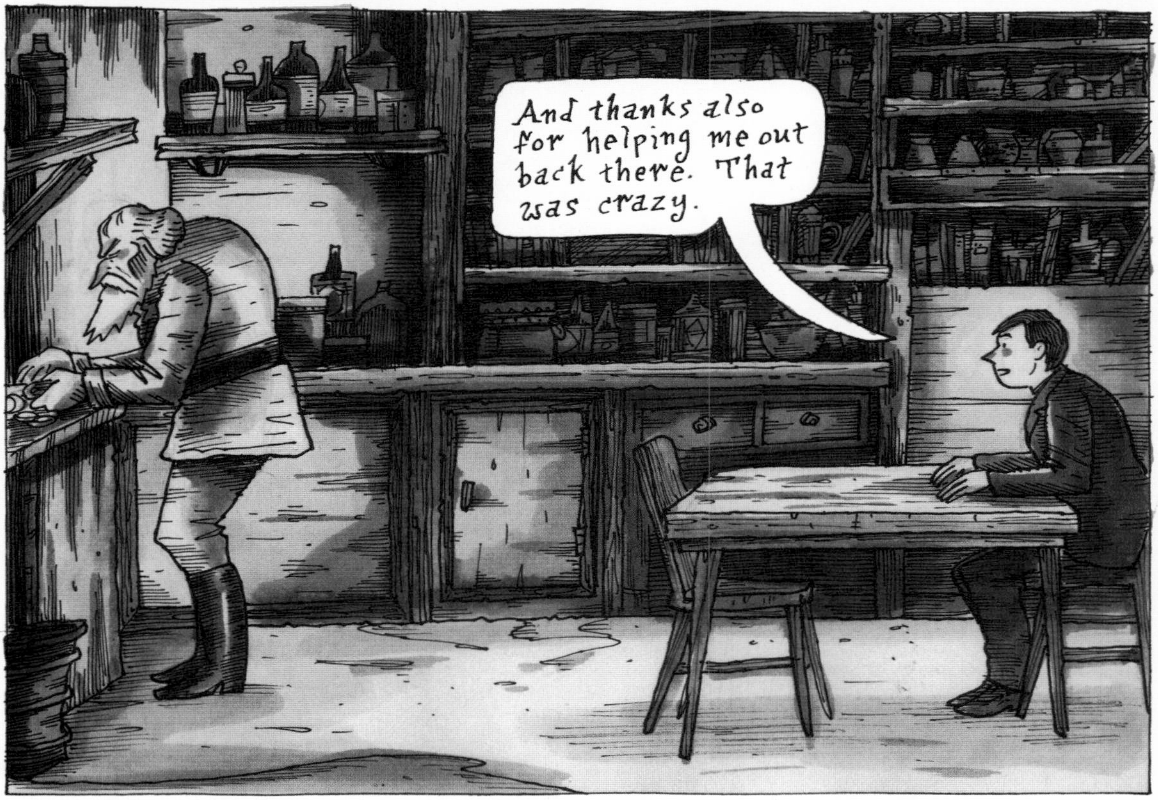
And thanks also for helping me out back there. That was crazy.

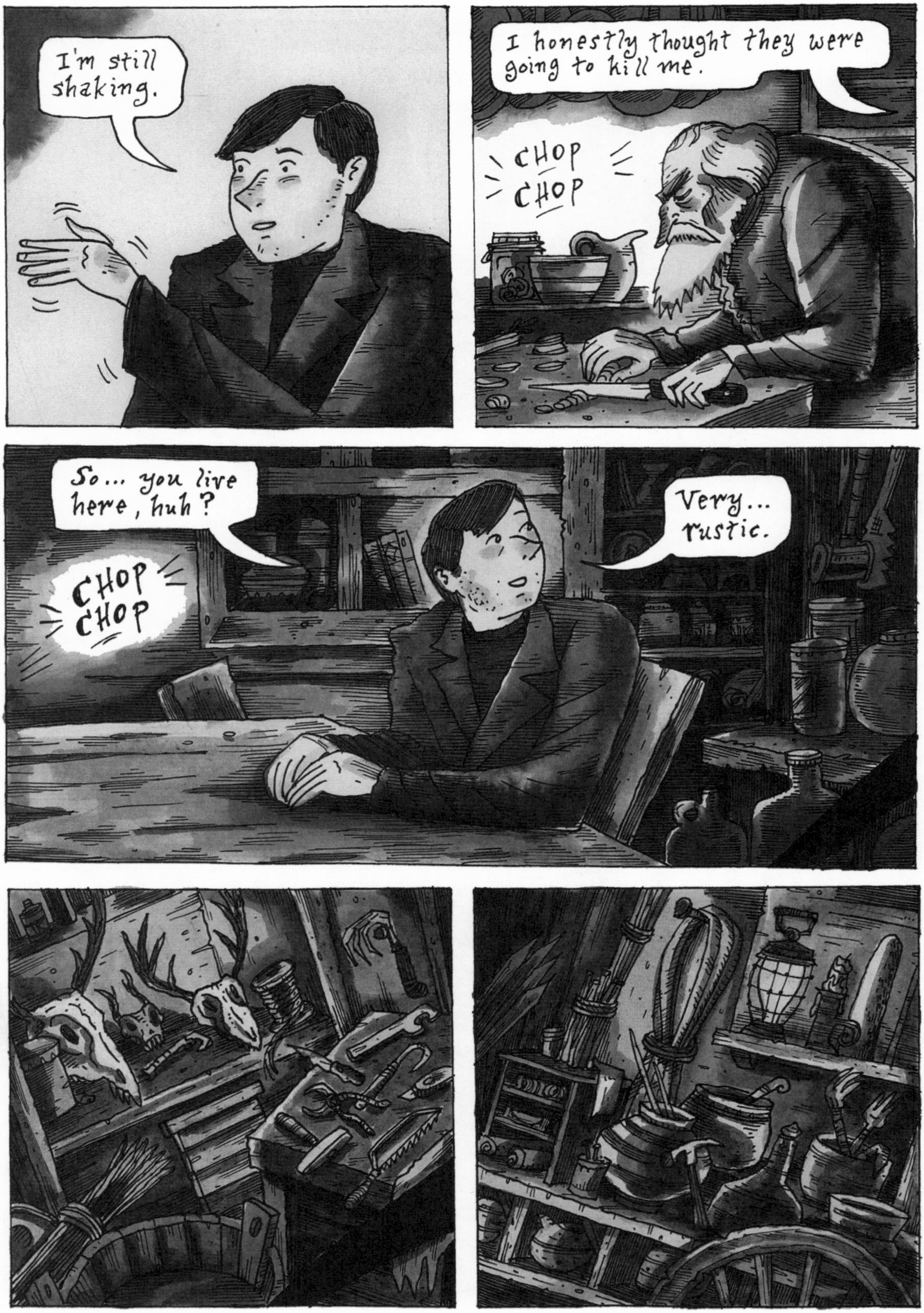
I'm still shaking.
I honestly thought they were going to kill me.
CHOP CHOP
So... you live here, huh?
CHOP CHOP
Very... rustic.

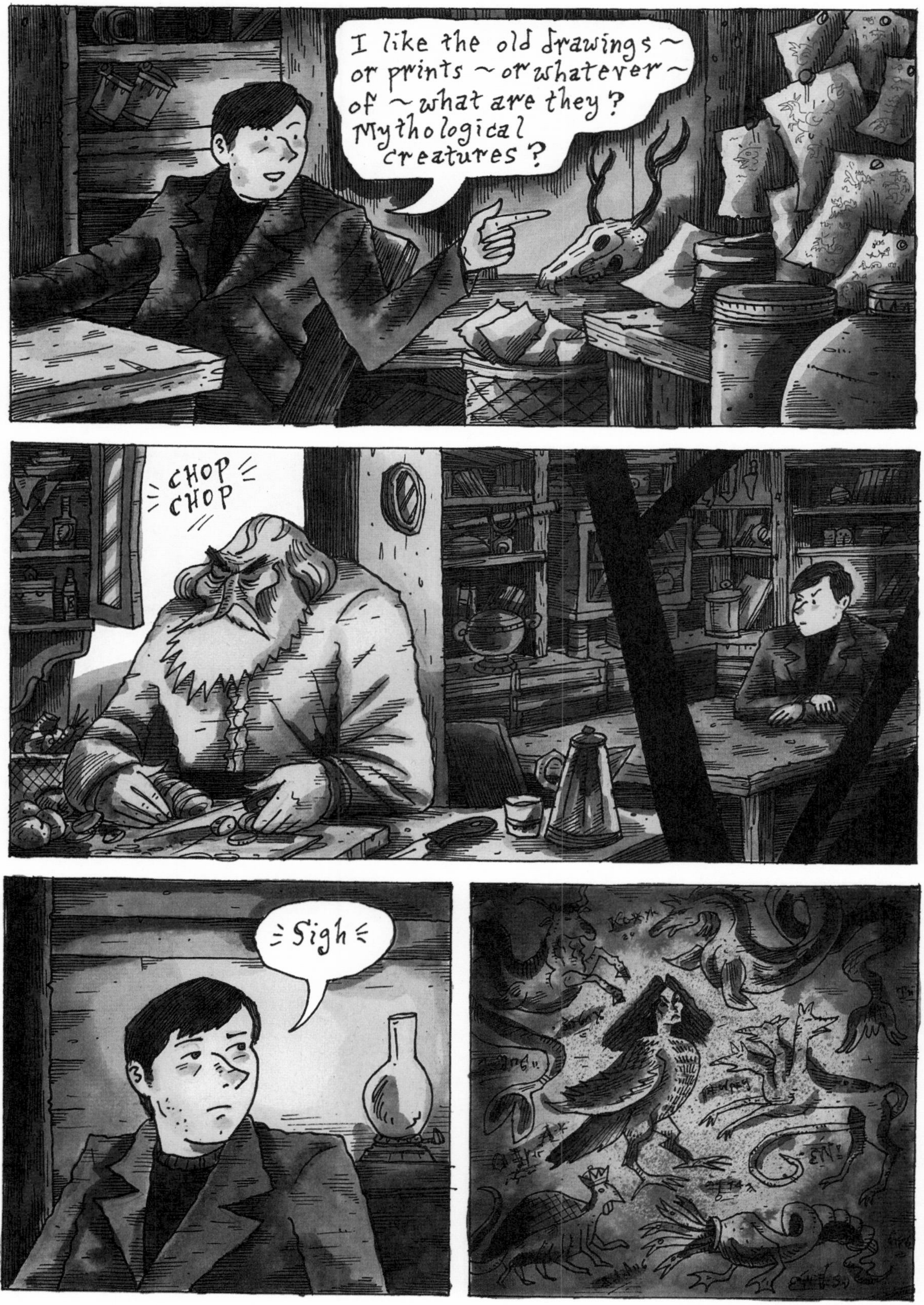
I like the old drawings ~ or prints ~ or whatever ~ of ~ what are they? Mythological creatures?
CHOP CHOP
Sigh

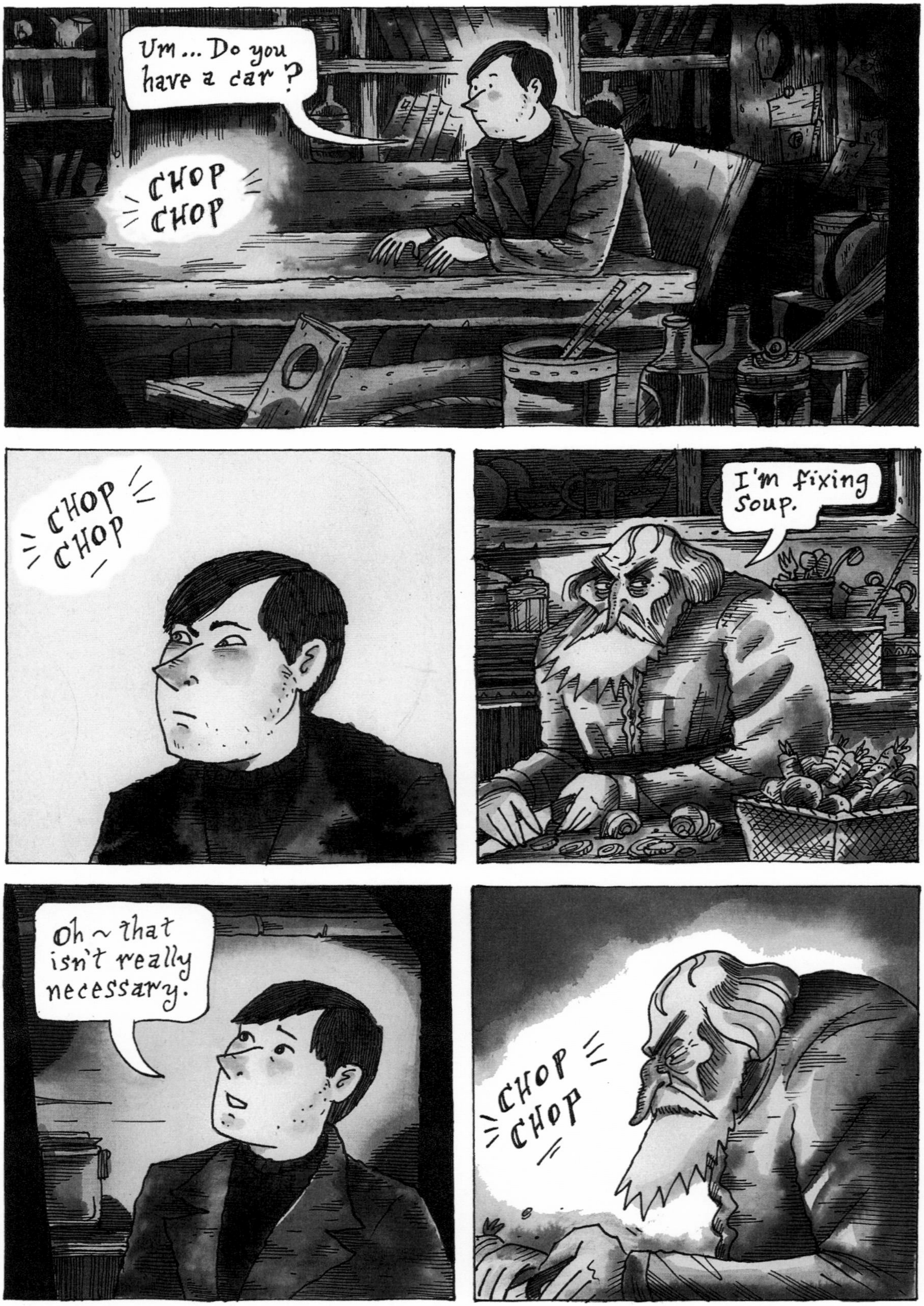
Um... Do you have a car?
CHOP CHOP
CHOP CHOP
I'm fixing soup.
Oh ~ that isn't really necessary.
CHOP CHOP

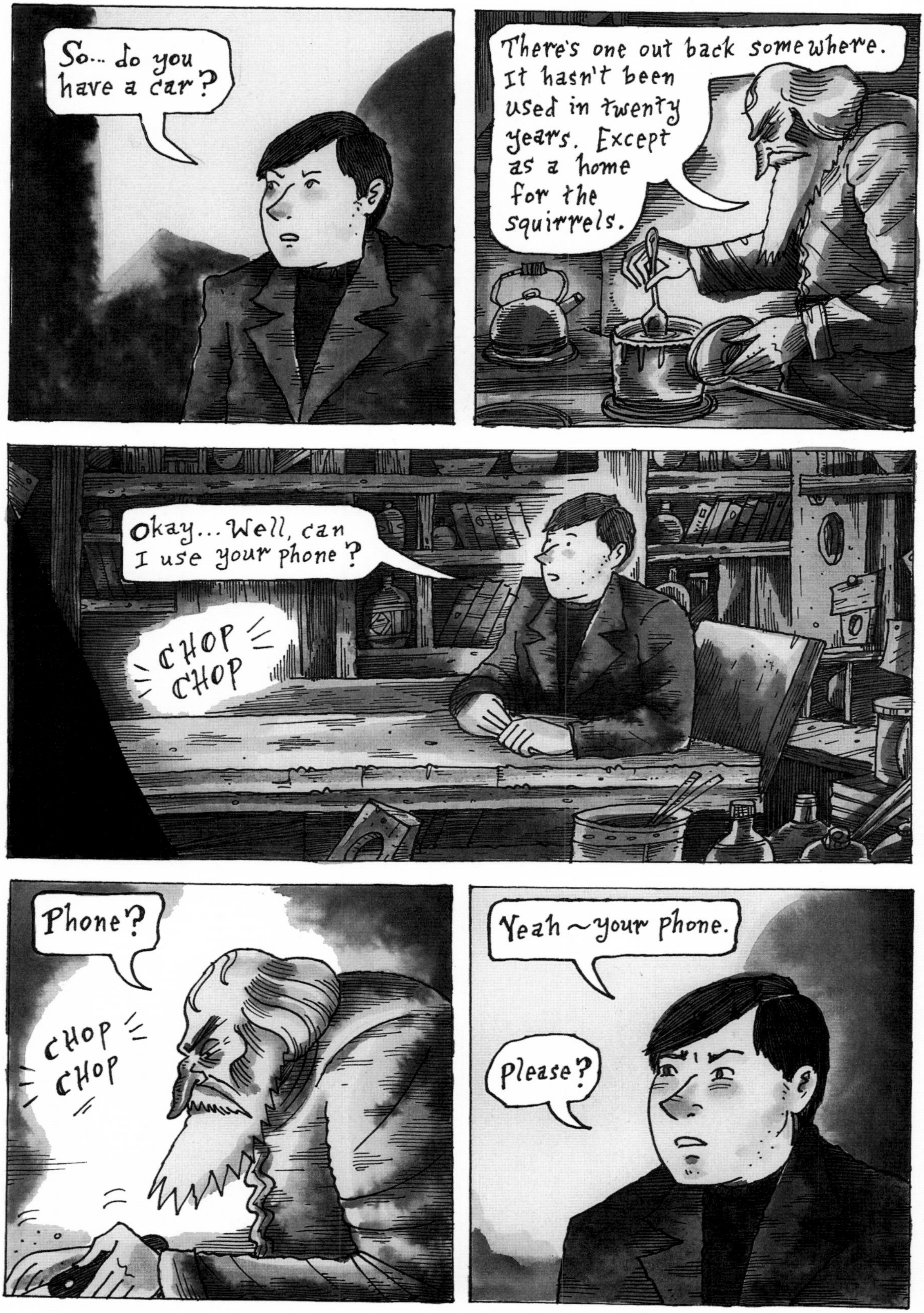
So... do you have a car?
There's one out back somewhere. It hasn't been used in twenty years. Except as a home for the squirrels.
Okay... Well, can I use your phone?
CHOP CHOP
Phone?
CHOP CHOP
Yeah ~ your phone.
Please?

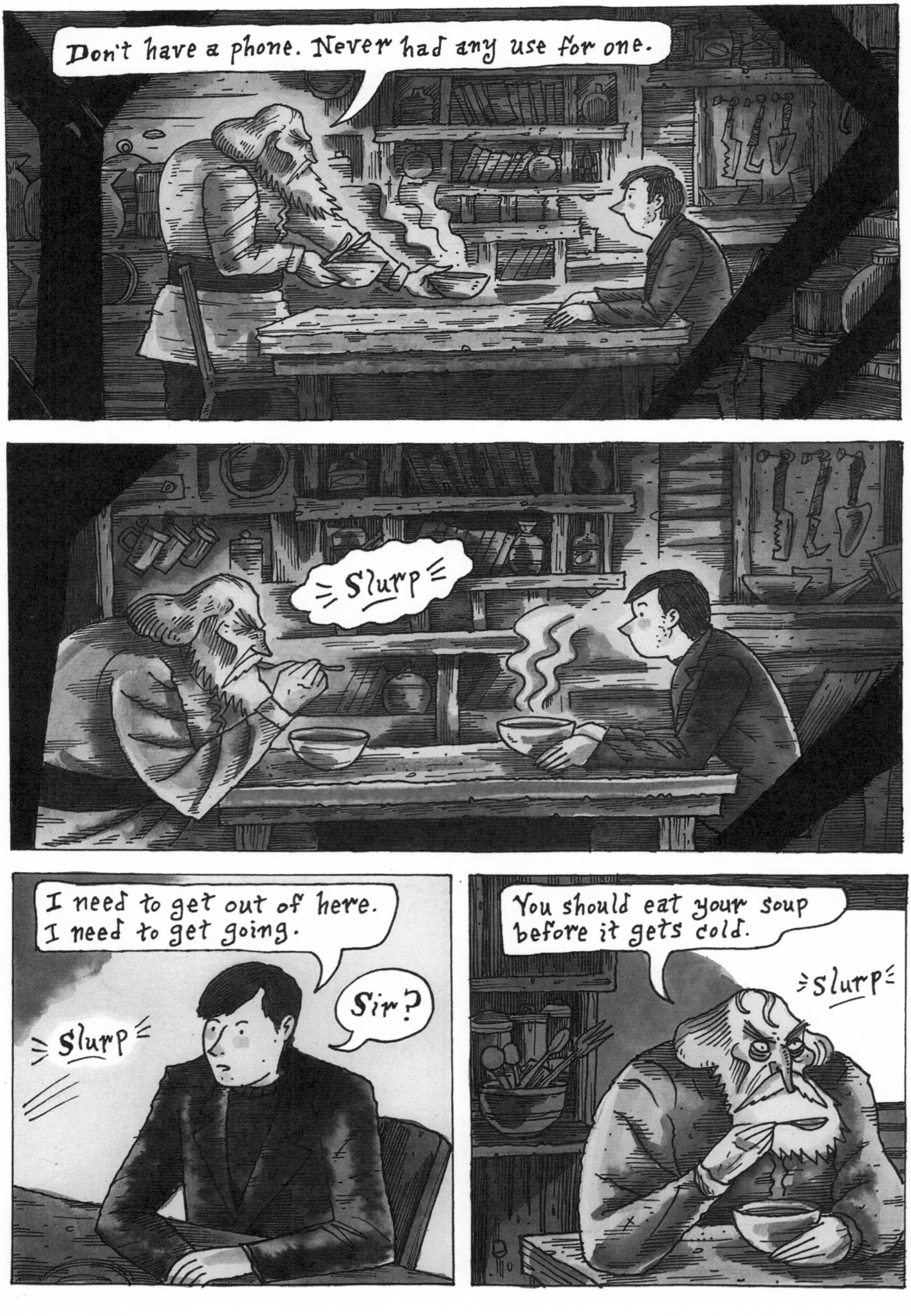
Don't have a phone. Never had any use for one.
Slurp
I need to get out of here.
I need to get going.
Slurp
Sir?
You should eat your soup before it gets cold.
Slurp

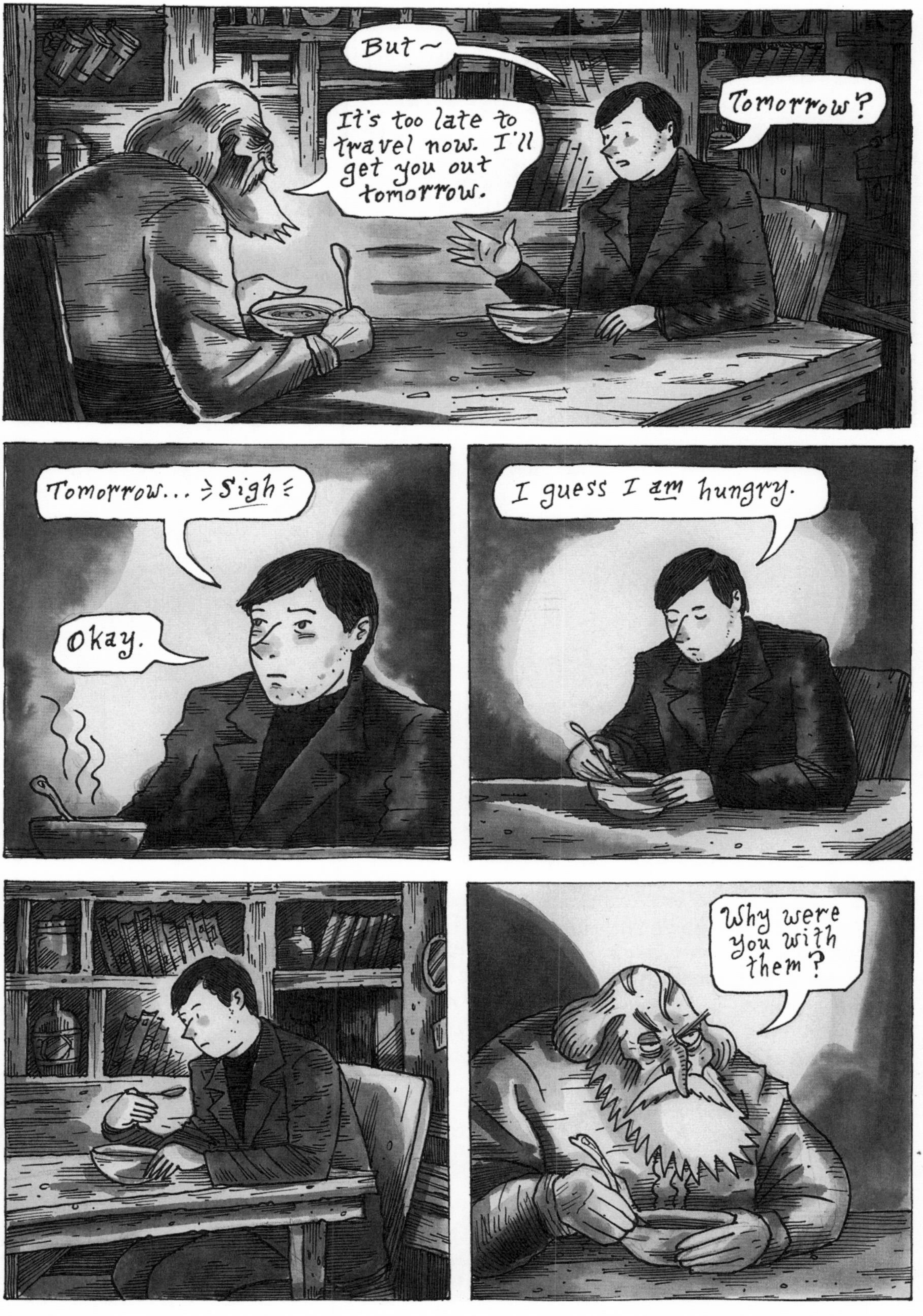
But~
It's too late to travel now. I'll get you out tomorrow.
Tomorrow?
Tomorrow... ≥sigh≤
Okay.
I guess I am hungry.
Why were you with them?

Who? Oh, those people? They were supposed to give me a ride into town.

≥ Slurp! ≤

Into town.

Um, yeah. I came here to ~ I'm trying to ~ I mean, I'm looking for someone I went to school with. It's been a few years. I lost touch with her.

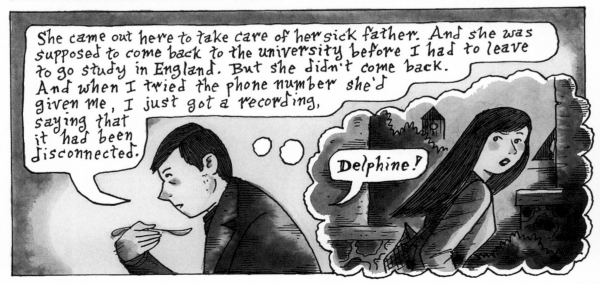

She came out here to take care of her sick father. And she was supposed to come back to the university before I had to leave to go study in England. But she didn't come back. And when I tried the phone number she'd given me, I just got a recording, saying that it had been disconnected.

Delphine!

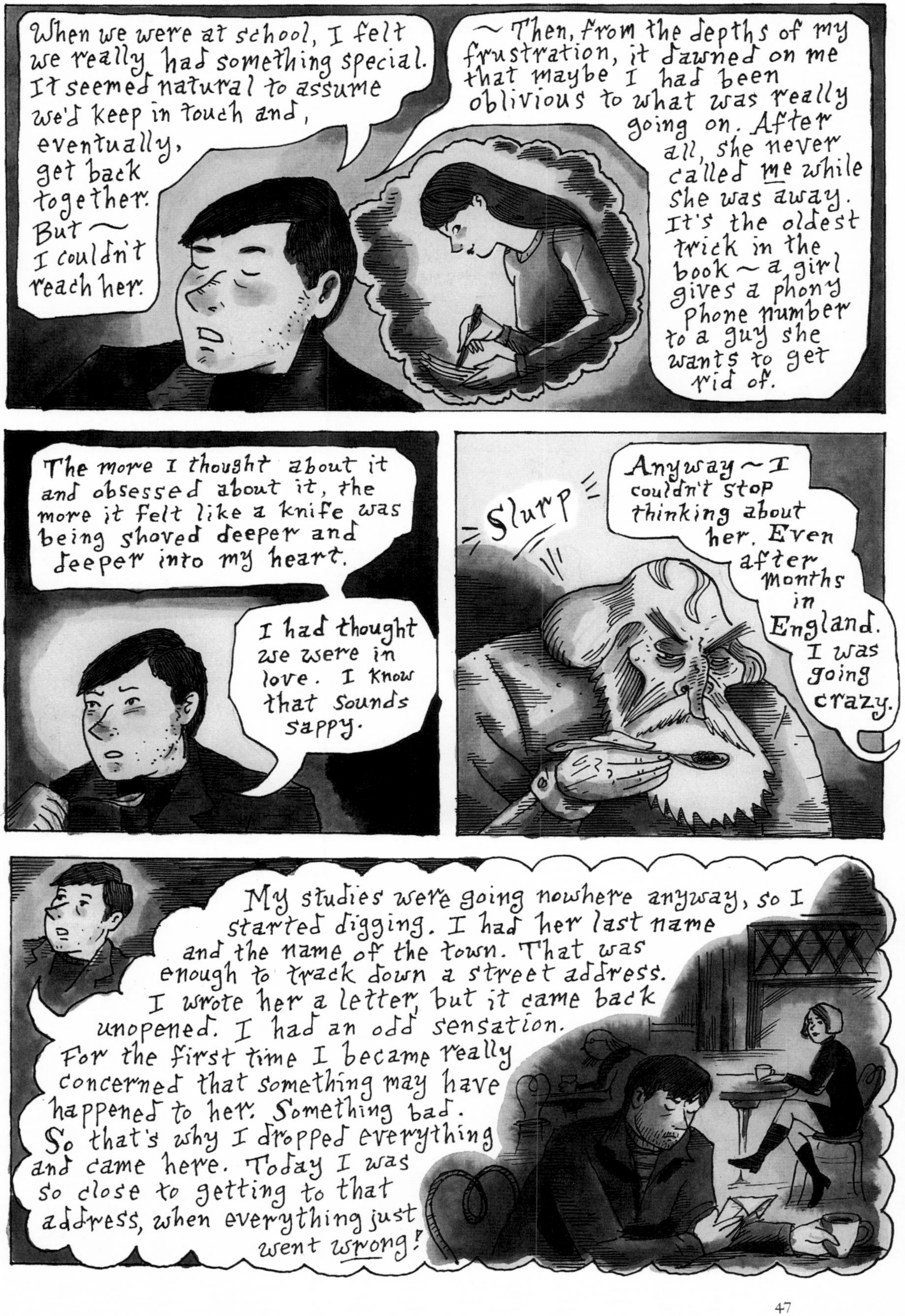
When we were at school, I felt we really had something special. It seemed natural to assume we'd keep in touch and, eventually, get back together. But ~ I couldn't reach her.
~ Then, from the depths of my frustration, it dawned on me that maybe I had been oblivious to what was really going on. After all, she never called me while she was away. It's the oldest trick in the book ~ a girl gives a phony phone number to a guy she wants to get rid of.
The more I thought about it and obsessed about it, the more it felt like a knife was being shoved deeper and deeper into my heart.
I had thought we were in love. I know that sounds sappy.
Slurp
Anyway ~ I couldn't stop thinking about her. Even after months in England. I was going crazy.
My studies were going nowhere anyway, so I started digging. I had her last name and the name of the town. That was enough to track down a street address. I wrote her a letter, but it came back unopened. I had an odd sensation. For the first time I became really concerned that something may have happened to her. Something bad. So that's why I dropped everything and came here. Today I was so close to getting to that address, when everything just went wrong!

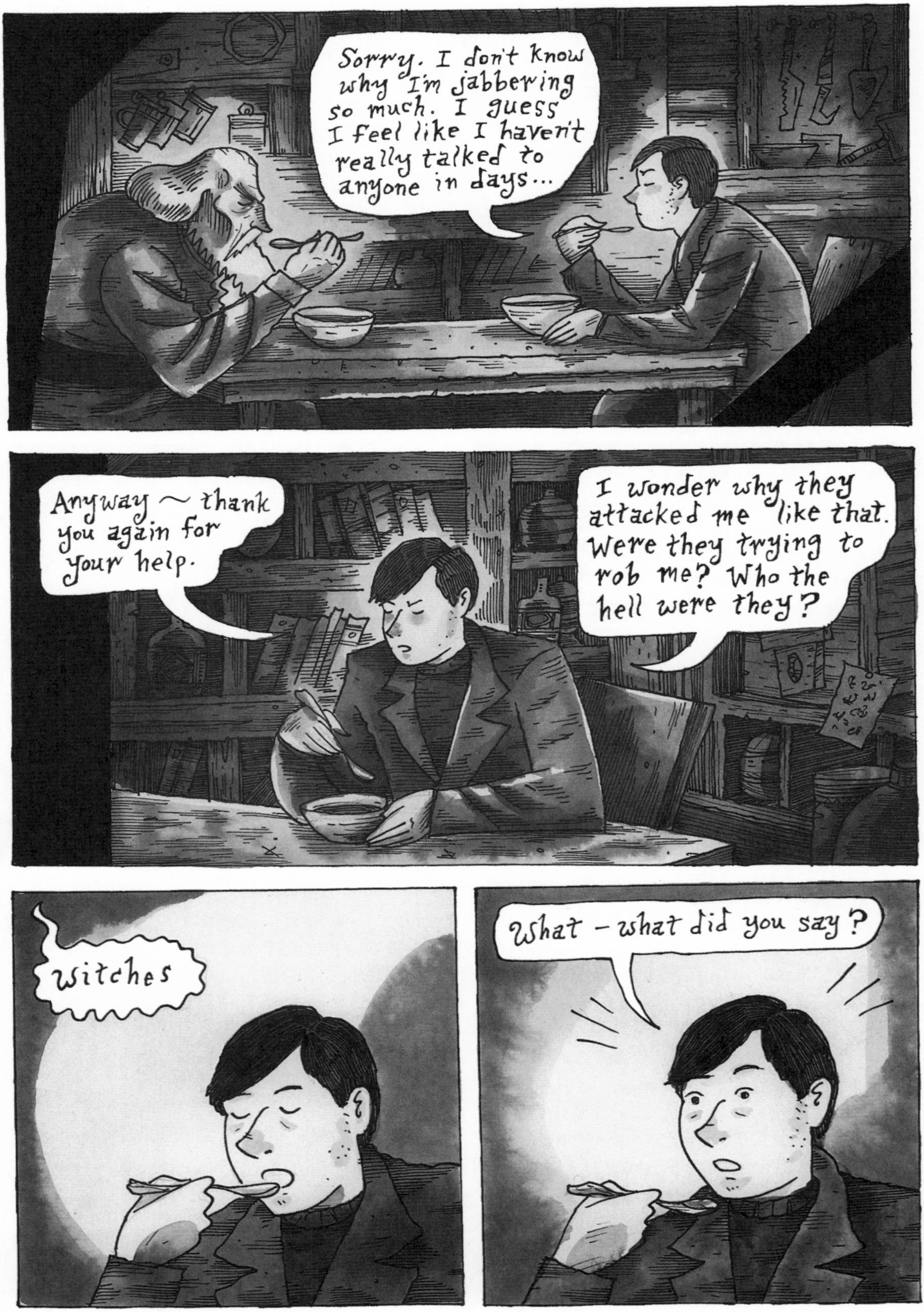
Sorry. I don't know why I'm jabbering so much. I guess I feel like I haven't really talked to anyone in days...
Anyway ~ thank you again for your help.
I wonder why they attacked me like that. Were they trying to rob me? Who the hell were they?
witches
What - what did you say?

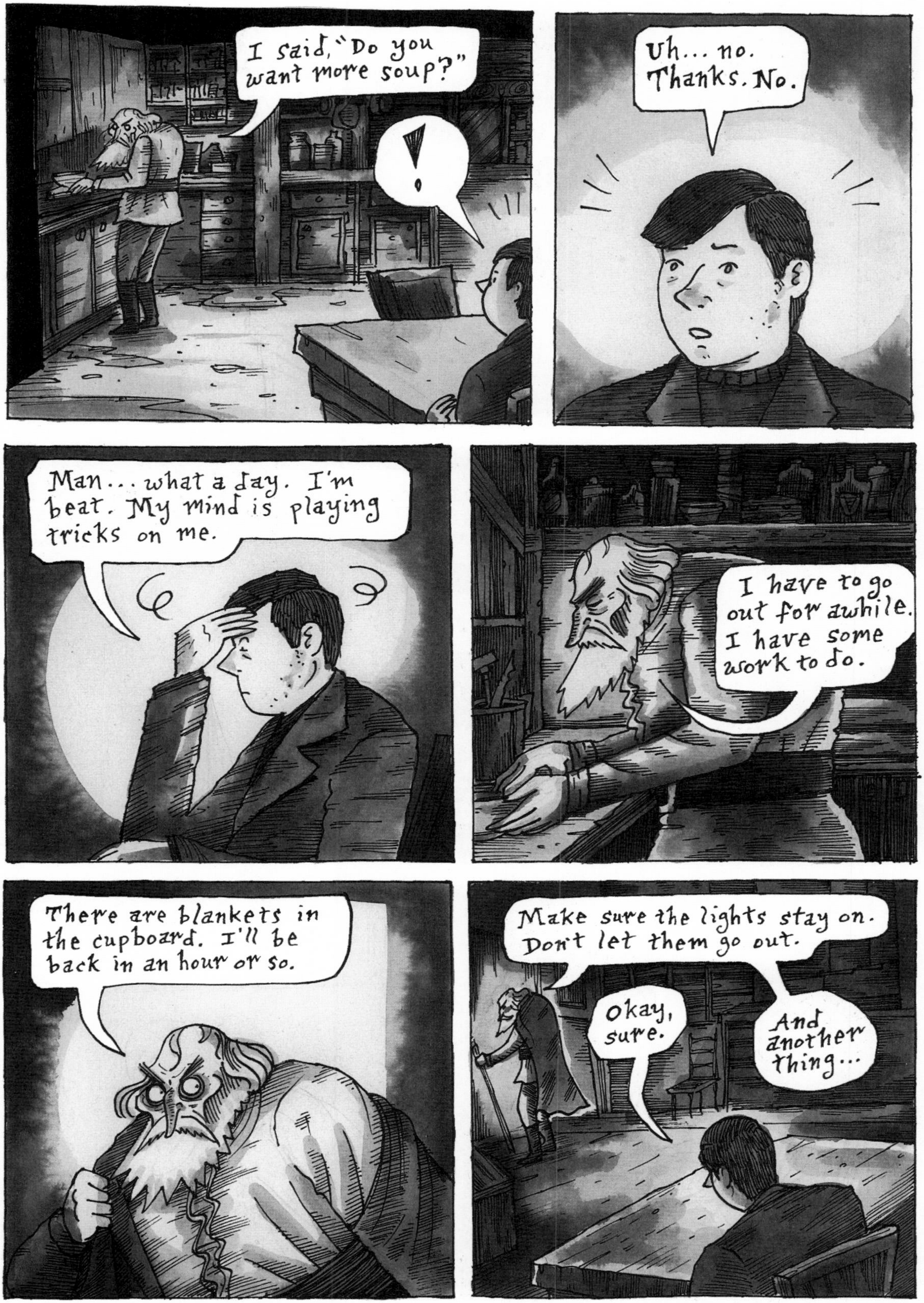
I said, "Do you want more soup?"
!
Uh... no. Thanks. No.
Man... what a day. I'm beat. My mind is playing tricks on me.
I have to go out for awhile. I have some work to do.
There are blankets in the cupboard. I'll be back in an hour or so.
Make sure the lights stay on. Don't let them go out.
Okay, sure.
And another thing...

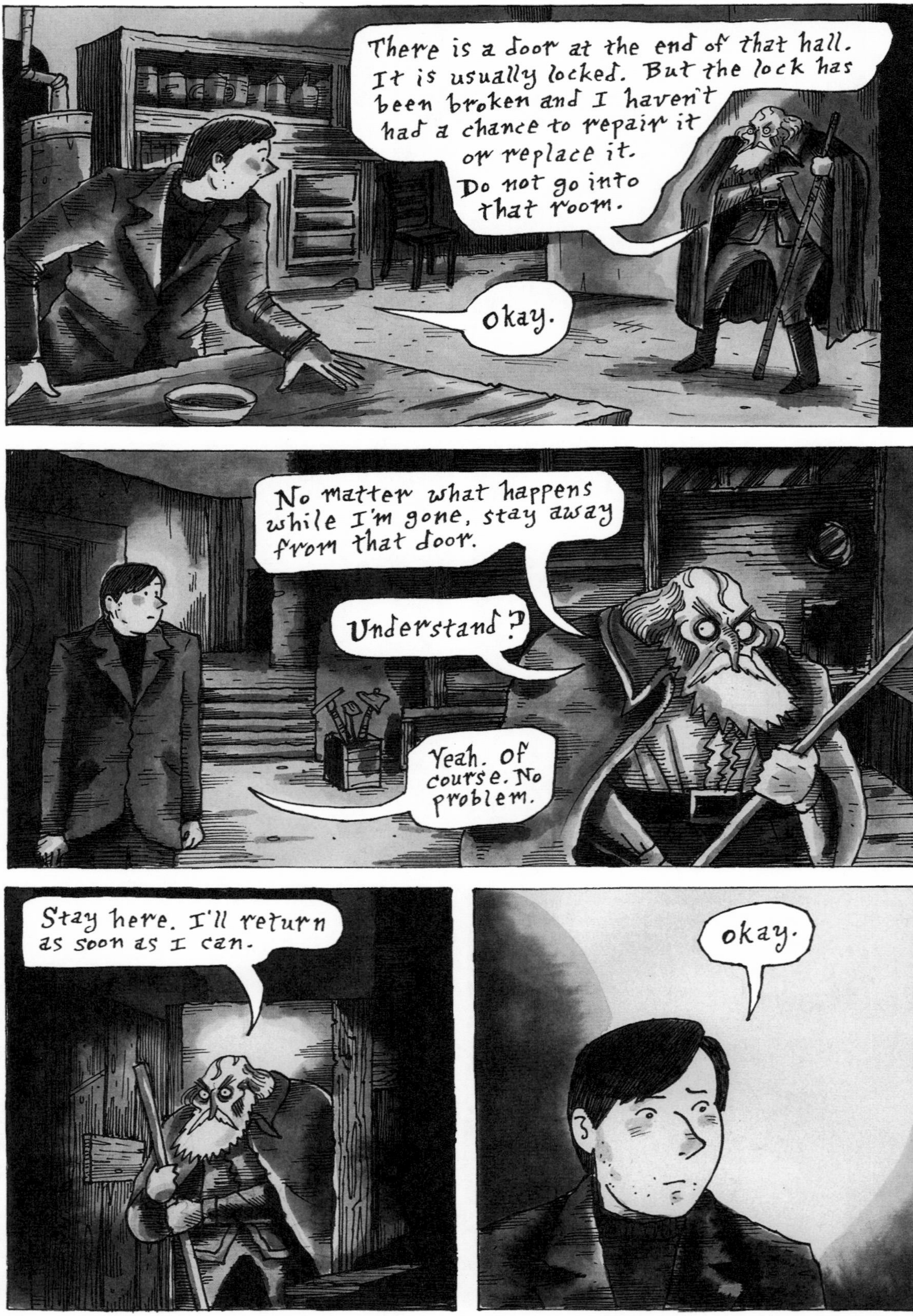
There is a door at the end of that hall. It is usually locked. But the lock has been broken and I haven't had a chance to repair it or replace it.
Do not go into that room.
Okay.
No matter what happens while I'm gone, stay away from that door.
Understand?
Yeah. Of course. No problem.
Stay here. I'll return as soon as I can.
Okay.

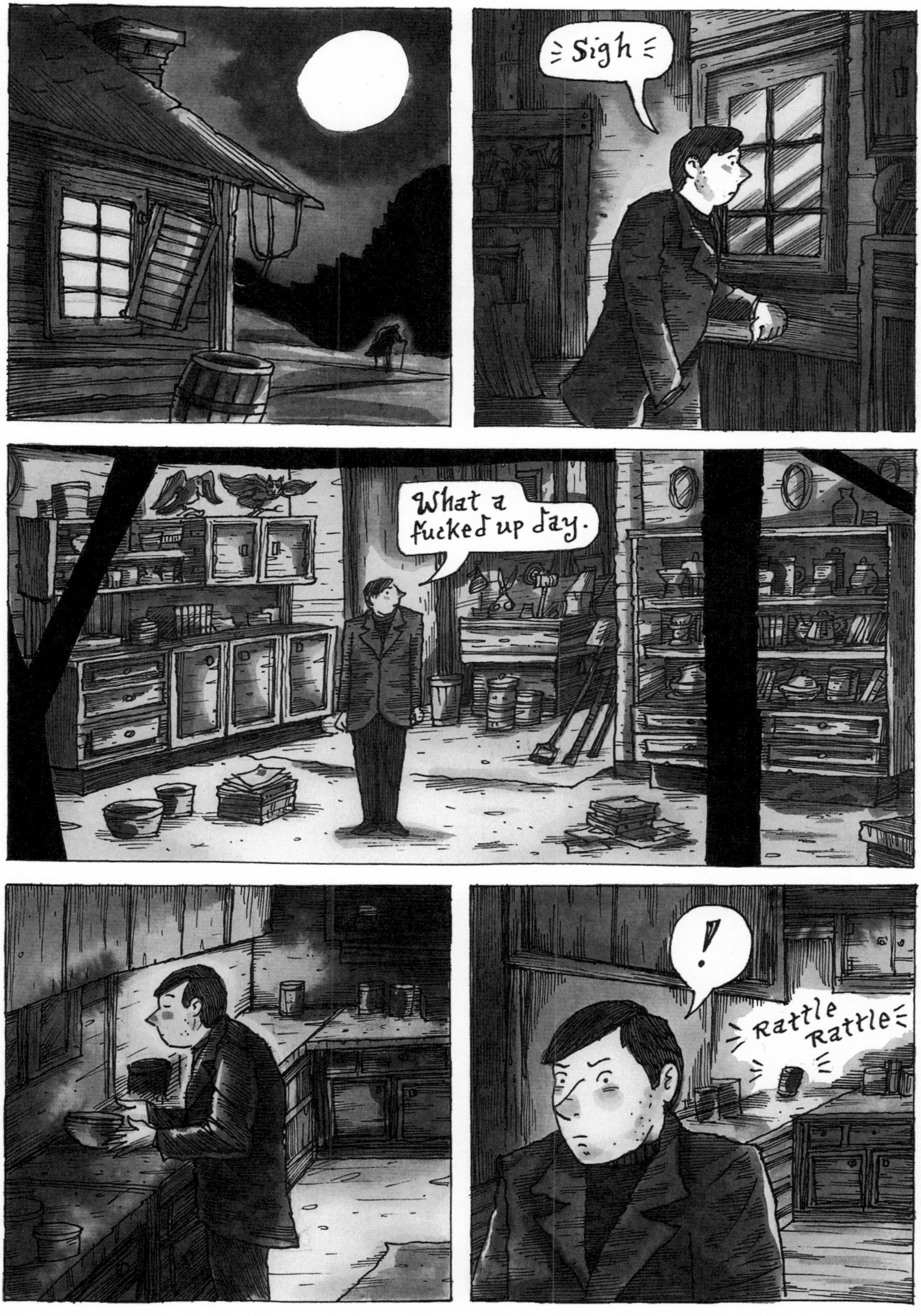
Sigh
What a fucked up day.
!
Rattle Rattle

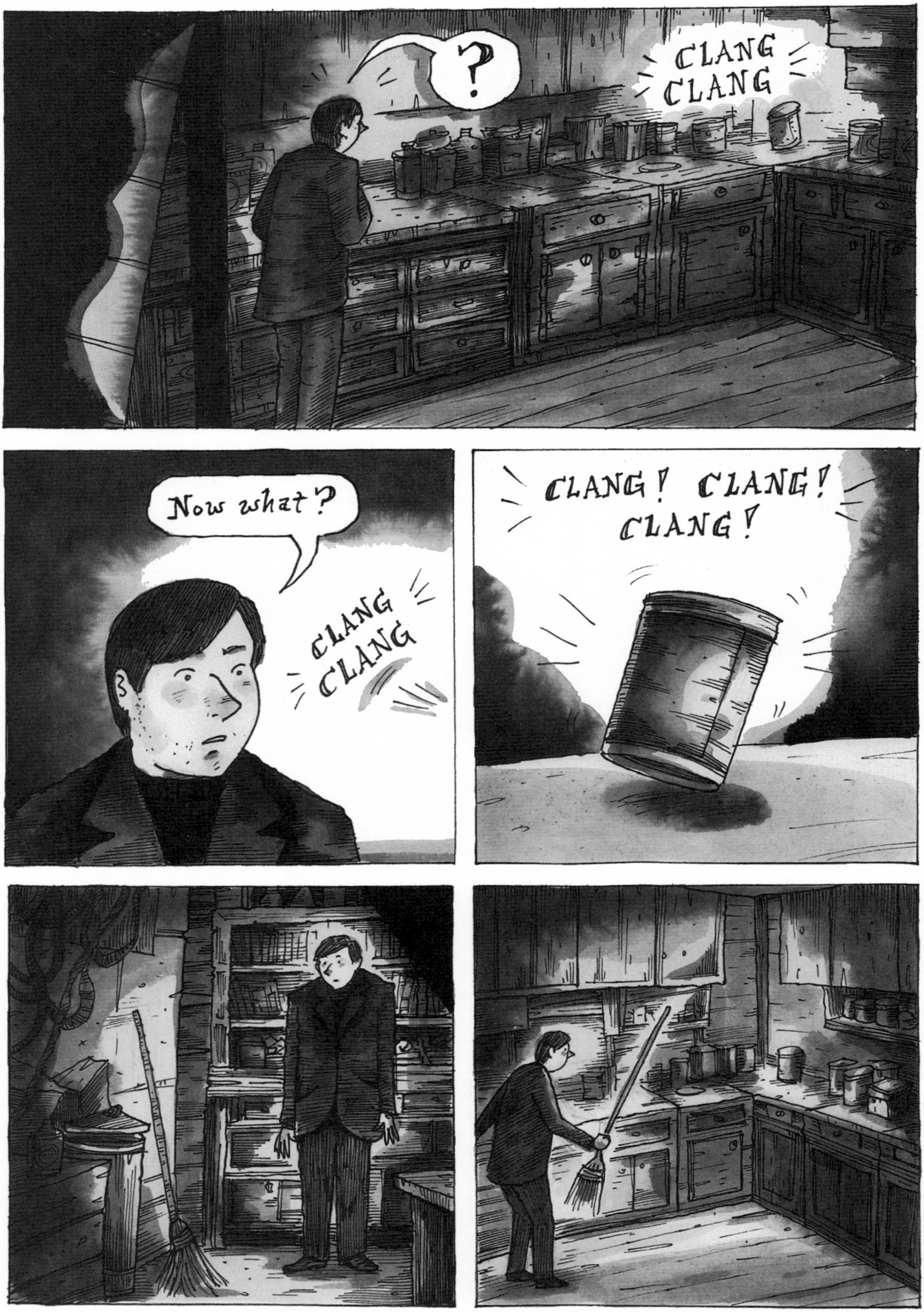
?
CLANG
CLANG
Now what?
CLANG
CLANG
CLANG! CLANG!
CLANG!

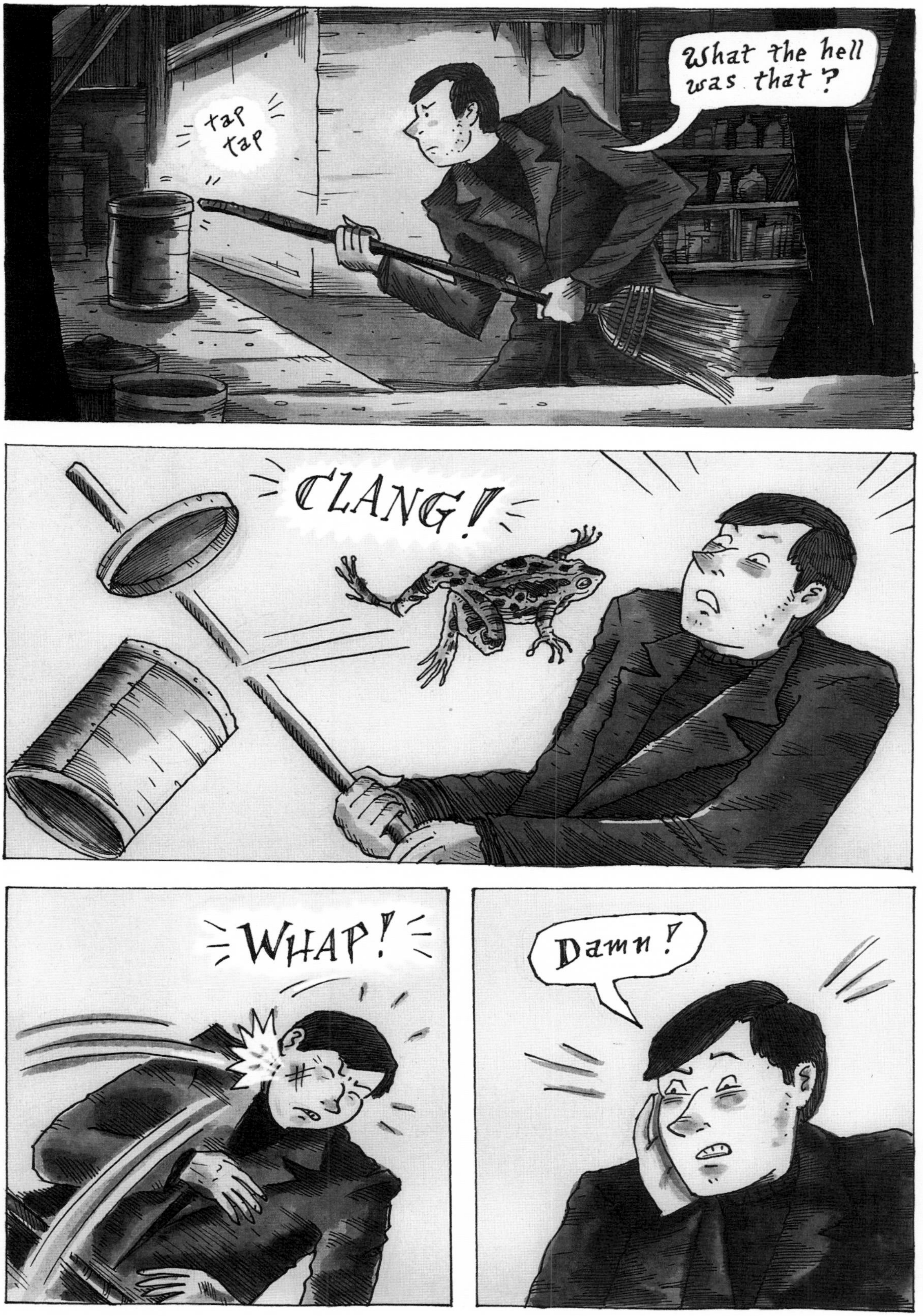
What the hell was that?
tap tap
CLANG!
WHAP!
Damn!

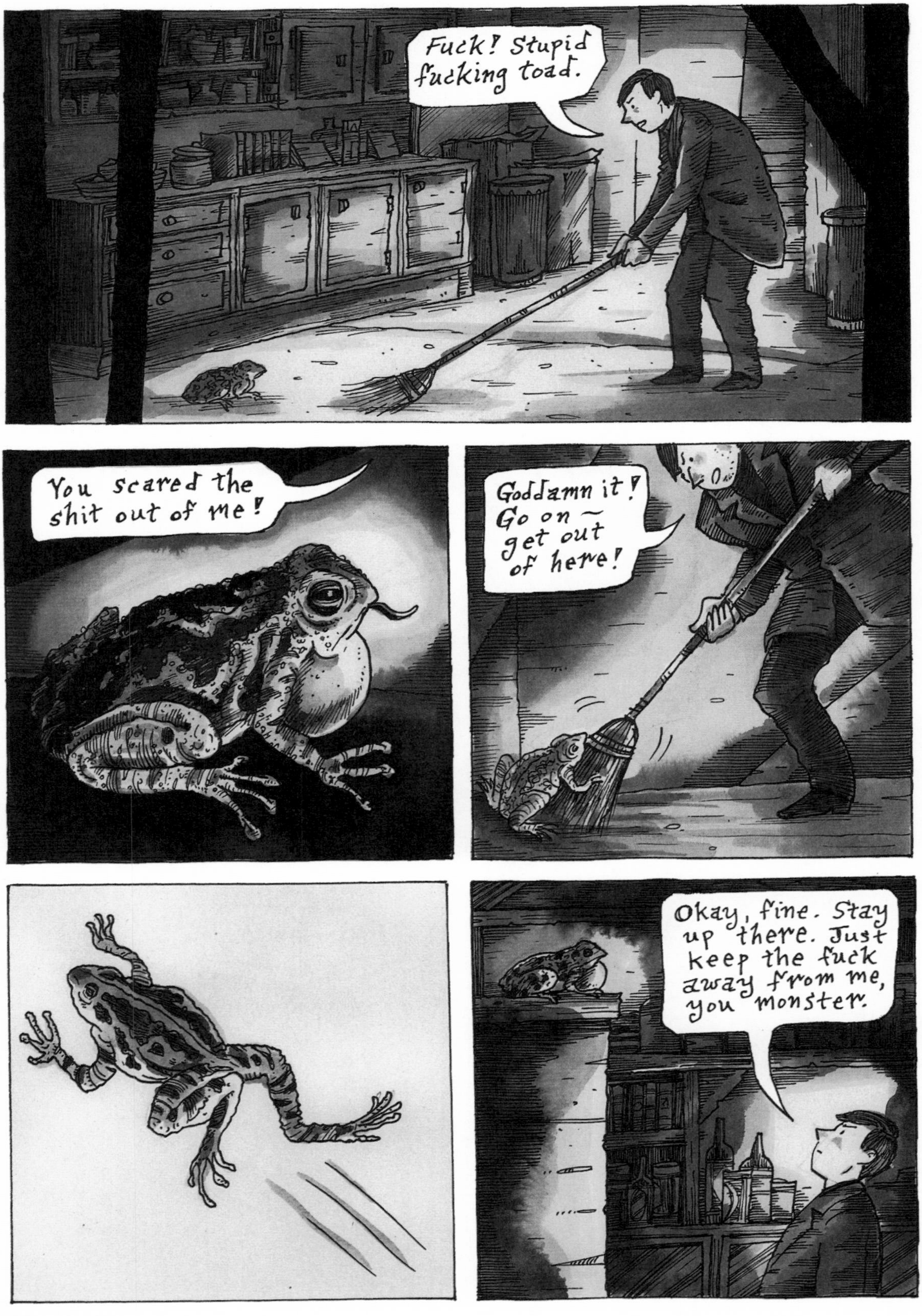
Fuck! Stupid fucking toad.
You scared the shit out of me!
Goddamn it! Go on ~ get out of here!
Okay, fine. Stay up there. Just keep the fuck away from me, you monster.

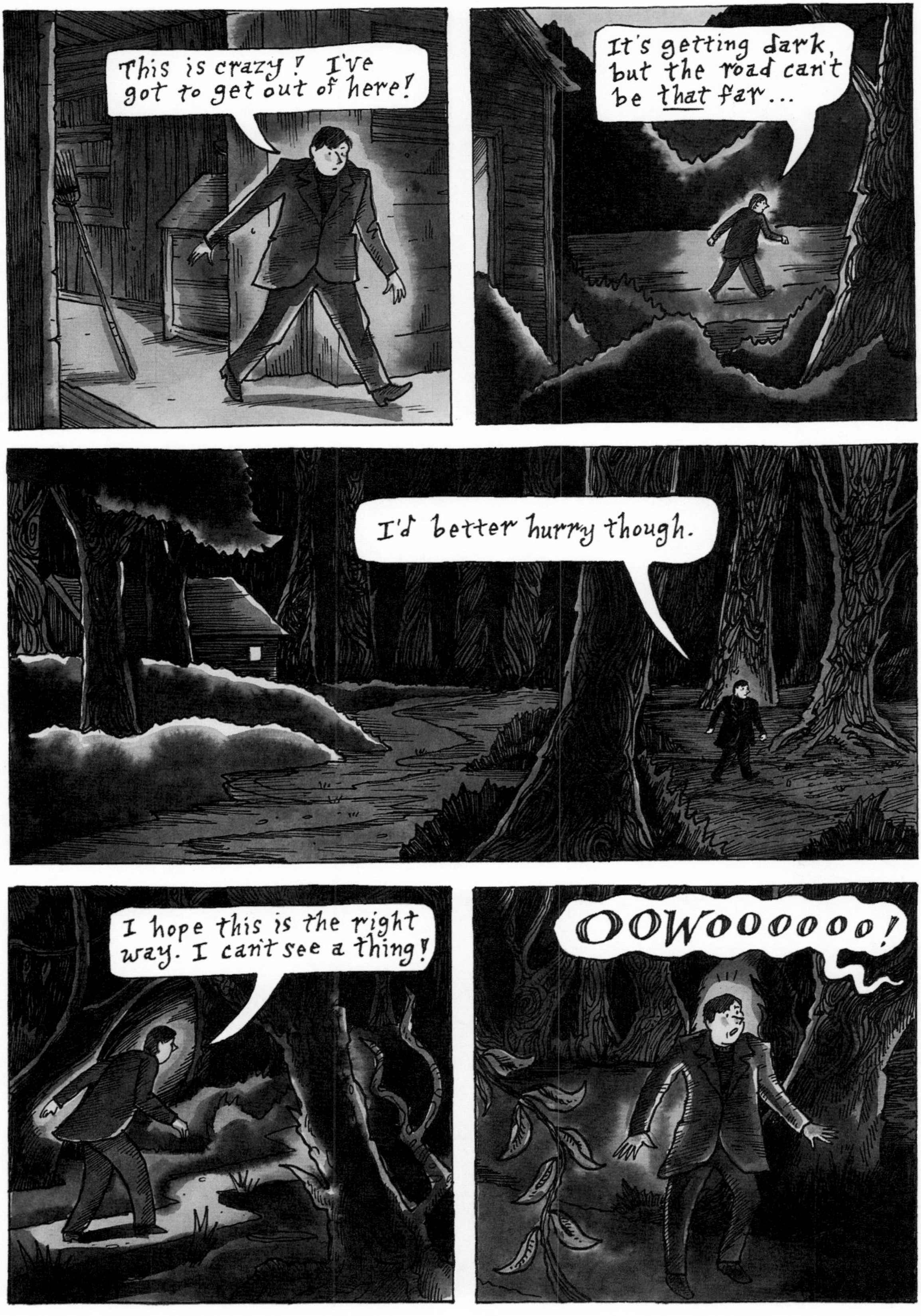
This is crazy! I've got to get out of here!
It's getting dark, but the road can't be that far...
I'd better hurry though.
I hope this is the right way. I can't see a thing!
OOWoooooo!

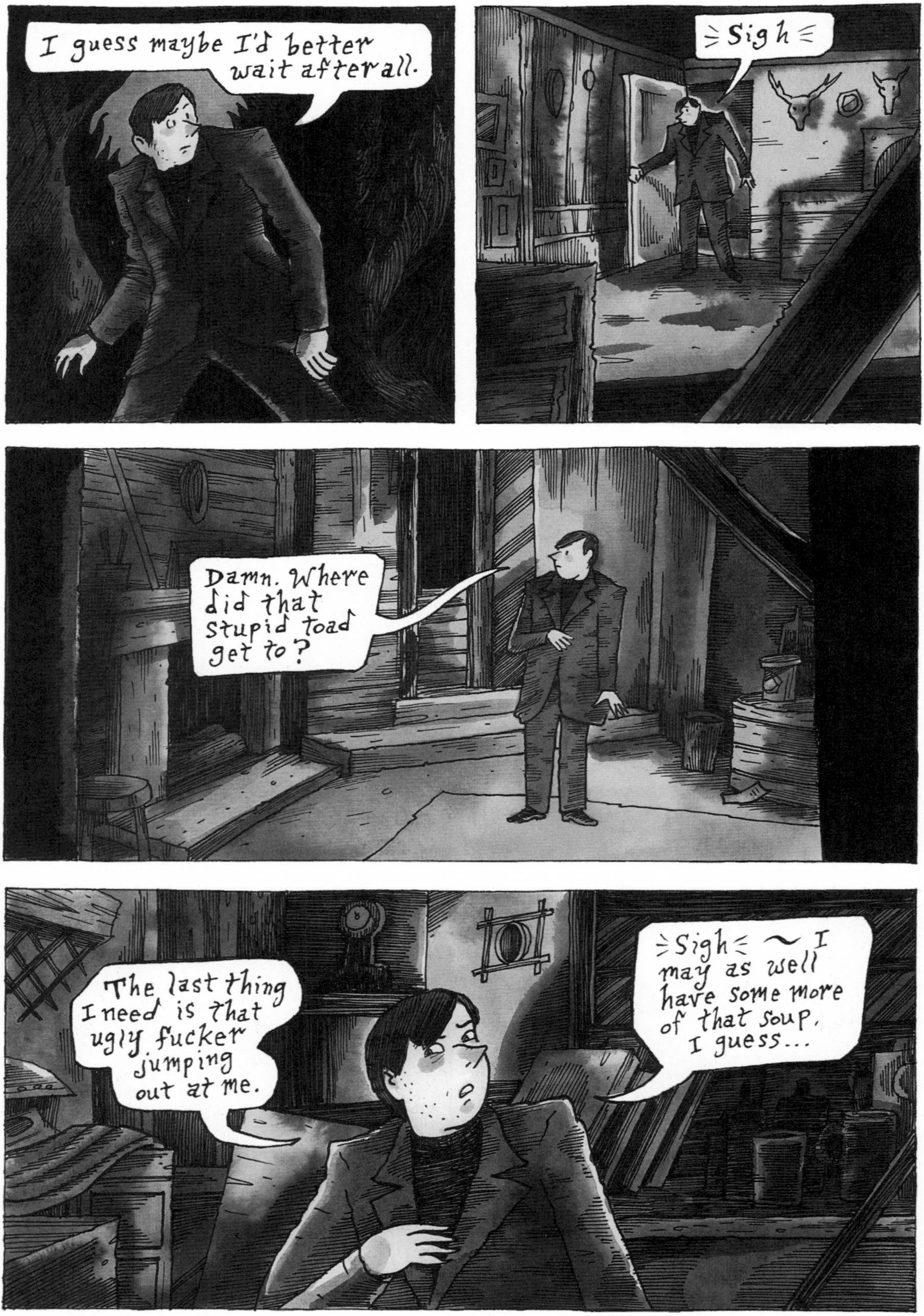
I guess maybe I'd better wait after all.
Sigh
Damn. Where did that stupid toad get to?
The last thing I need is that ugly fucker jumping out at me.
Sigh ~ I may as well have some more of that soup, I guess...

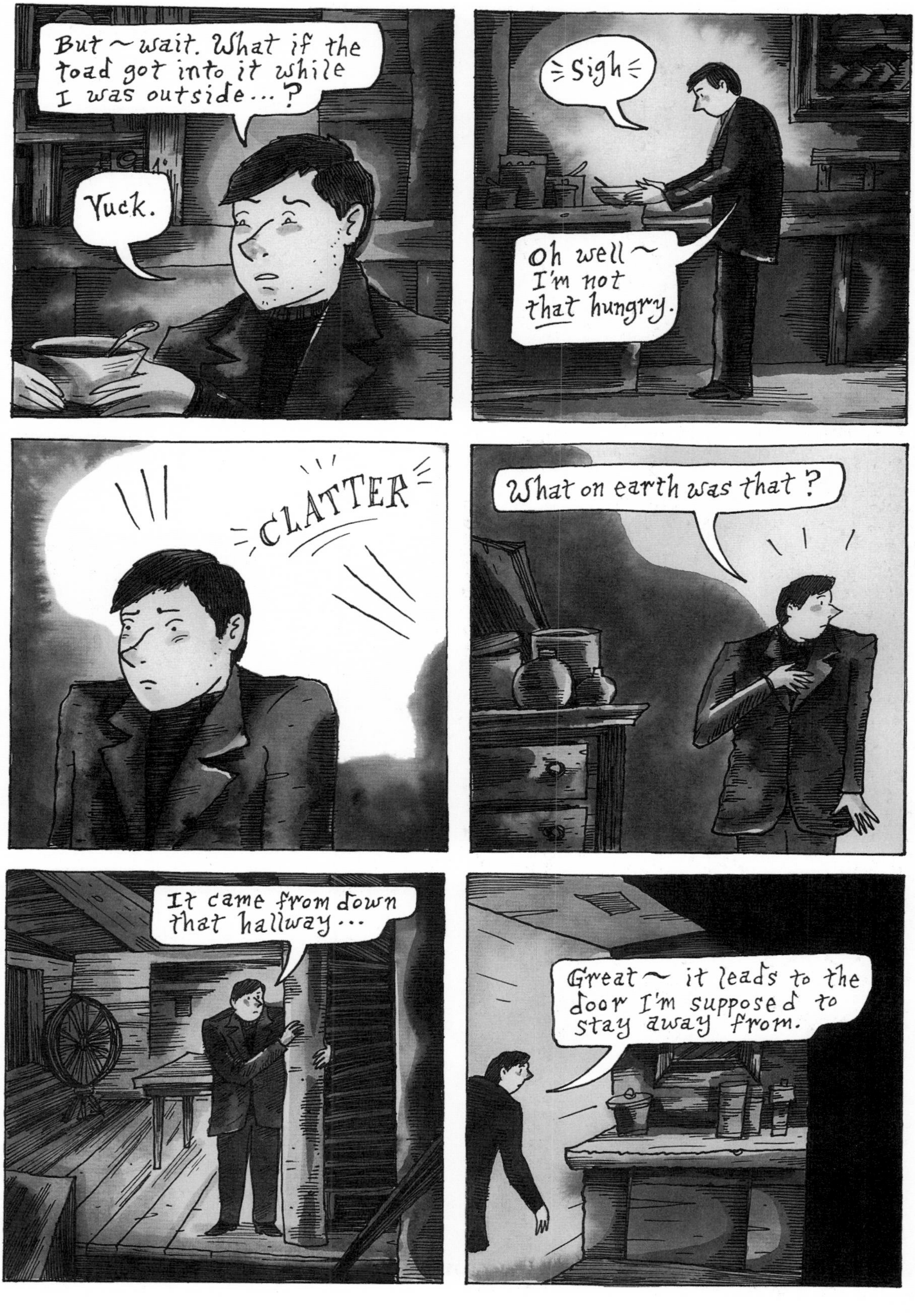
But ~ wait. What if the toad got into it while I was outside...?
Yuck.
Sigh
Oh well ~ I'm not that hungry.
CLATTER
What on earth was that?
It came from down that hallway...
Great ~ it leads to the door I'm supposed to stay away from.

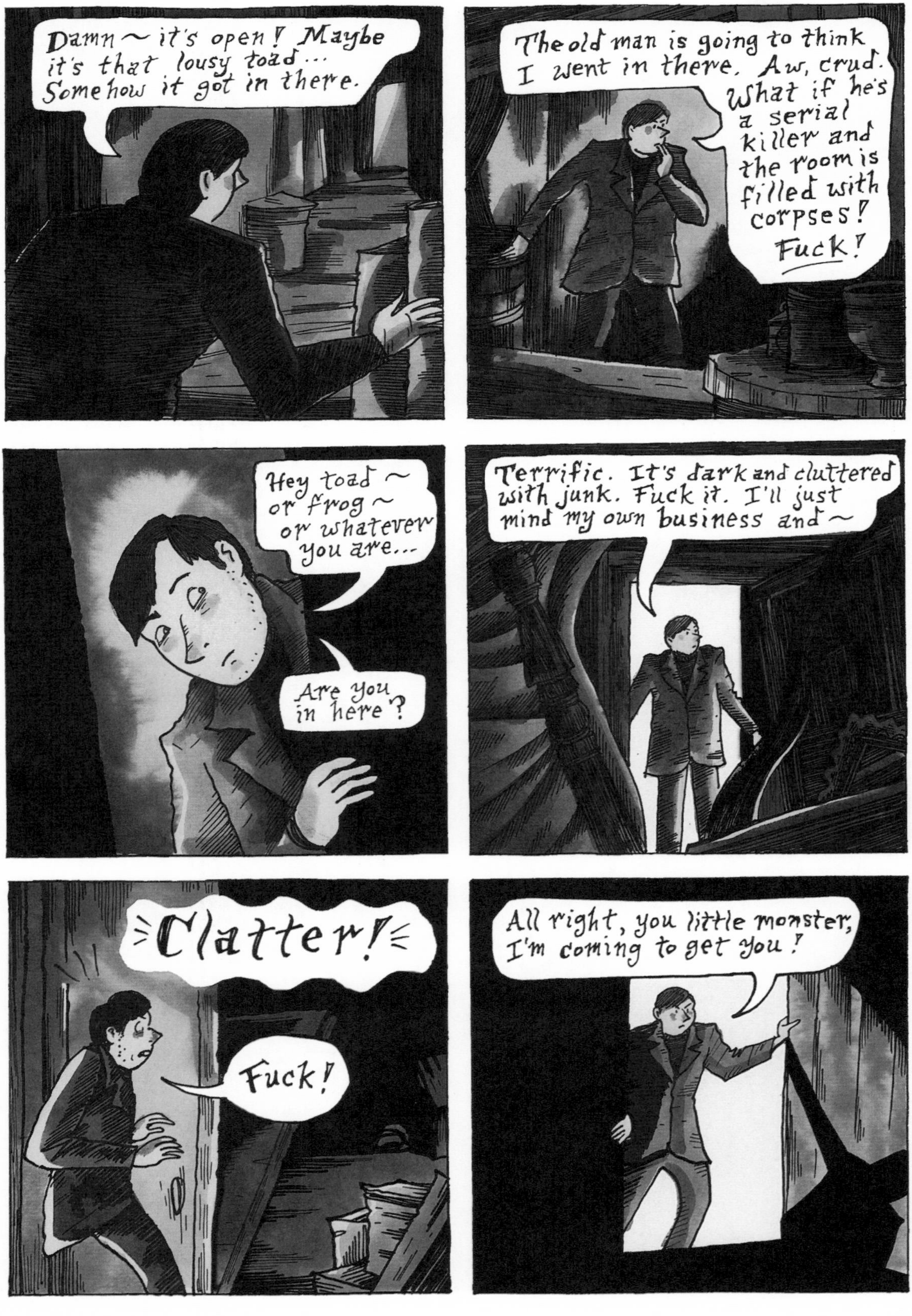
Damn ~ it's open! Maybe it's that lousy toad... Somehow it got in there.
The old man is going to think I went in there. Aw, crud.
What if he's a serial killer and the room is filled with corpses!
Fuck!
Hey toad ~ or frog ~ or whatever you are...
Are you in here?
Terrific. It's dark and cluttered with junk. Fuck it. I'll just mind my own business and ~
Clatter!
Fuck!
All right, you little monster, I'm coming to get you!

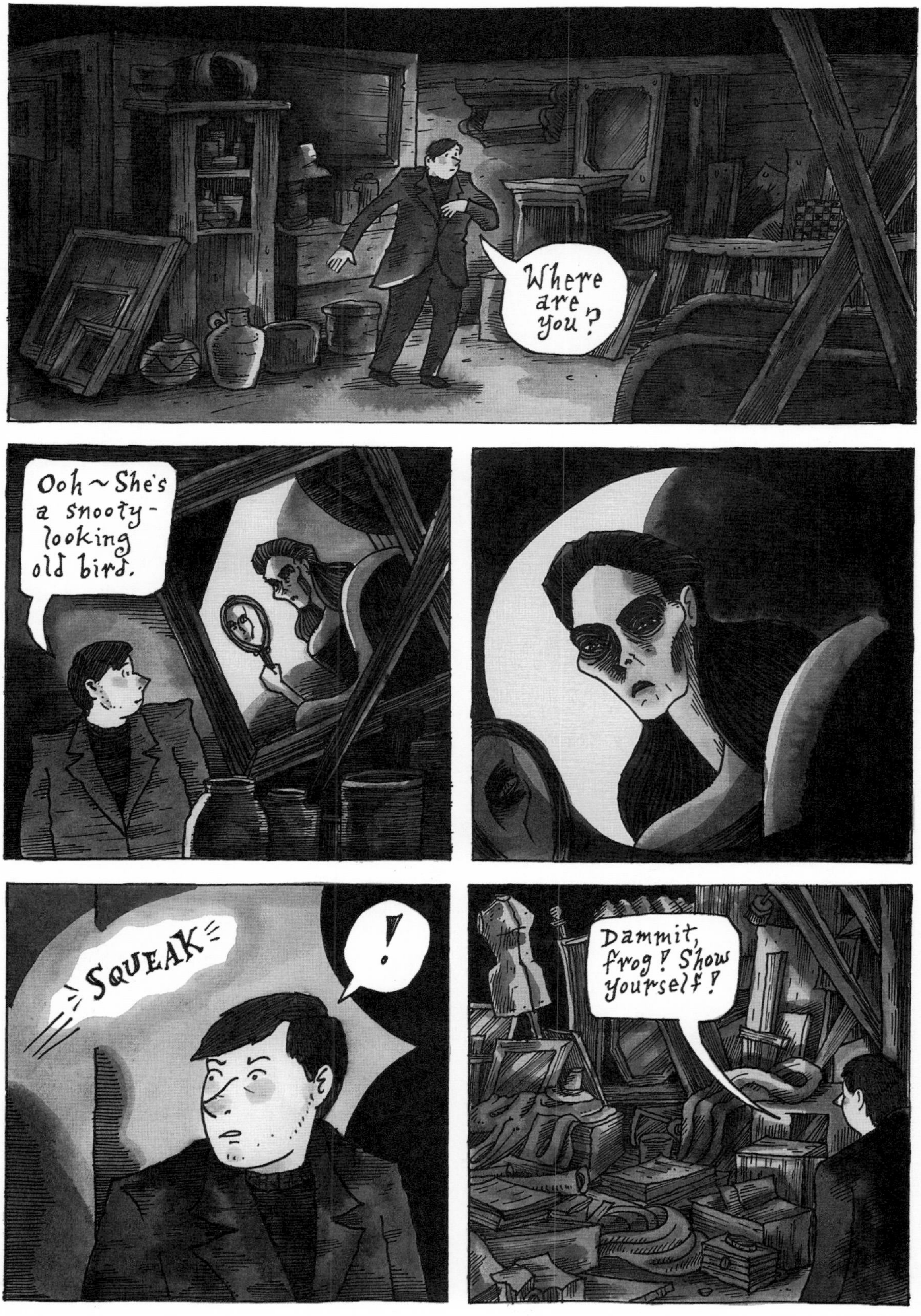
Where are you?
Ooh ~ She's a snooty-looking old bird.
SQUEAK
!
Dammit, frog! Show yourself!

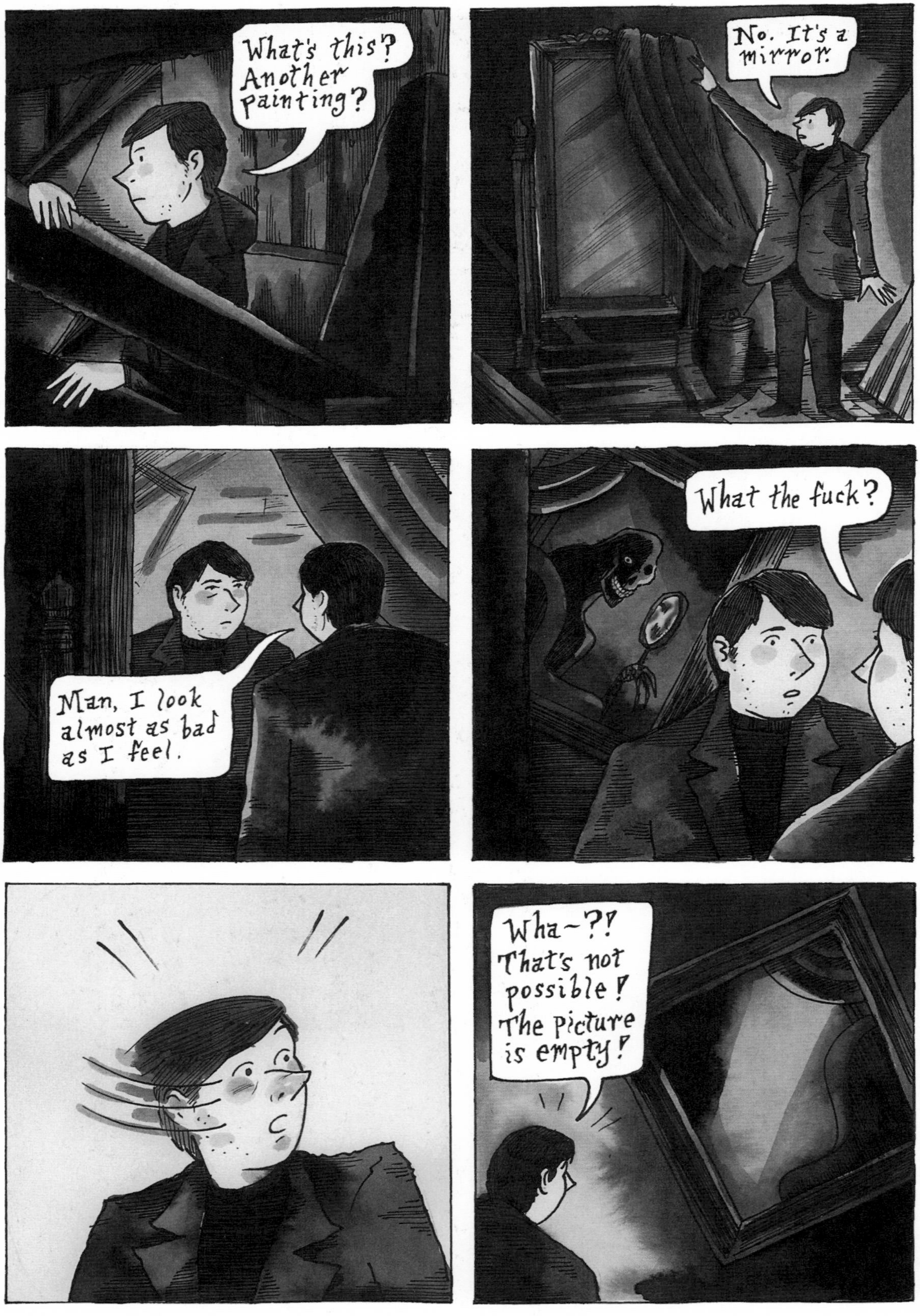
What's this? Another painting?
No. It's a mirror.
Man, I look almost as bad as I feel.
What the fuck?
Wha-?! That's not possible! The picture is empty!

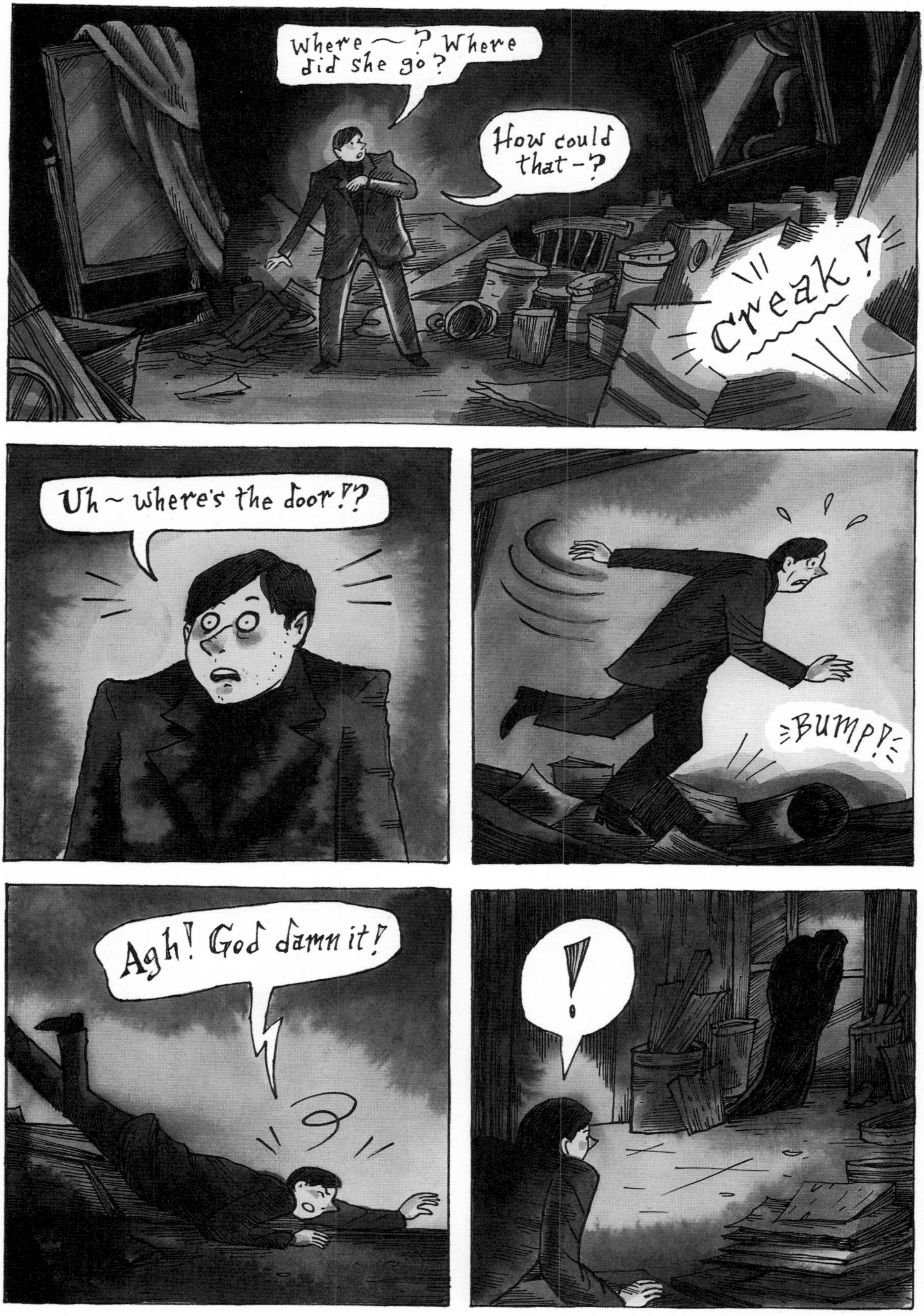
Where—? Where did she go?
How could that—?
Creak!
Uh—where's the door!?
Bump!
Agh! God damn it!
!

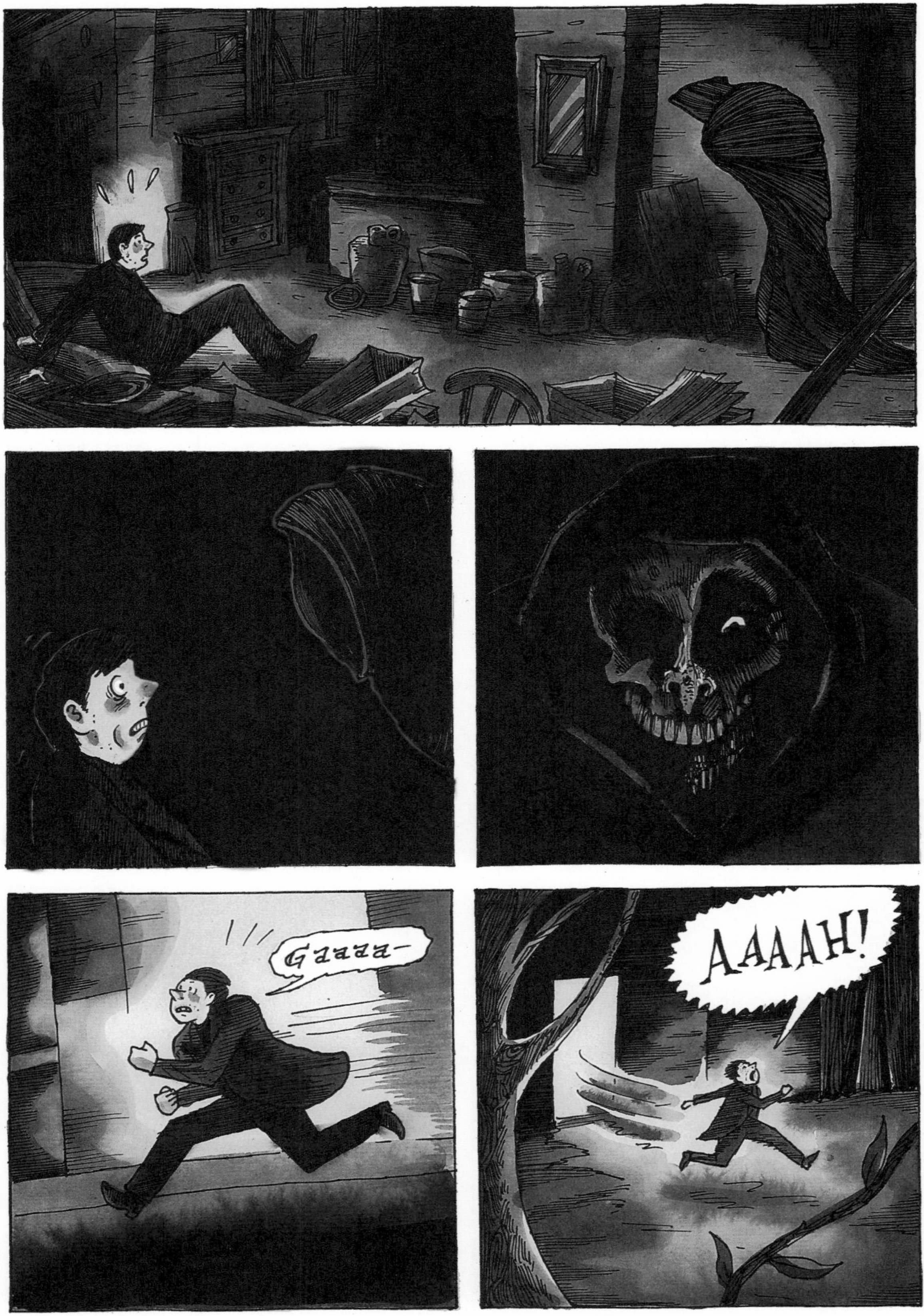
Gaaaa–
AAAAH!

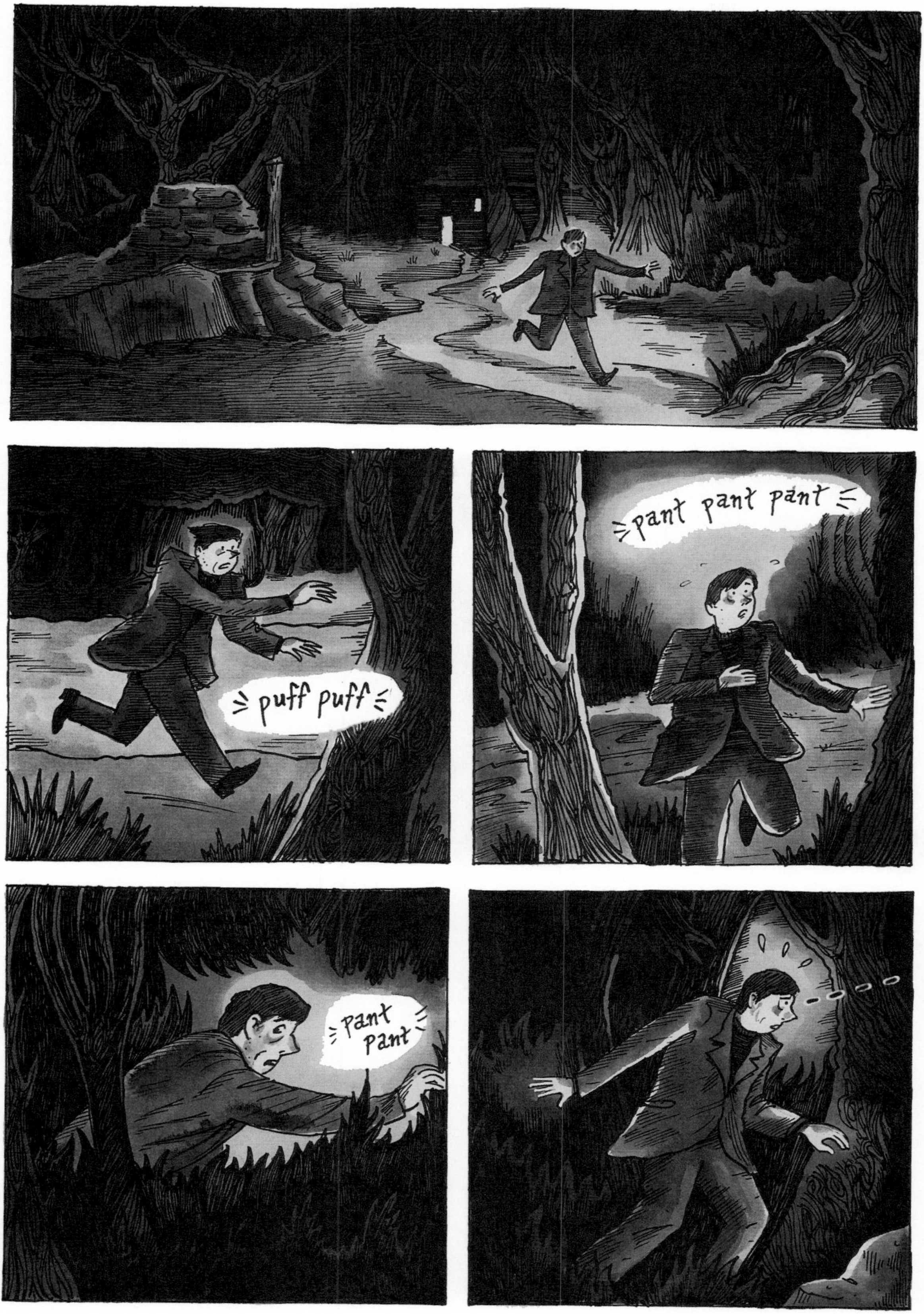
puff puff
pant pant pant
pant
pant

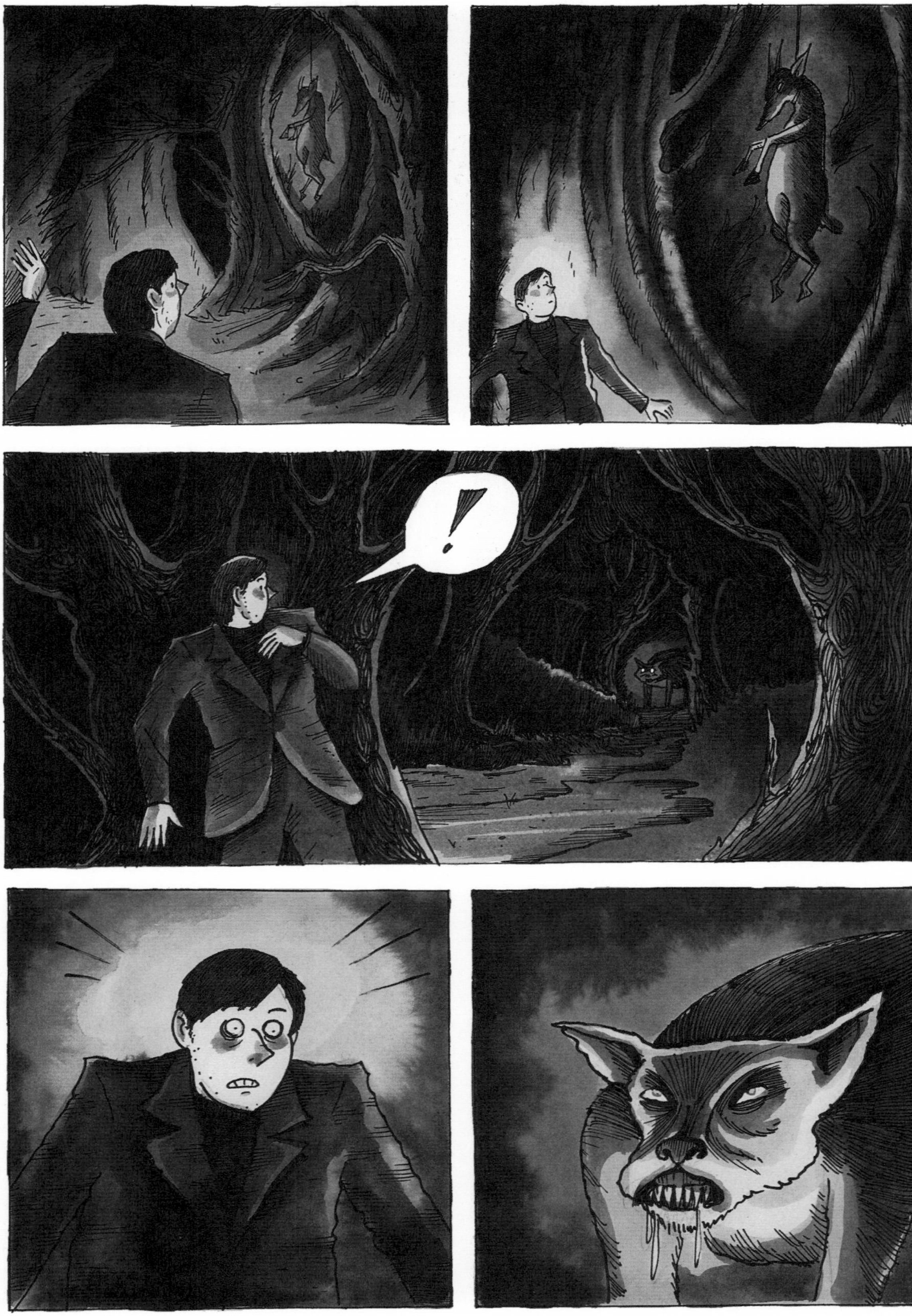
!

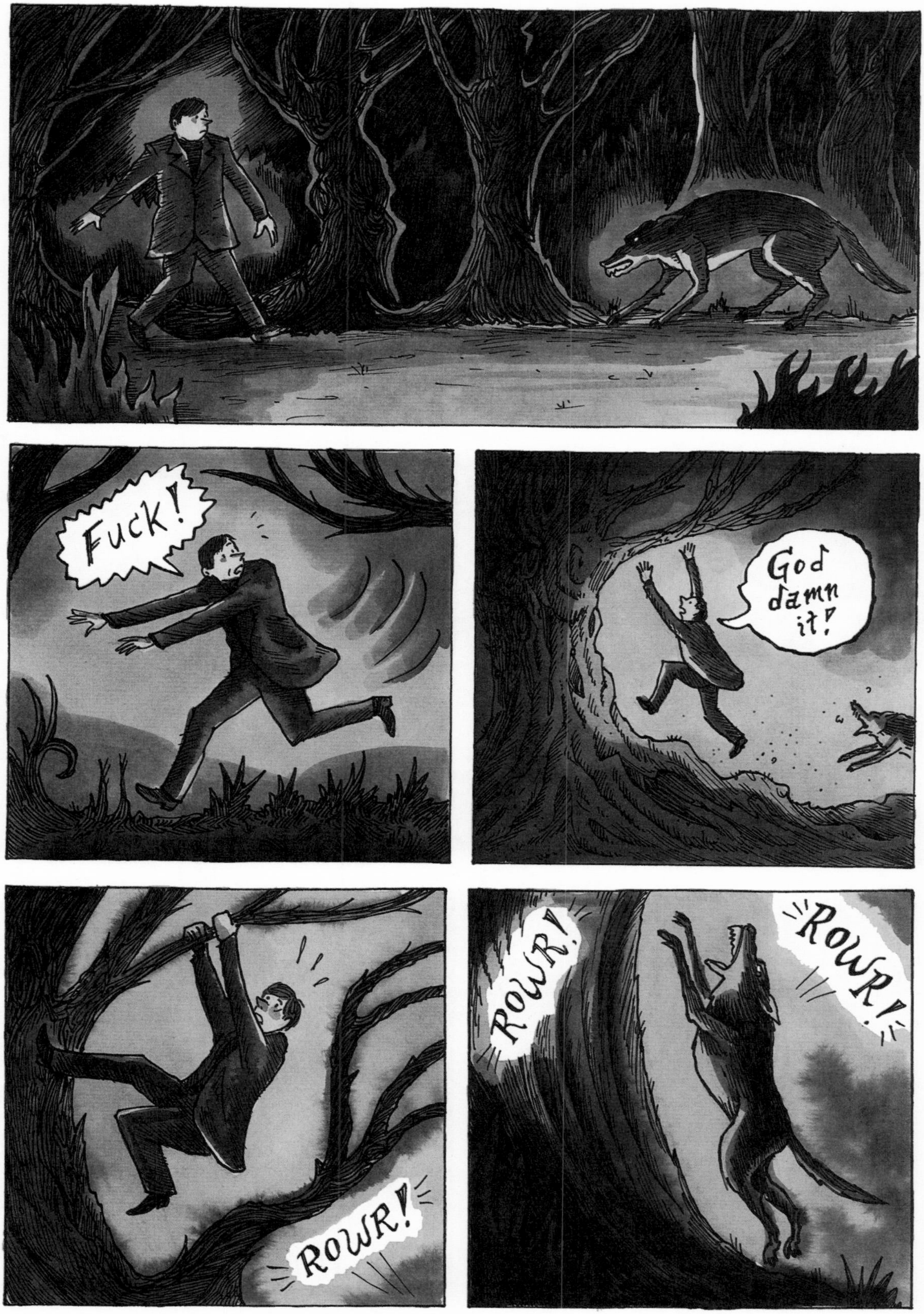
Fuck!
God damn it!
ROWR!
ROWR!
ROWR!

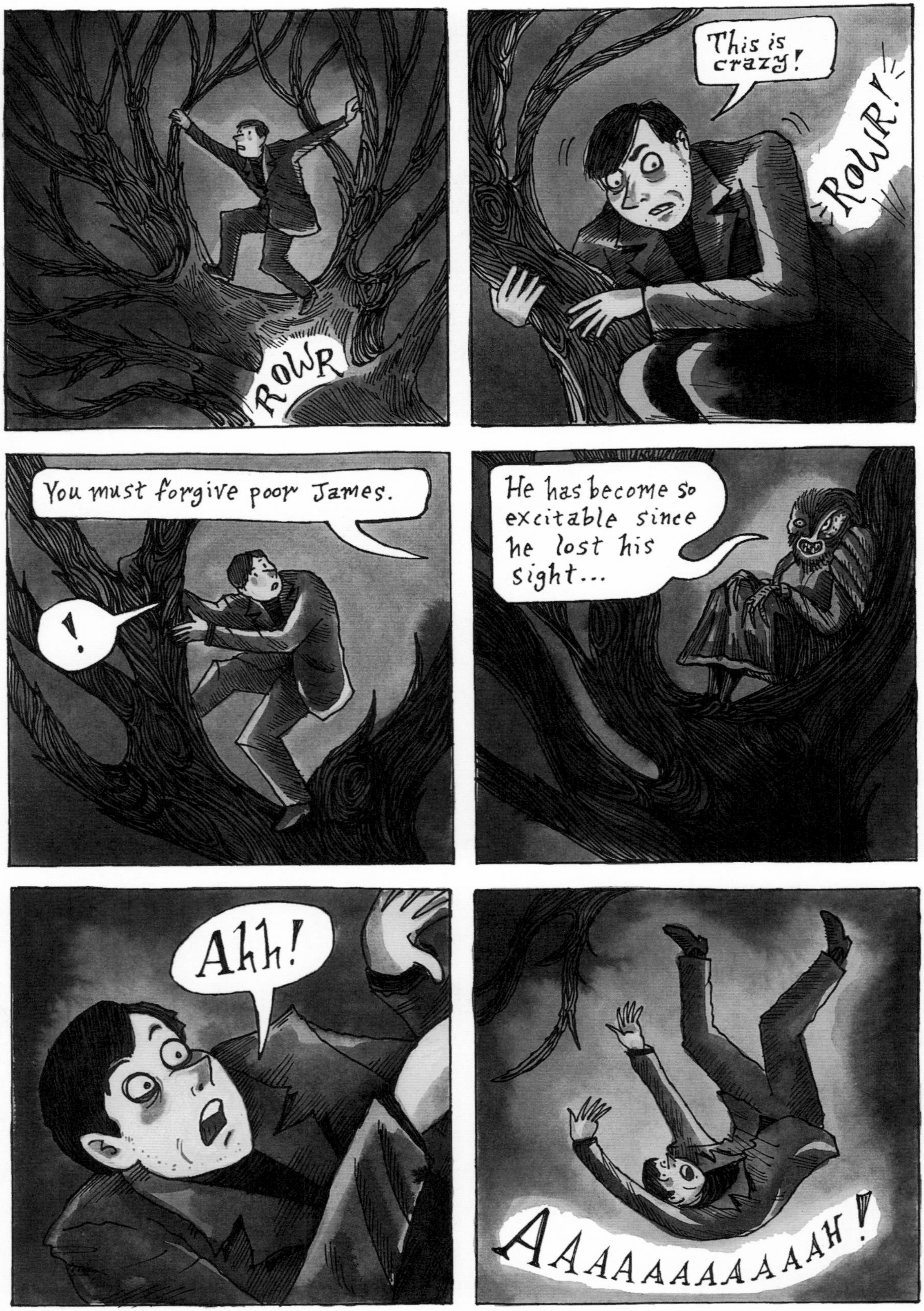
ROWR
This is crazy!
ROWR!
You must forgive poor James.
!
He has become so excitable since he lost his sight...
Ahh!
AAAAAAAAAAAH!

3.
The Dog

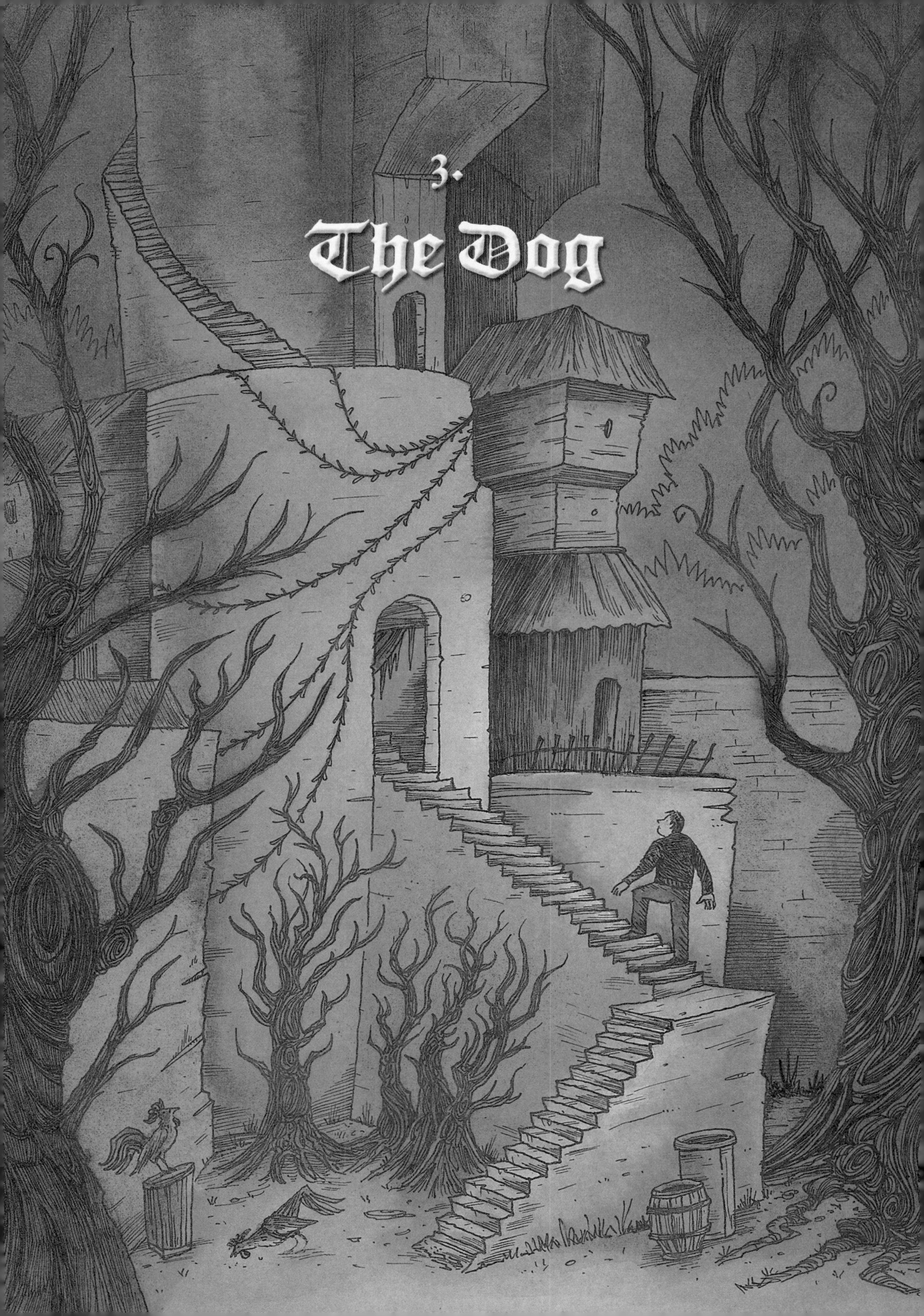

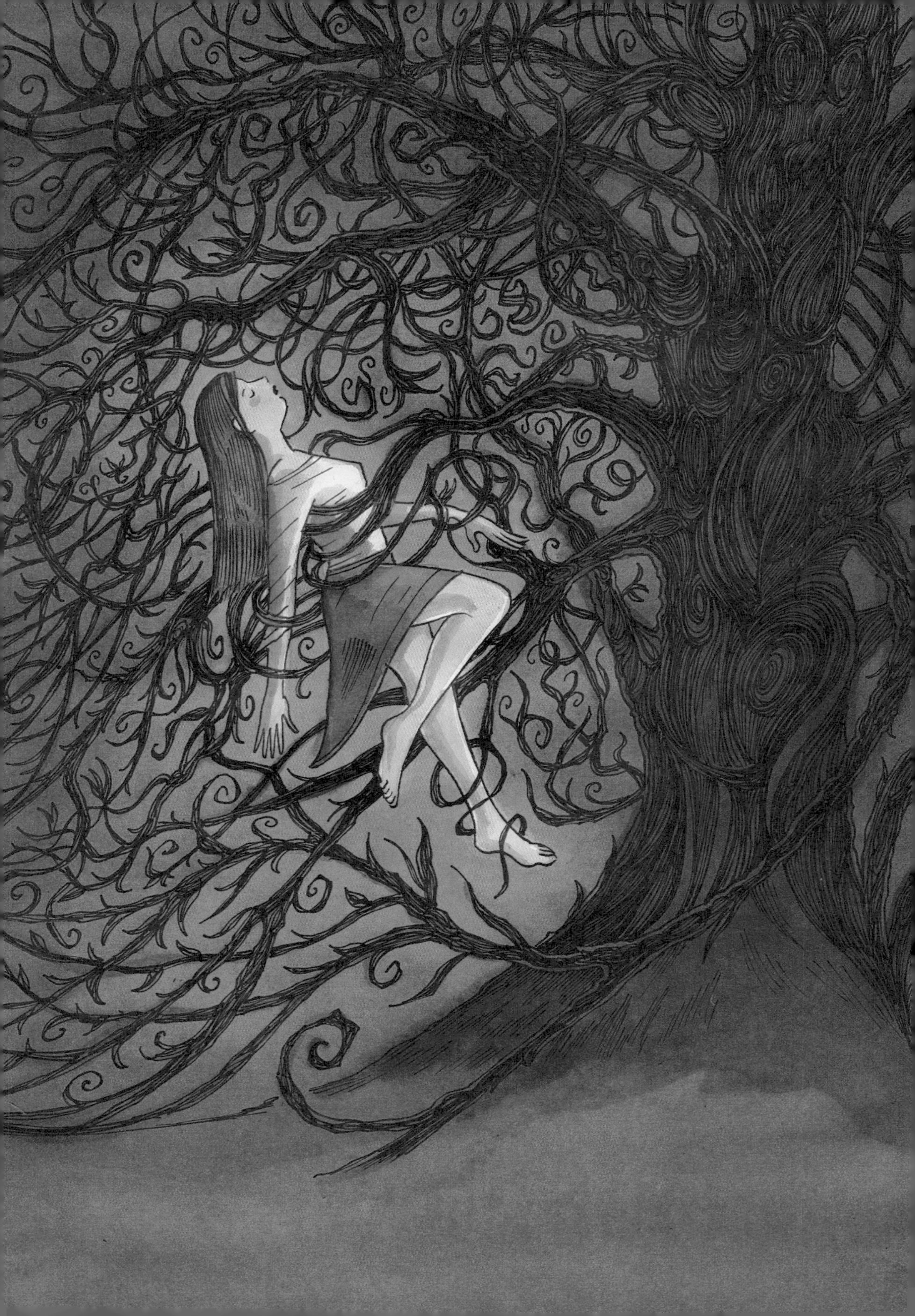

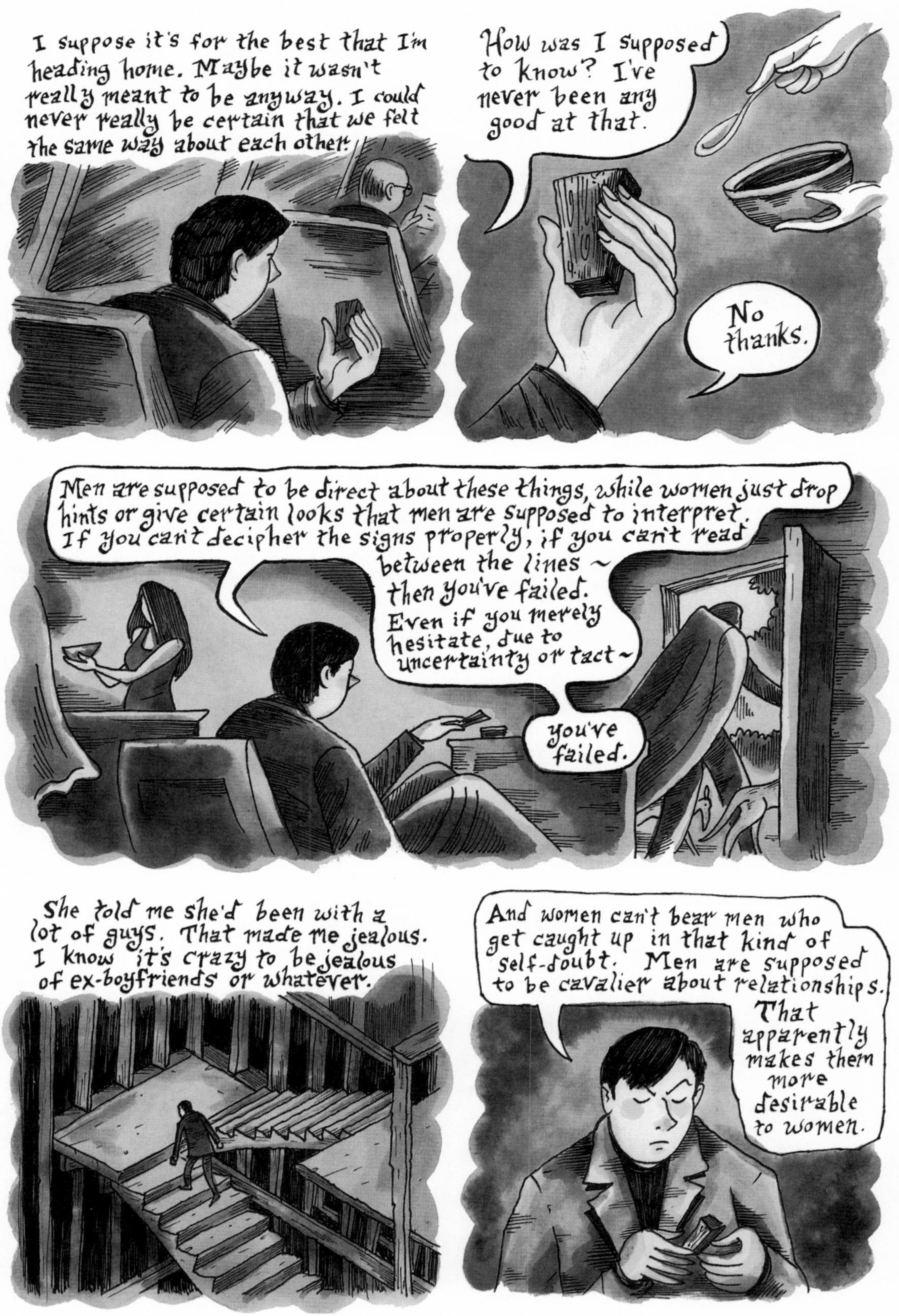
I suppose it's for the best that I'm heading home. Maybe it wasn't really meant to be anyway. I could never really be certain that we felt the same way about each other.
How was I supposed to know? I've never been any good at that.
No thanks.
Men are supposed to be direct about these things, while women just drop hints or give certain looks that men are supposed to interpret. If you can't decipher the signs properly, if you can't read between the lines ~ then you've failed. Even if you merely hesitate, due to uncertainty or tact ~
you've failed.
She told me she'd been with a lot of guys. That made me jealous. I know it's crazy to be jealous of ex-boyfriends or whatever.
And women can't bear men who get caught up in that kind of self-doubt. Men are supposed to be cavalier about relationships.
That apparently makes them more desirable to women.

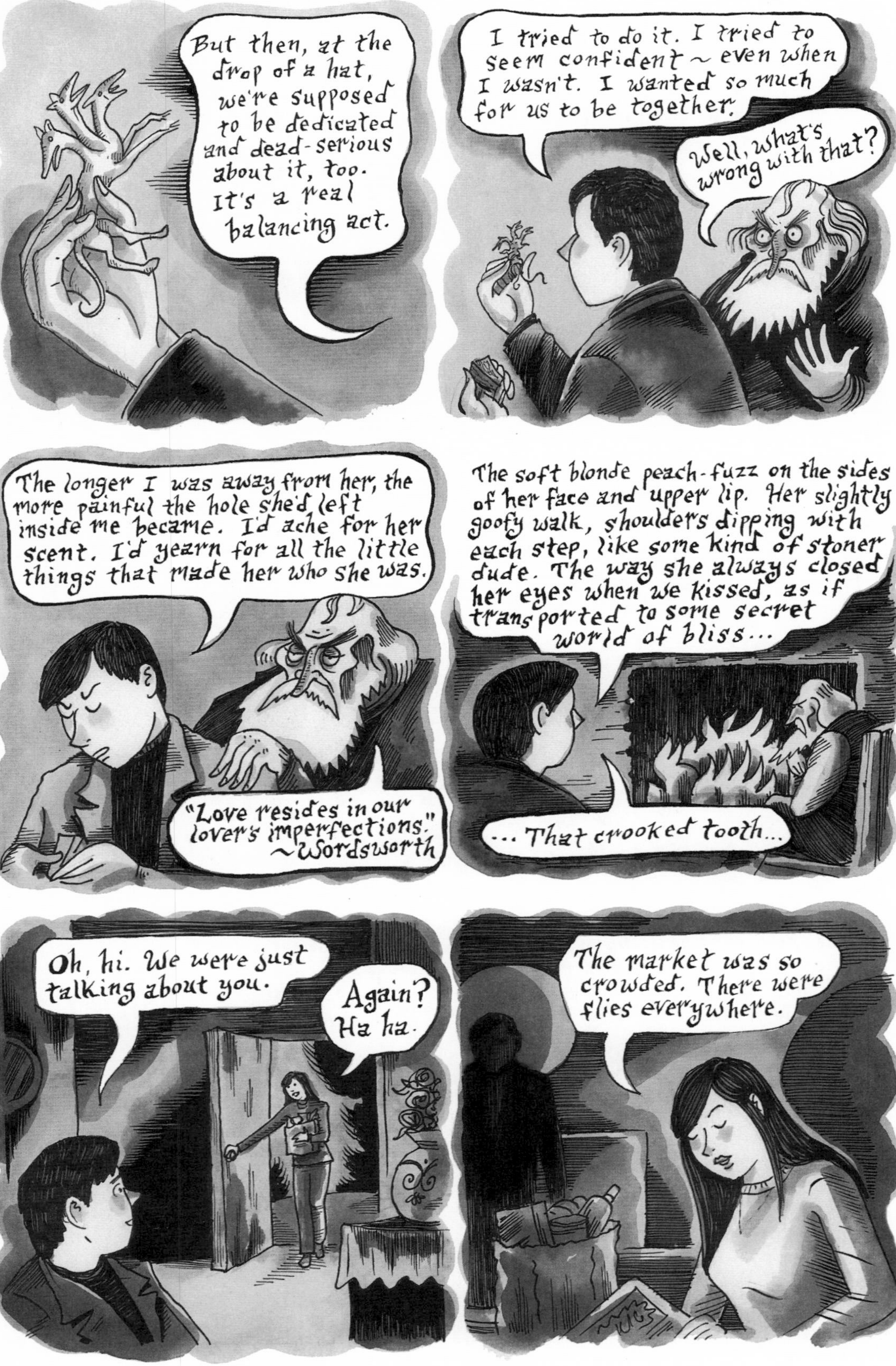
But then, at the drop of a hat, we're supposed to be dedicated and dead-serious about it, too. It's a real balancing act.
I tried to do it. I tried to seem confident ~ even when I wasn't. I wanted so much for us to be together.
Well, what's wrong with that?
The longer I was away from her, the more painful the hole she'd left inside me became. I'd ache for her scent. I'd yearn for all the little things that made her who she was.
"Love resides in our lover's imperfections." ~Wordsworth
The soft blonde peach-fuzz on the sides of her face and upper lip. Her slightly goofy walk, shoulders dipping with each step, like some kind of stoner dude. The way she always closed her eyes when we kissed, as if transported to some secret world of bliss...
... That crooked tooth...
Oh, hi. We were just talking about you.
Again? Ha ha.
The market was so crowded. There were flies everywhere.

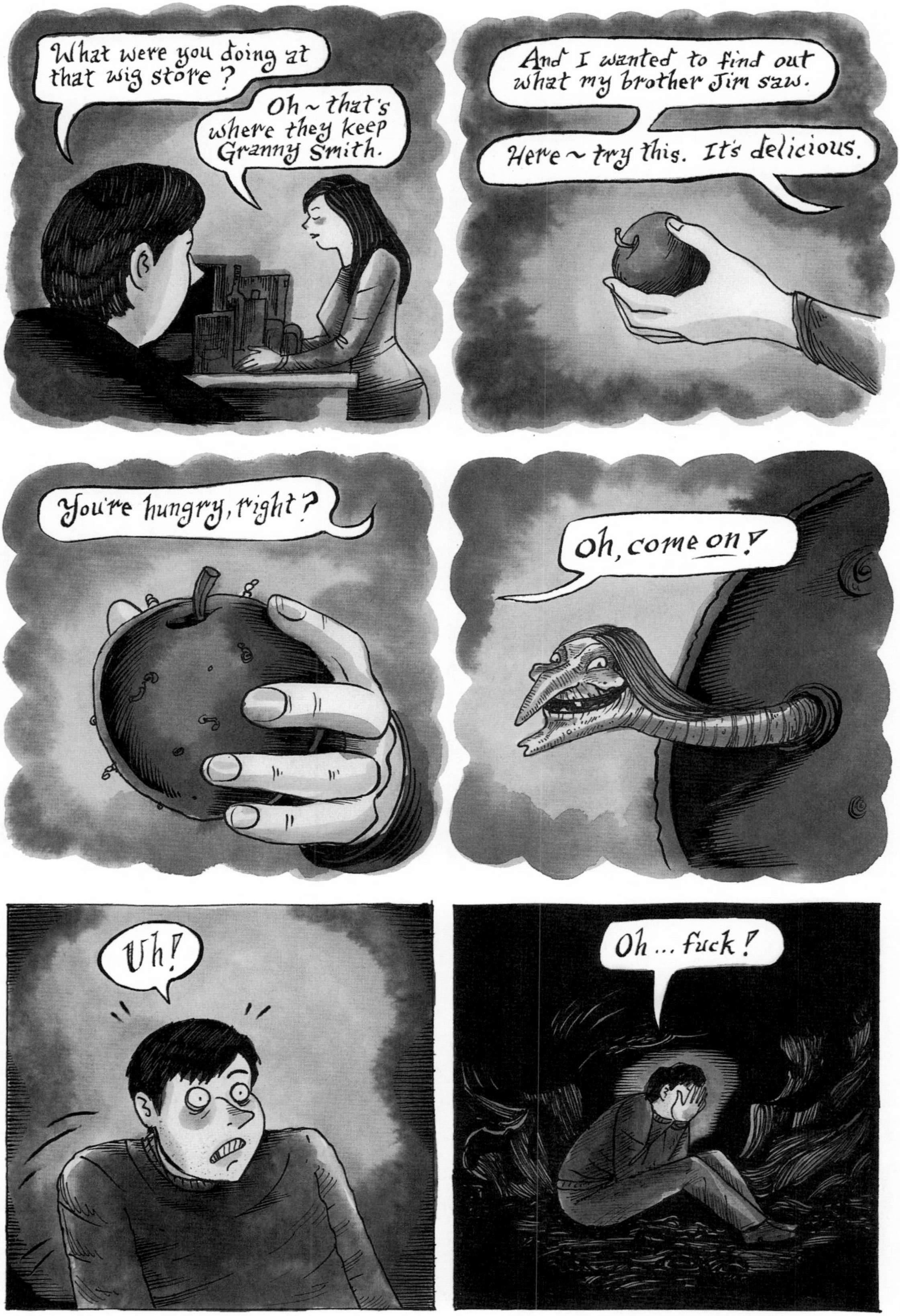
What were you doing at that wig store?
Oh ~ that's where they keep Granny Smith.
And I wanted to find out what my brother Jim saw.
Here ~ try this. It's delicious.
You're hungry, right?
Oh, come on!
Uh!
Oh ... fuck!

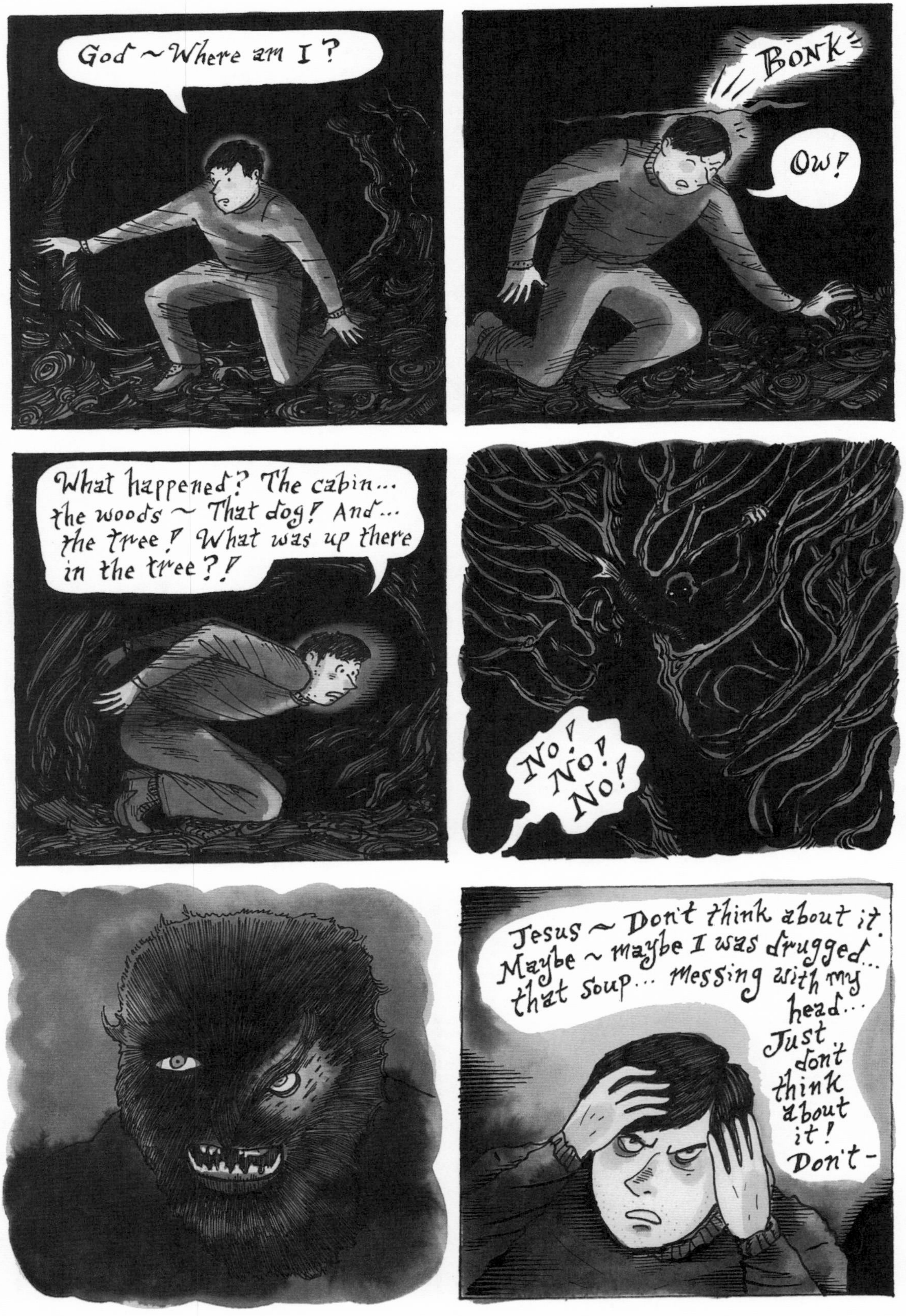
God ~ Where am I?
BONK
Ow!
What happened? The cabin... the woods ~ That dog! And... the tree! What was up there in the tree?!
No! No! No!
Jesus ~ Don't think about it. Maybe ~ maybe I was drugged... that soup... messing with my head... Just don't think about it! Don't-

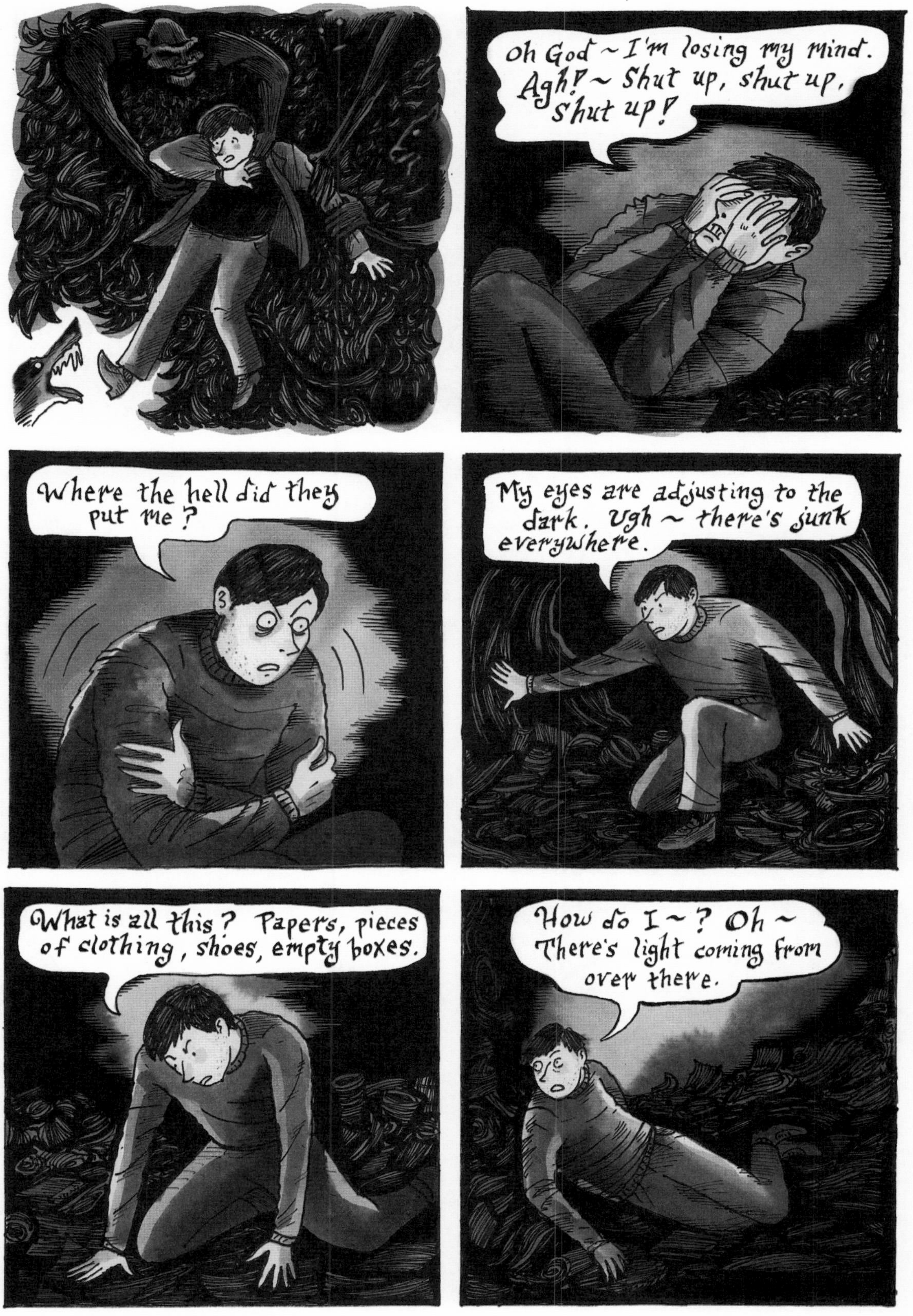
Oh God ~ I'm losing my mind. Agh! ~ Shut up, shut up, shut up!
Where the hell did they put me?
My eyes are adjusting to the dark. Ugh ~ there's junk everywhere.
What is all this? Papers, pieces of clothing, shoes, empty boxes.
How do I ~? Oh ~ There's light coming from over there.

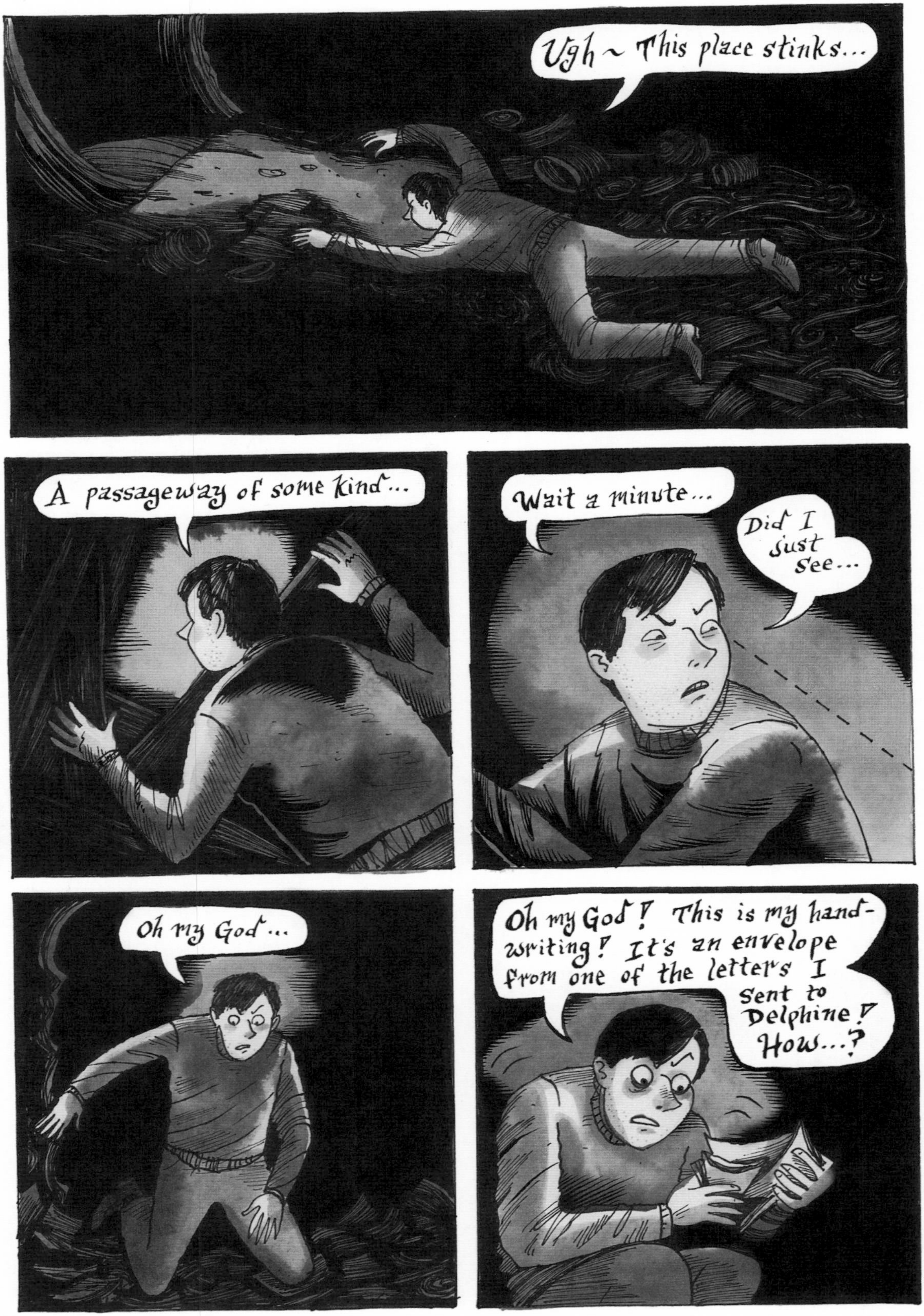
Ugh ~ This place stinks...
A passageway of some kind...
Wait a minute...
Did I just see...
Oh my God...
Oh my God! This is my hand-writing! It's an envelope from one of the letters I sent to Delphine! How...?

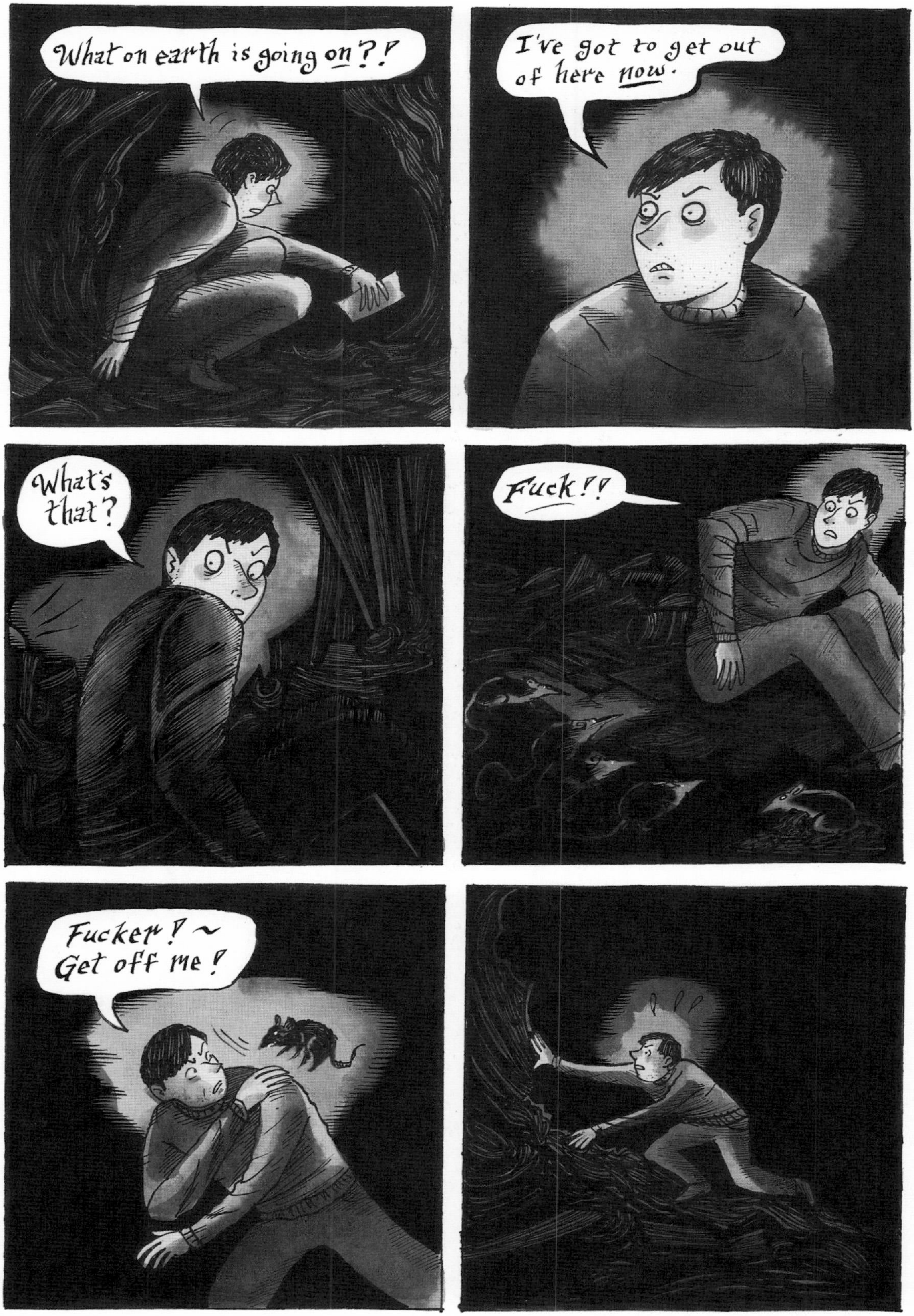
What on earth is going on?!
I've got to get out of here now.
What's that?
Fuck!!
Fucker! ~ Get off me!

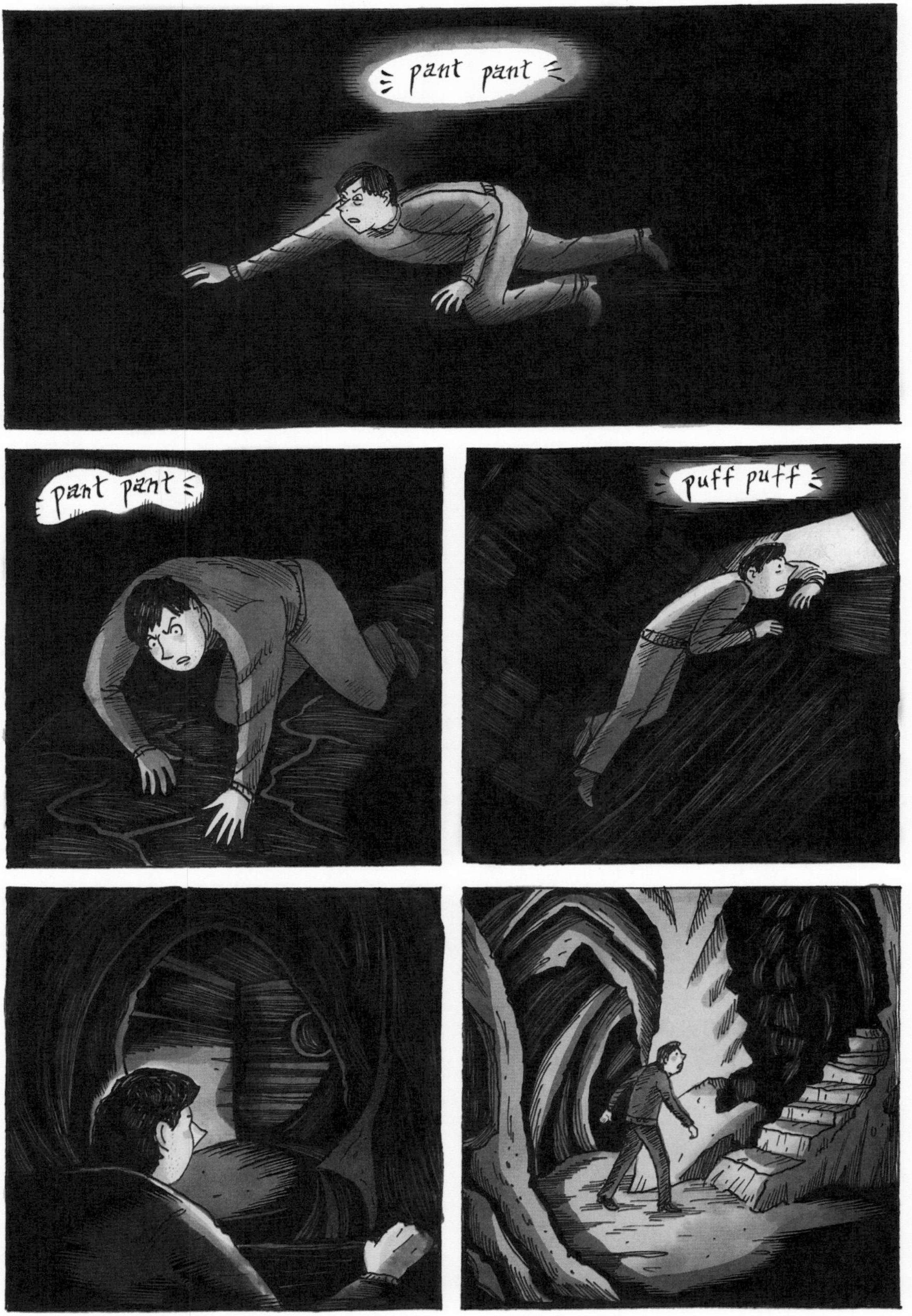
pant pant
pant pant
puff puff

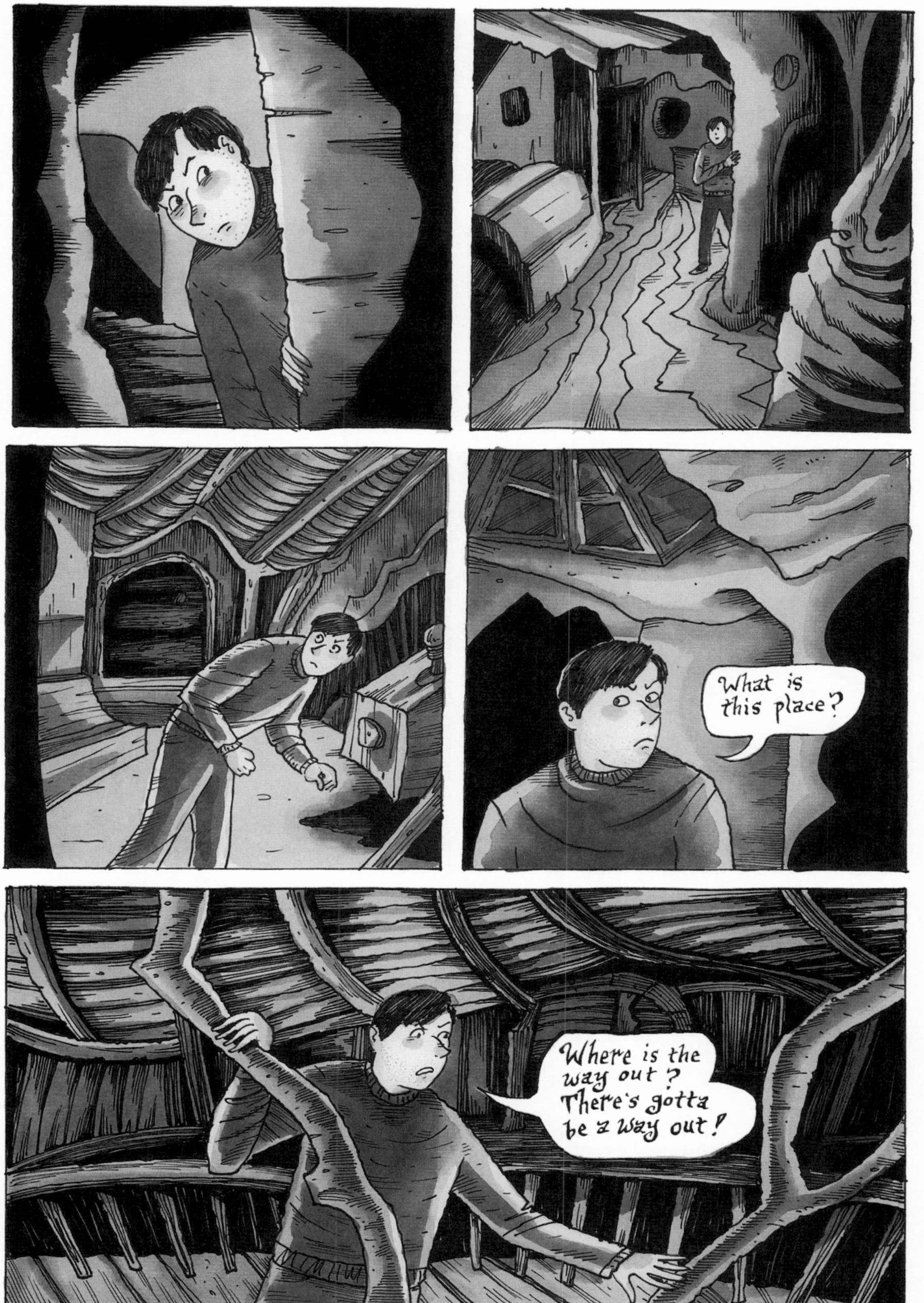
What is this place?
Where is the way out? There's gotta be a way out!

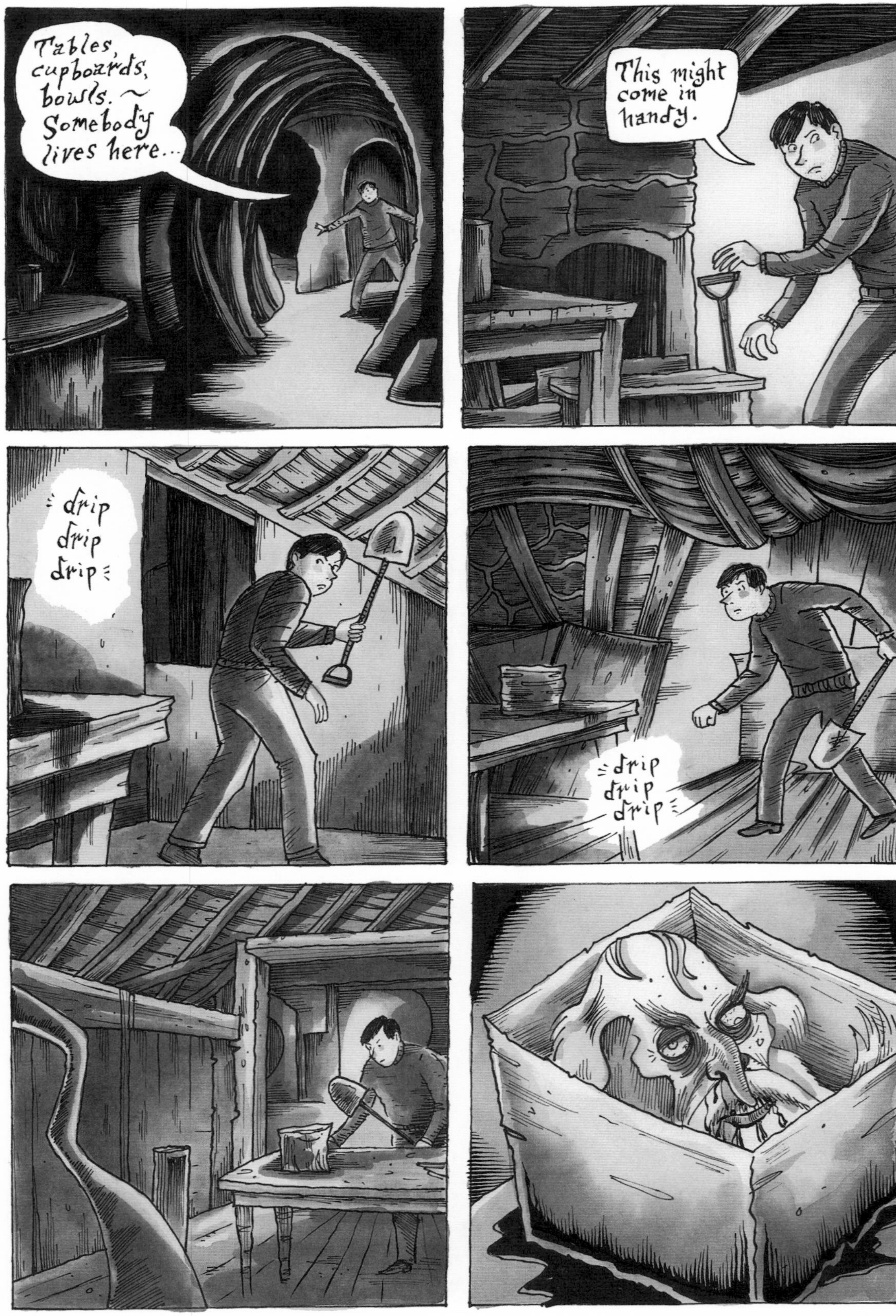
Tables, cupboards, bowls. ~ Somebody lives here...
This might come in handy.
drip drip drip
drip drip drip

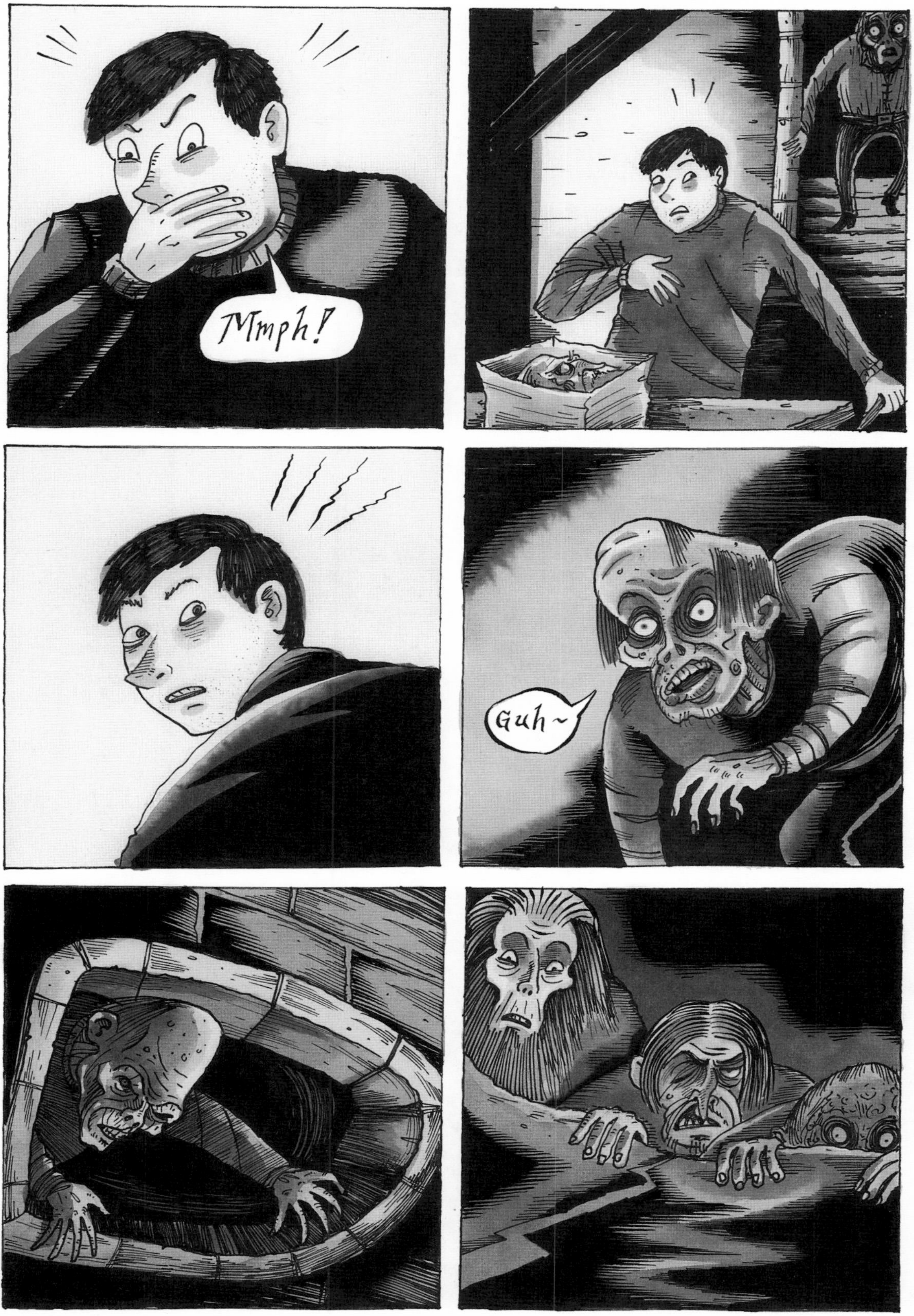
Mmph!
Guh~

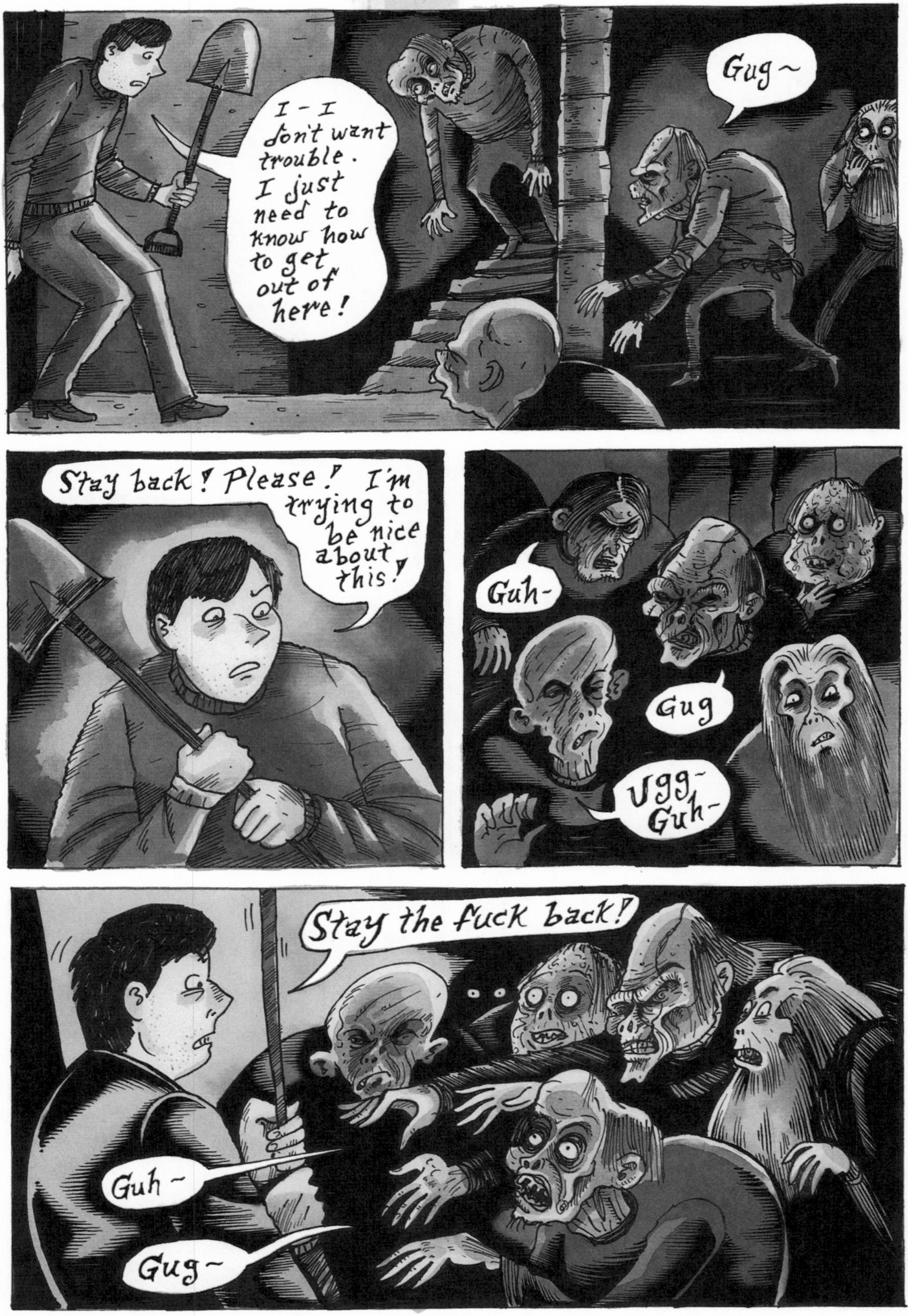
I - I don't want trouble. I just need to know how to get out of here!
Gug ~
Stay back! Please! I'm trying to be nice about this!
Guh-
Gug
Ugg-Guh-
Stay the fuck back!
Guh ~
Gug ~

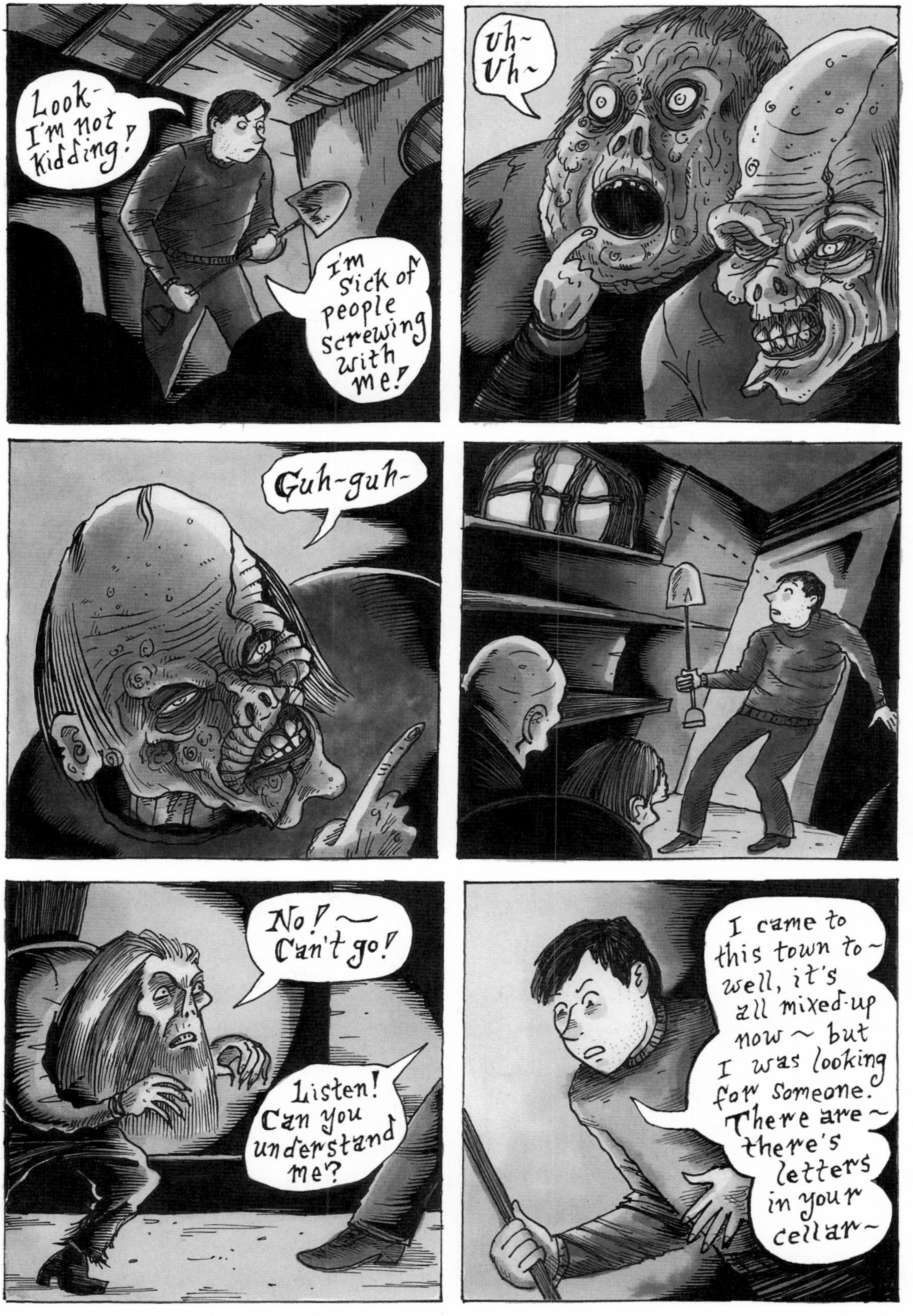
Look- I'm not kidding!
I'm sick of people screwing with me!
Uh- Uh-
Guh-guh-
No!~ Can't go!
Listen! Can you understand me?
I came to this town to~ well, it's all mixed-up now~ but I was looking for someone. There are~ there's letters in your cellar~

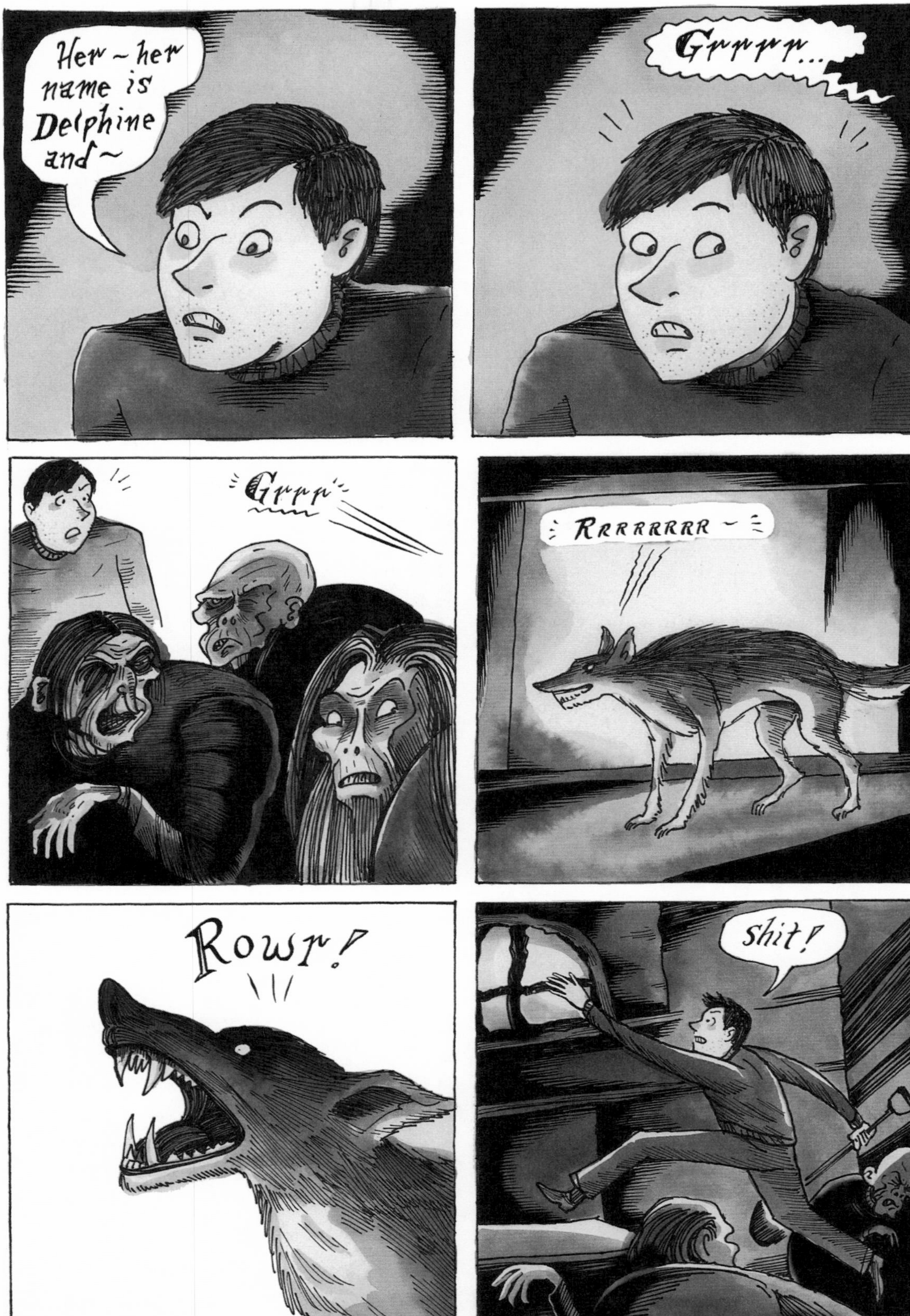
Her~her name is Delphine and~
Grrrrr...
Grrr
Rrrrrrrr~
Rowr!
shit!

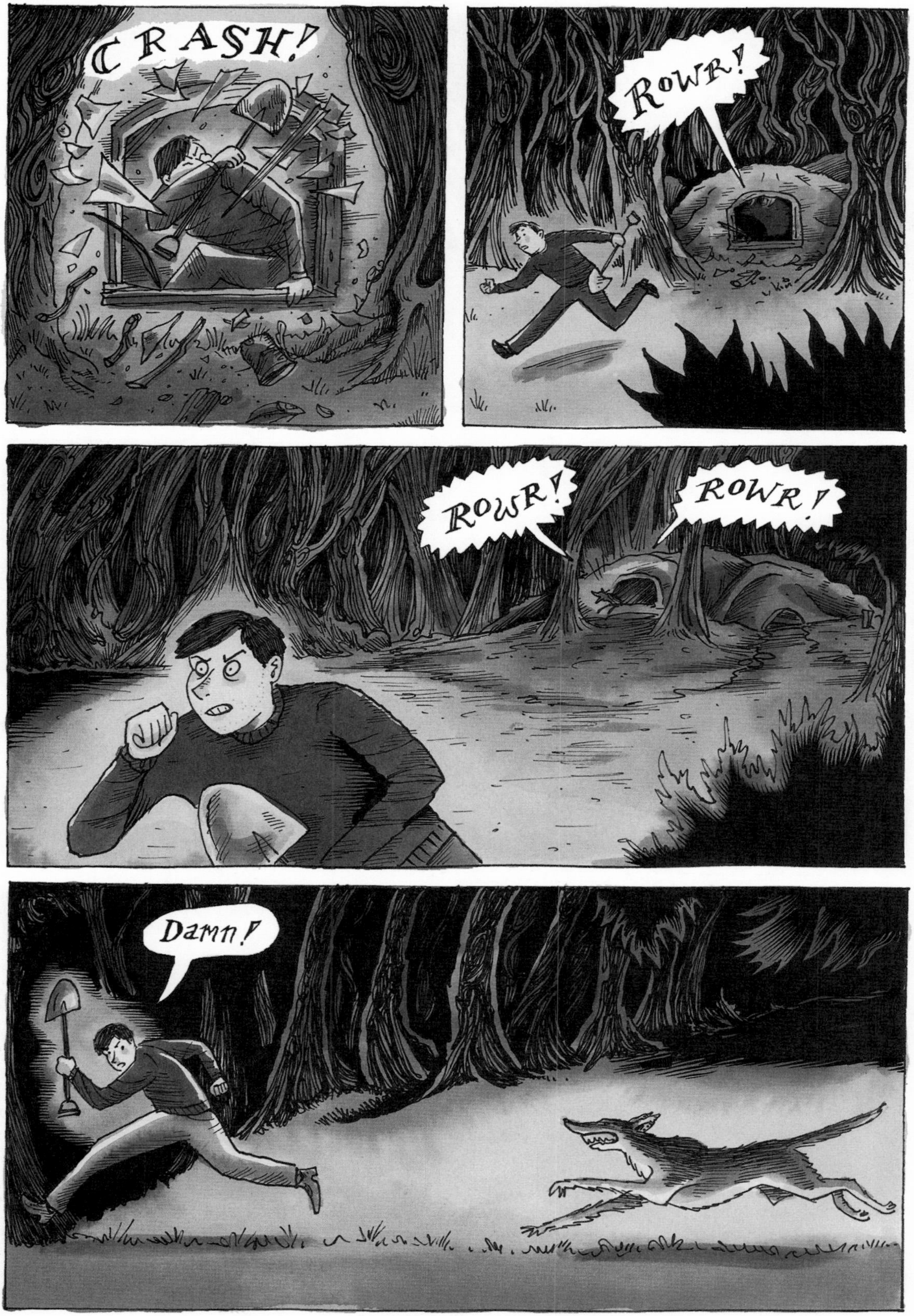
CRASH!
ROWR!
ROWR!
ROWR!
Damn!

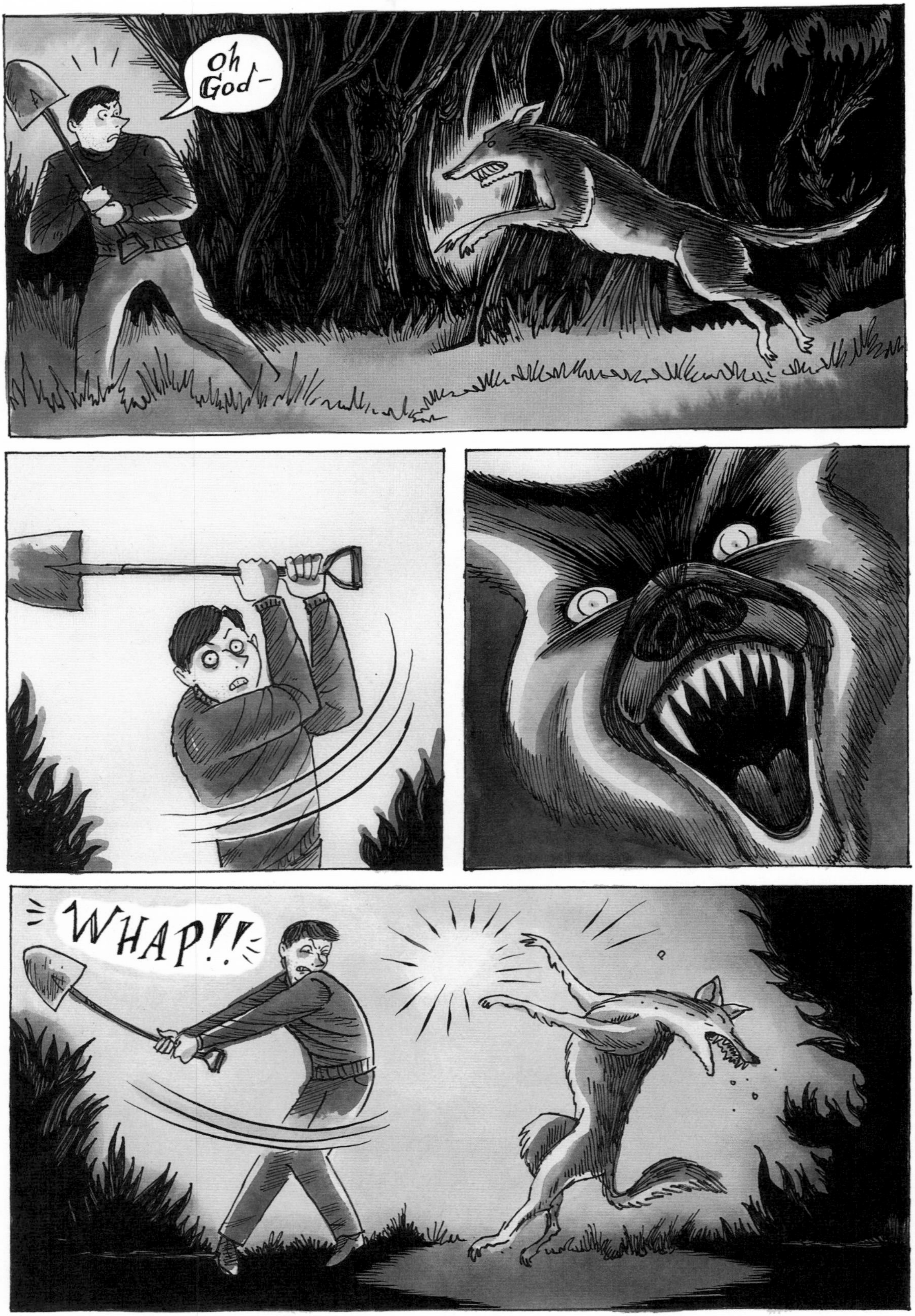
Oh God-
WHAP!!

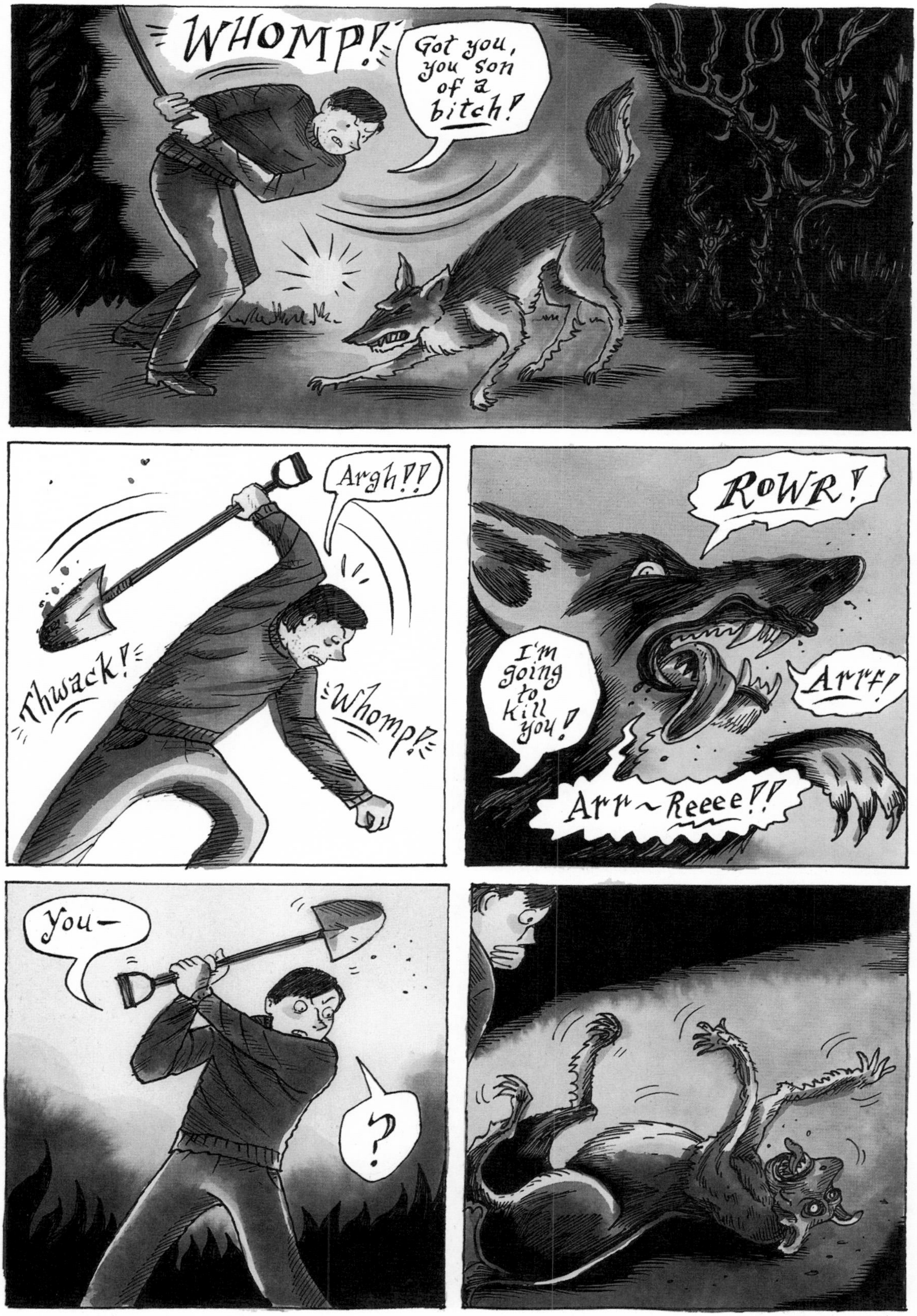
WHOMP!
Got you, you son of a bitch!
Argh!!
Thwack!
Whomp!
ROWR!
I'm going to kill you!
Arrf!
Arr~Reeee!!
You—
?

what the fuck?

Owooo!

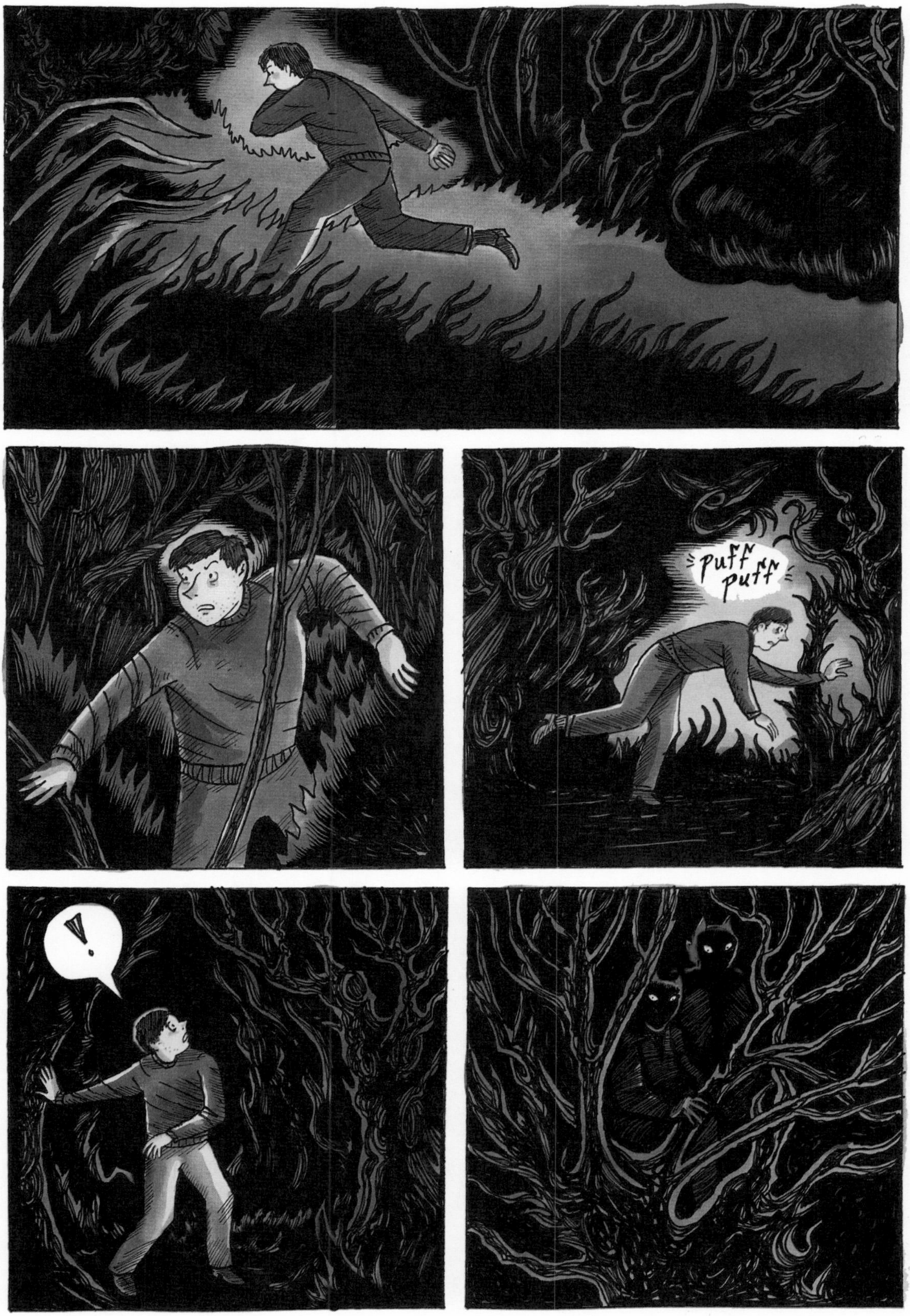
puff puff
!

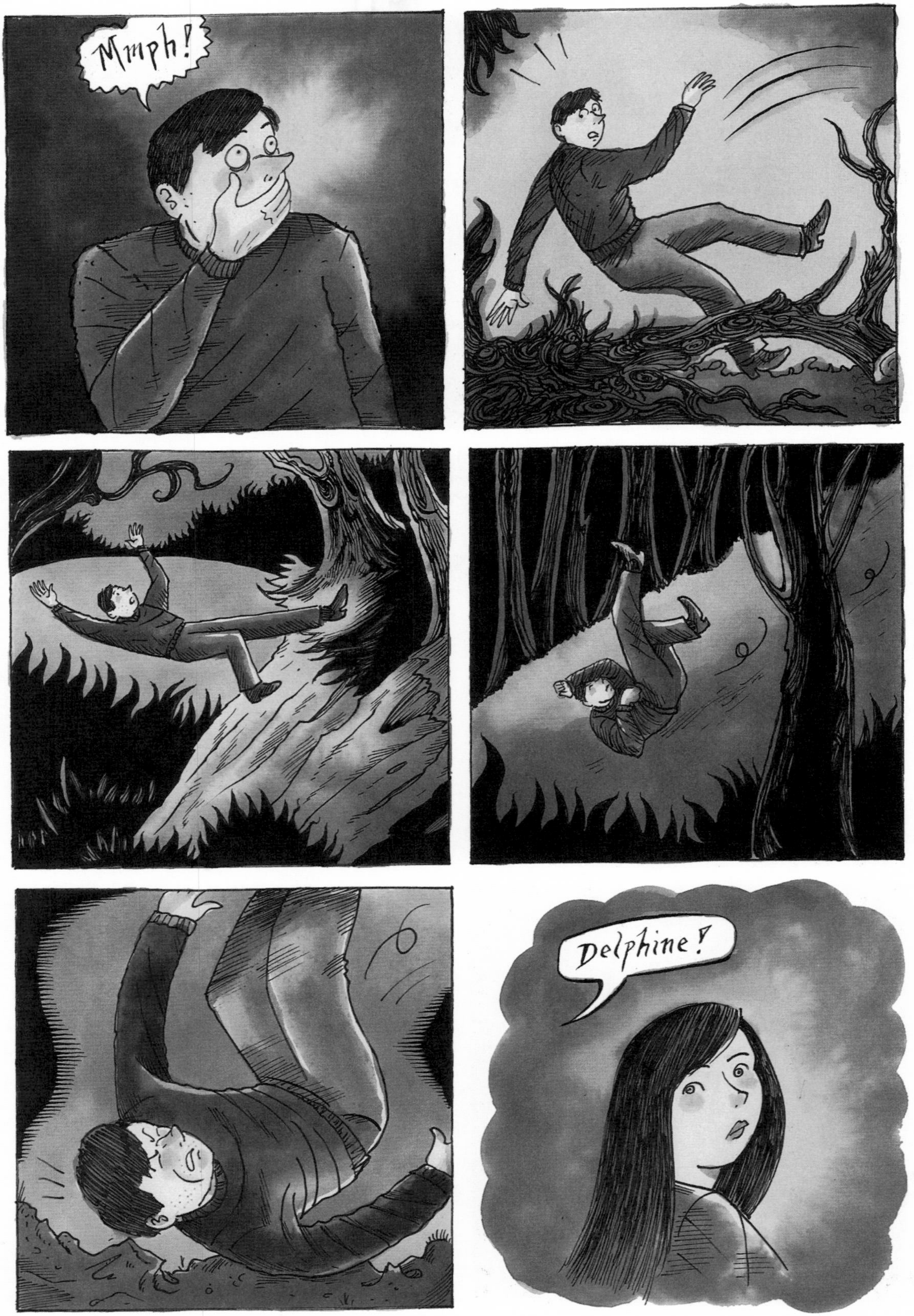
Mmph!
Delphine!

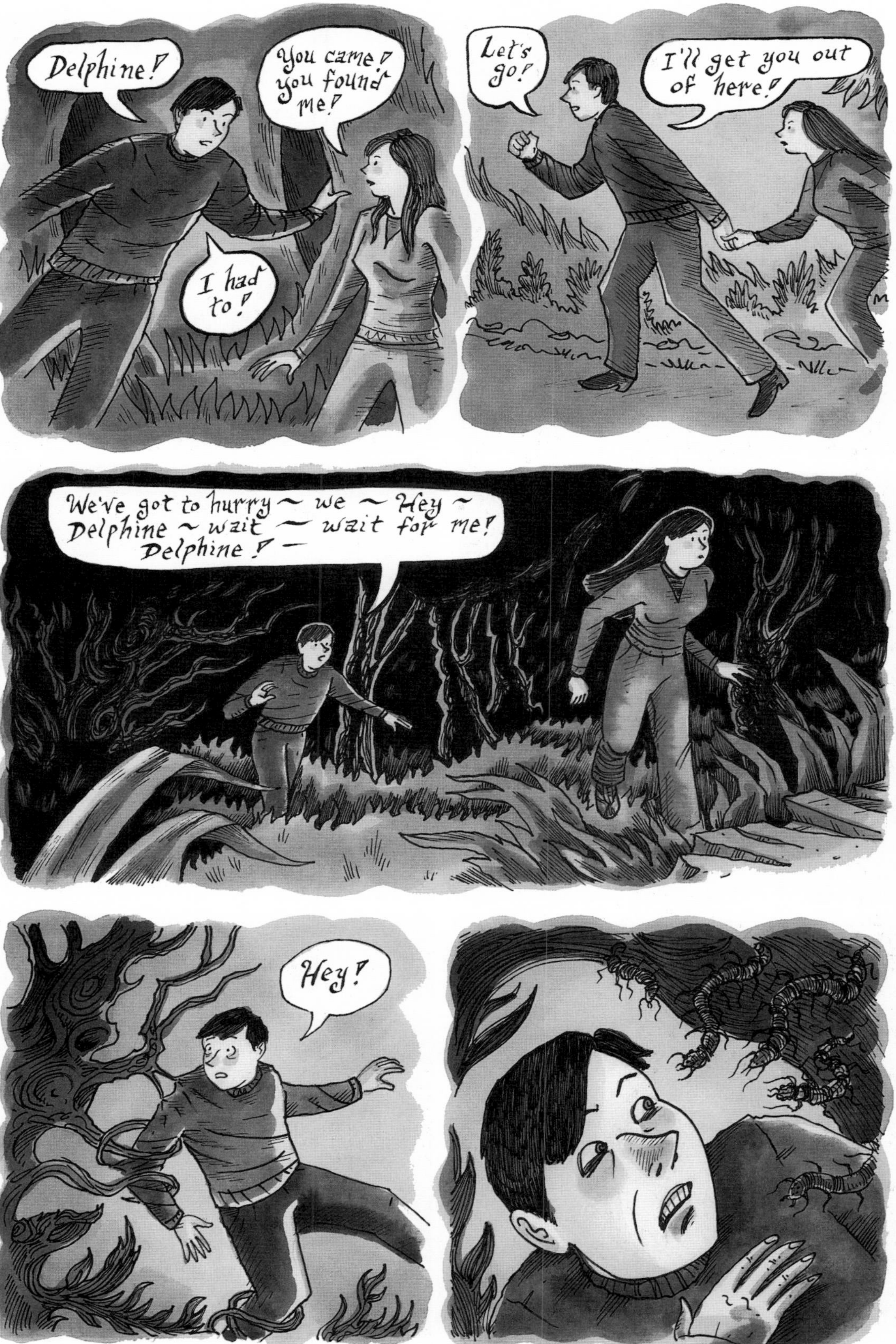
Delphine!
You came! you found me!
I had to!
Let's go!
I'll get you out of here!
We've got to hurry ~ we ~ Hey ~ Delphine ~ wait ~ wait for me! Delphine! ~
Hey!

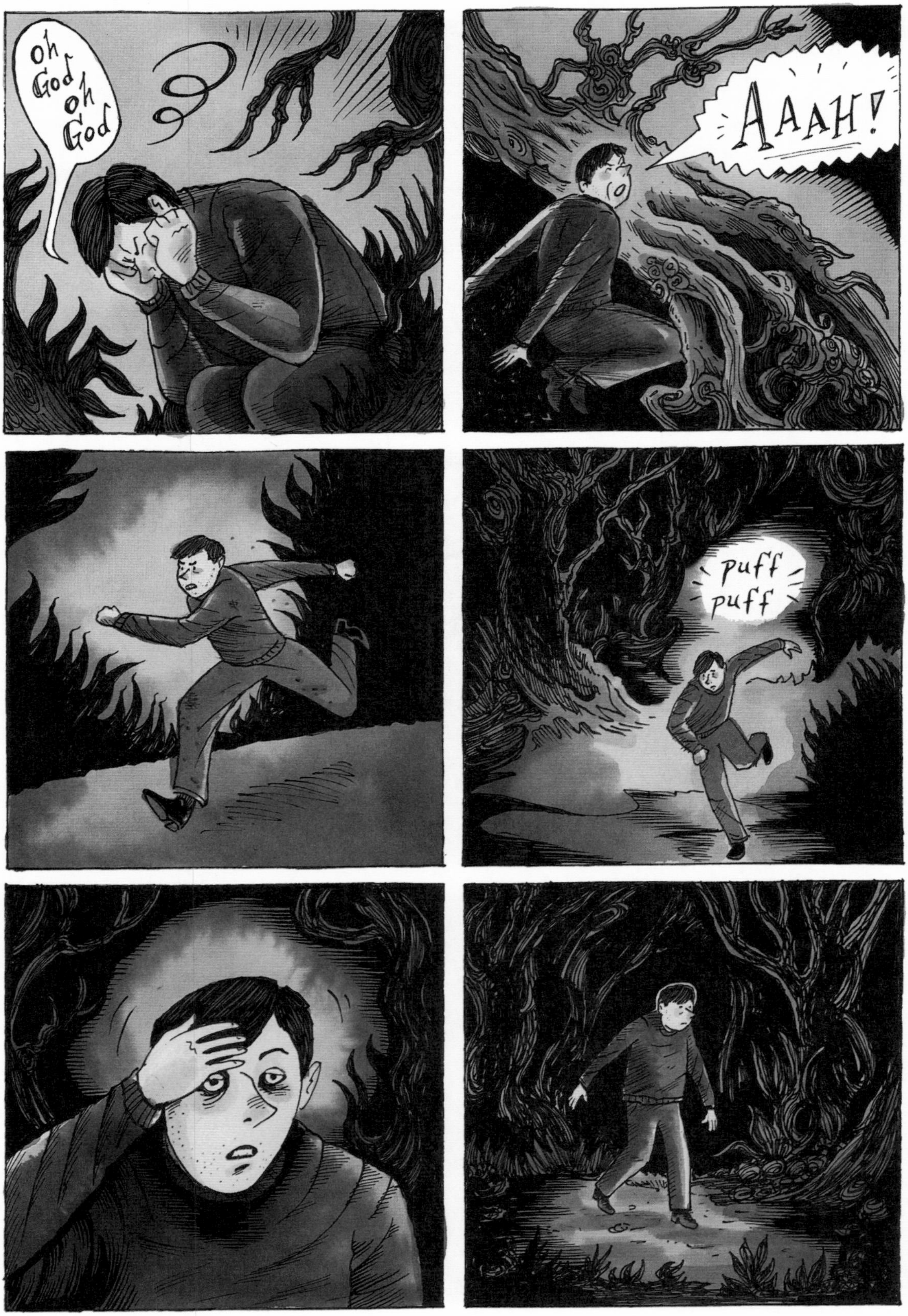
oh God oh God
AAAH!
puff puff

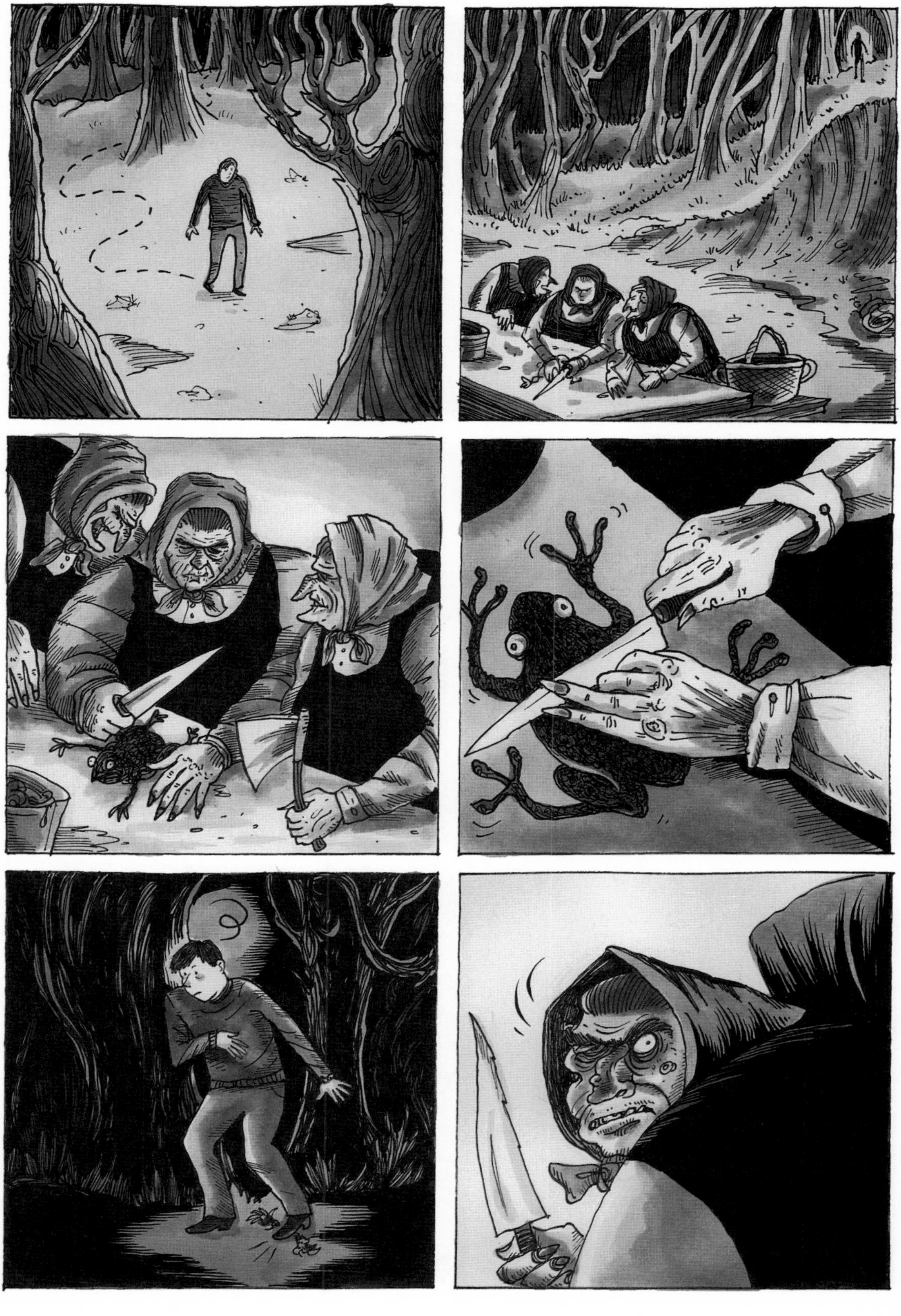

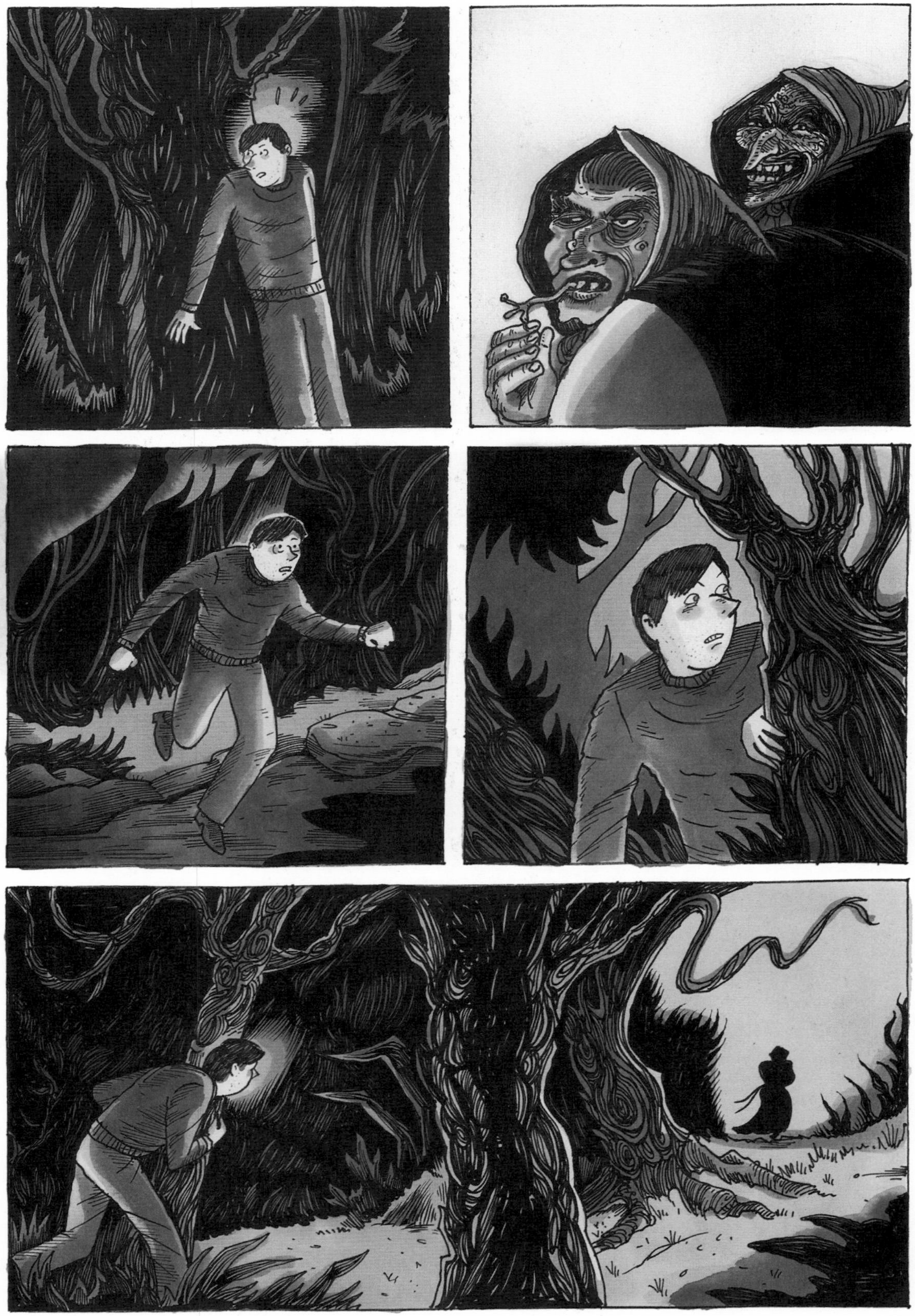

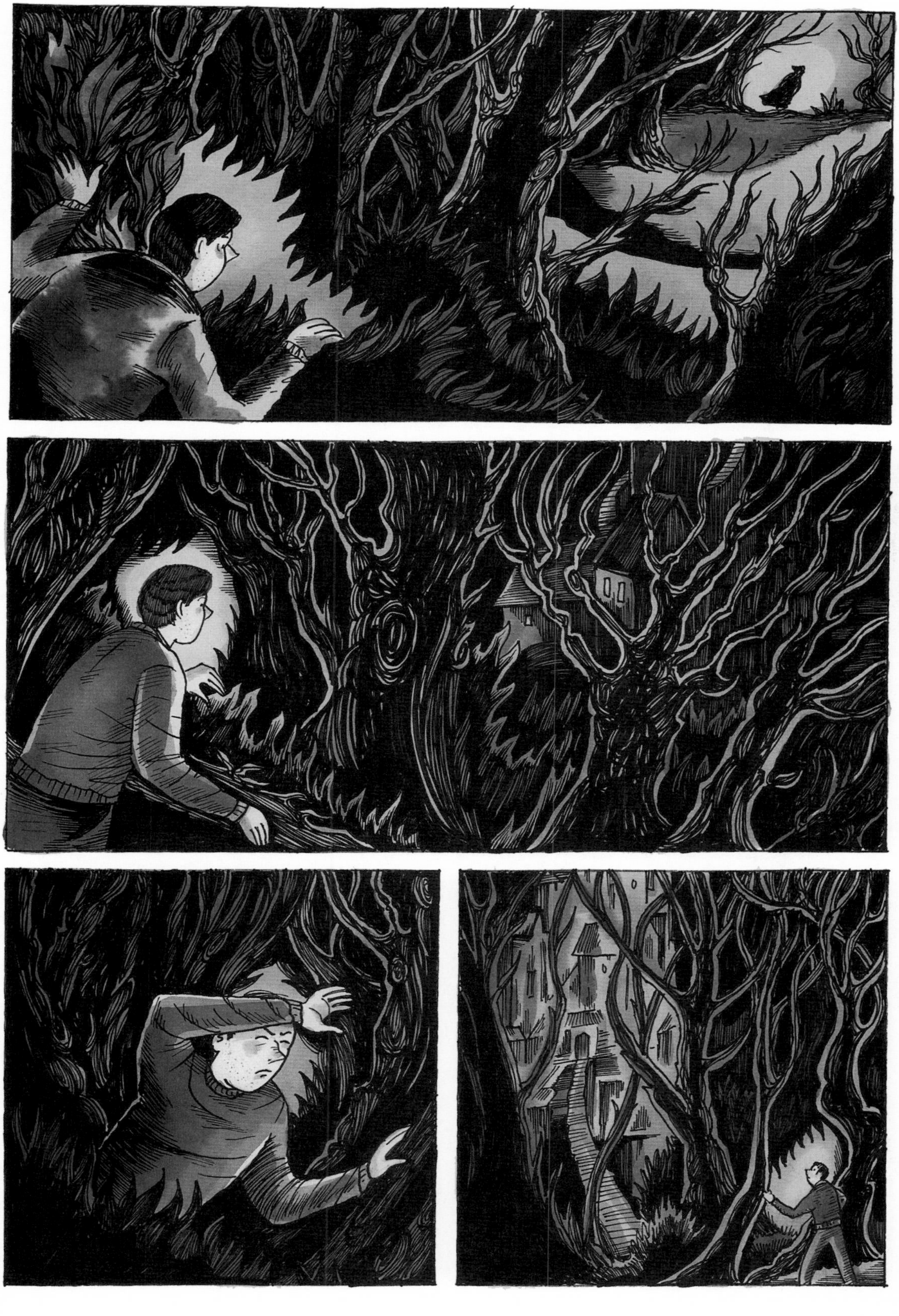

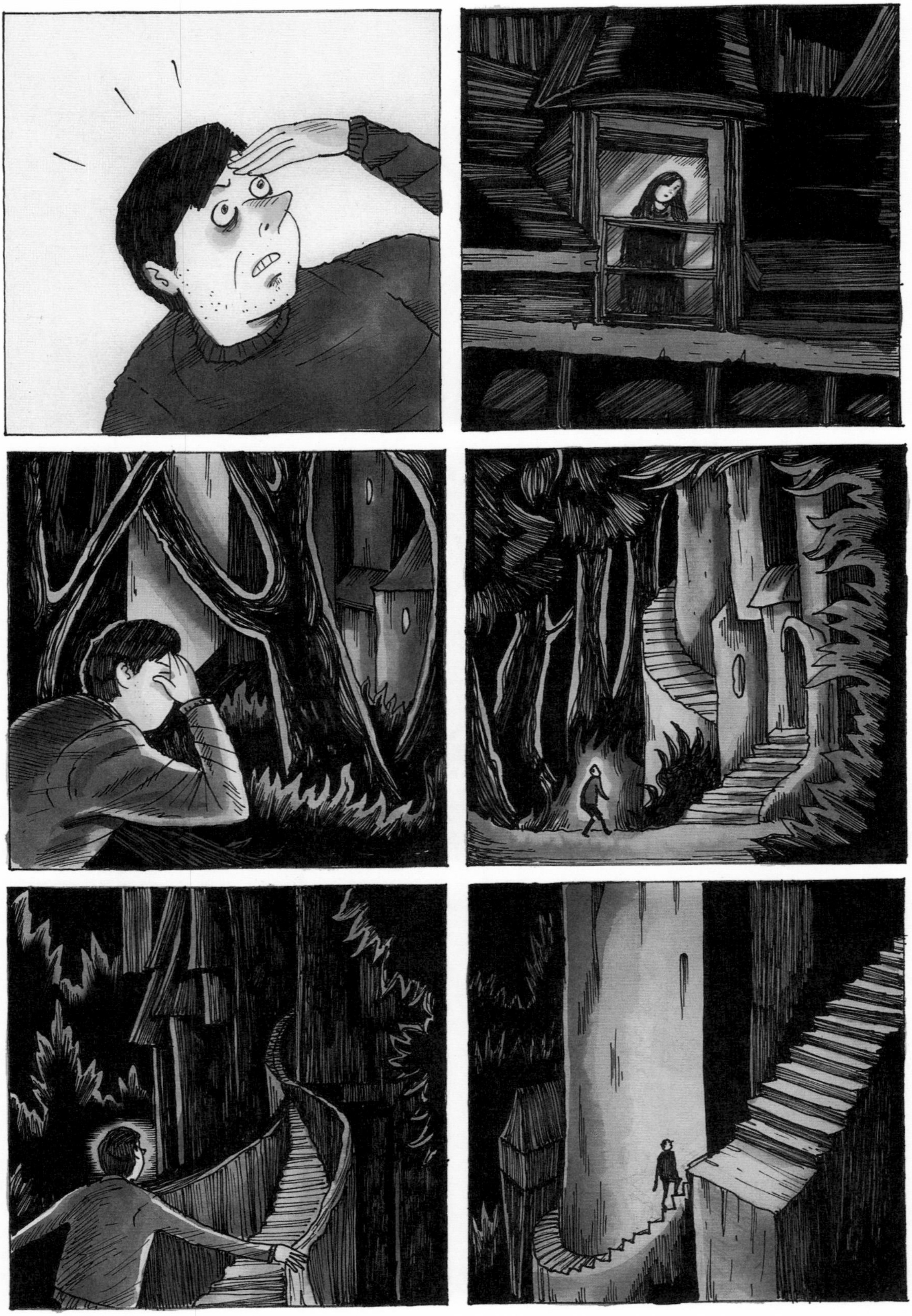

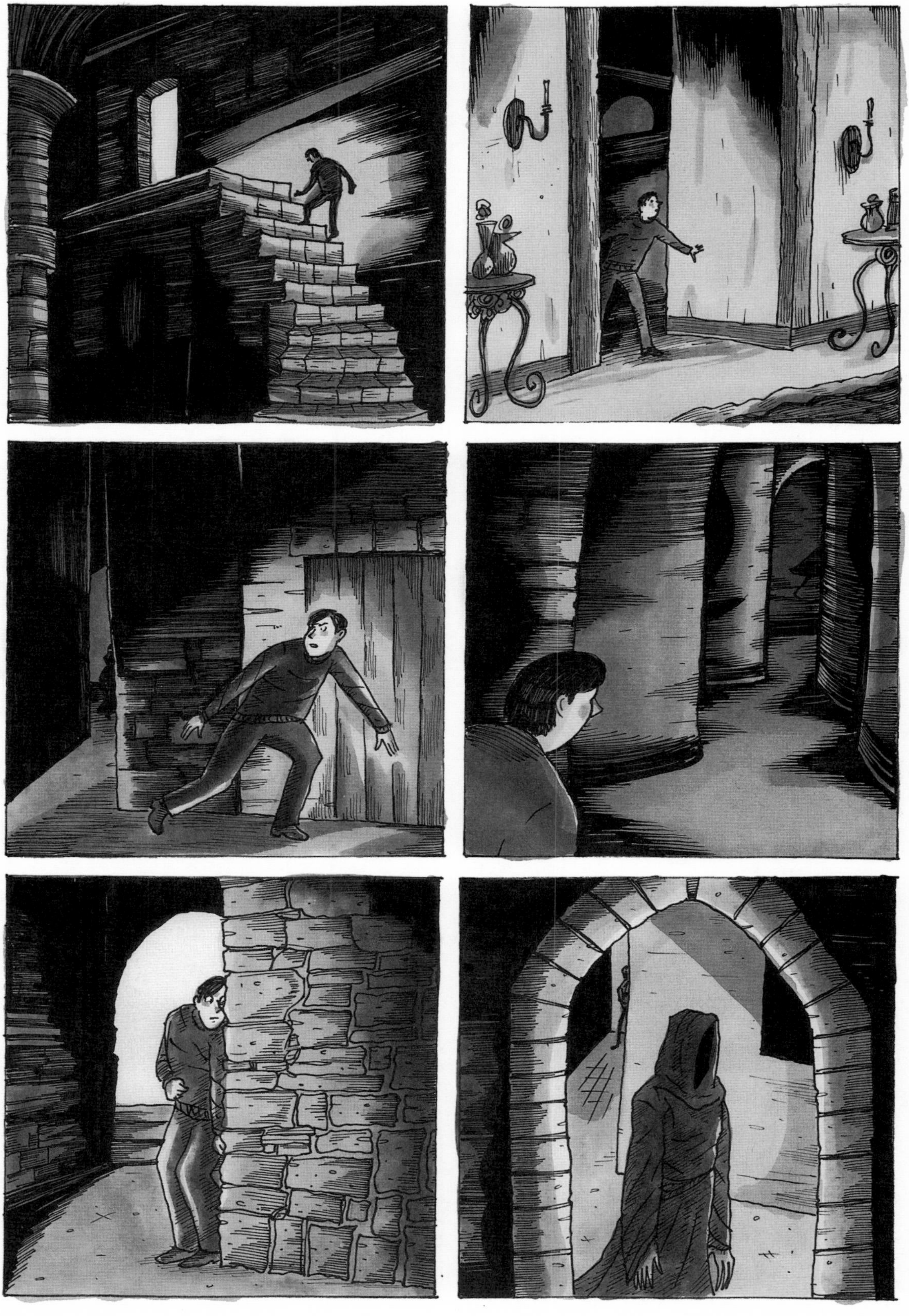

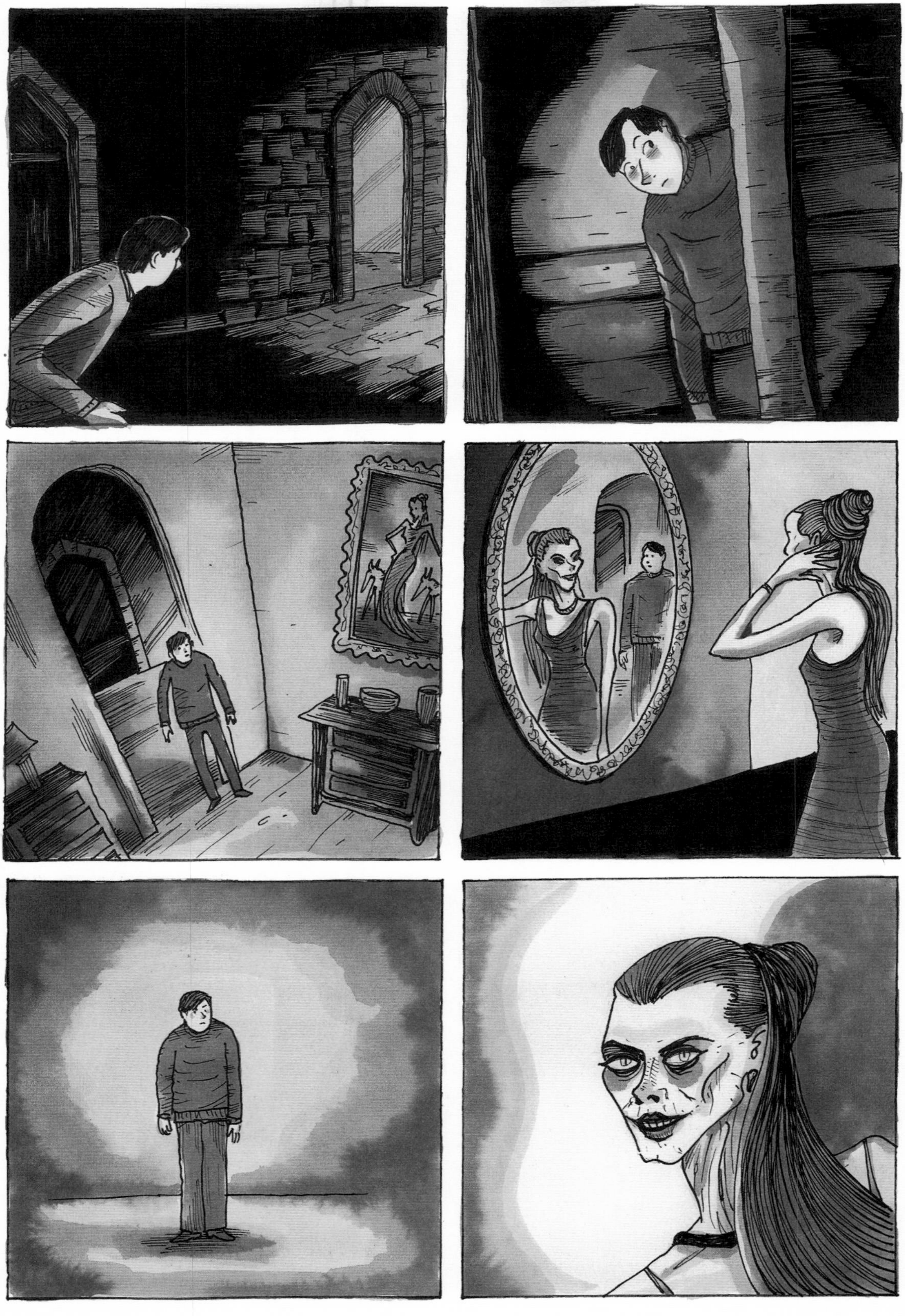

4.
The Spider

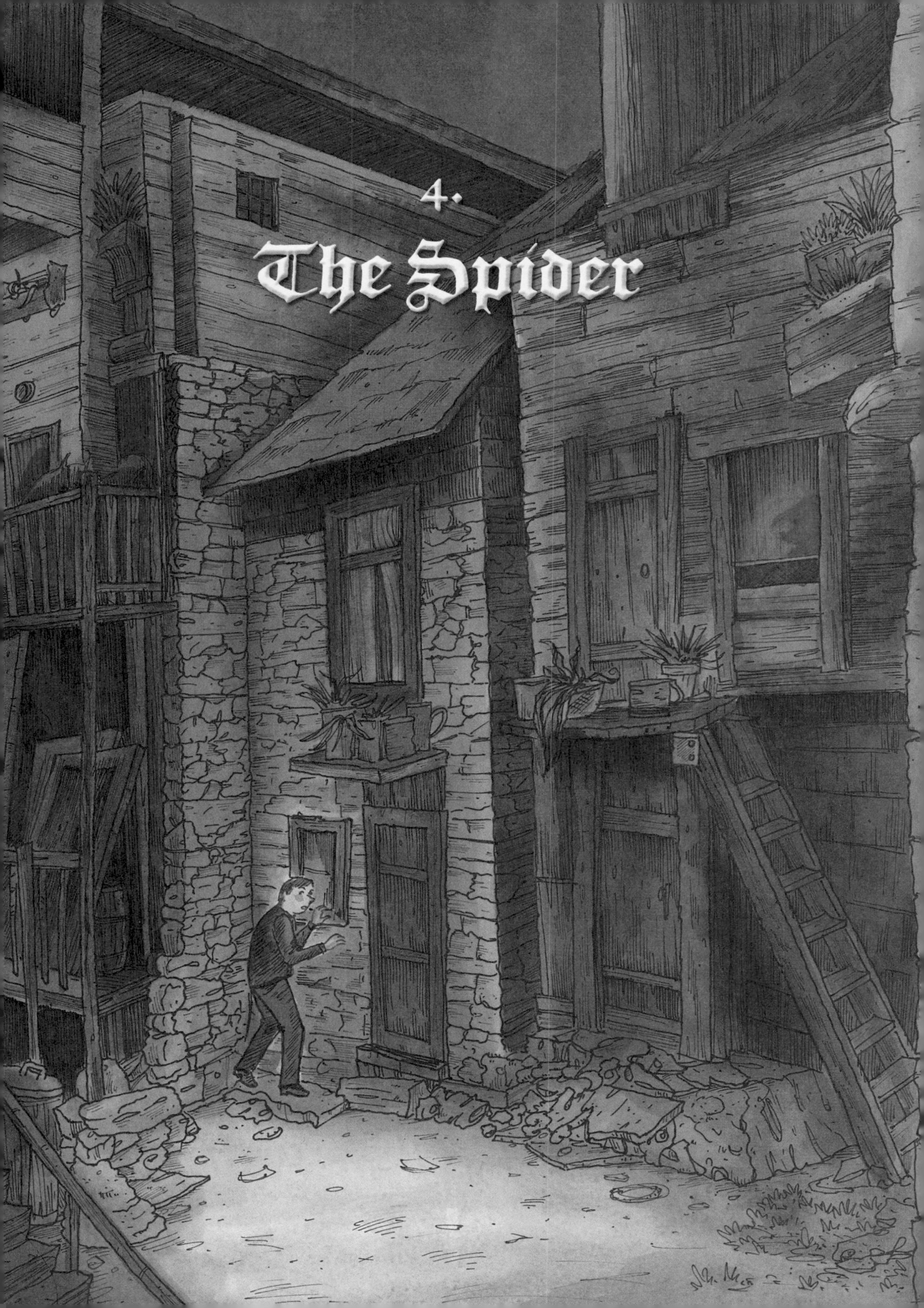

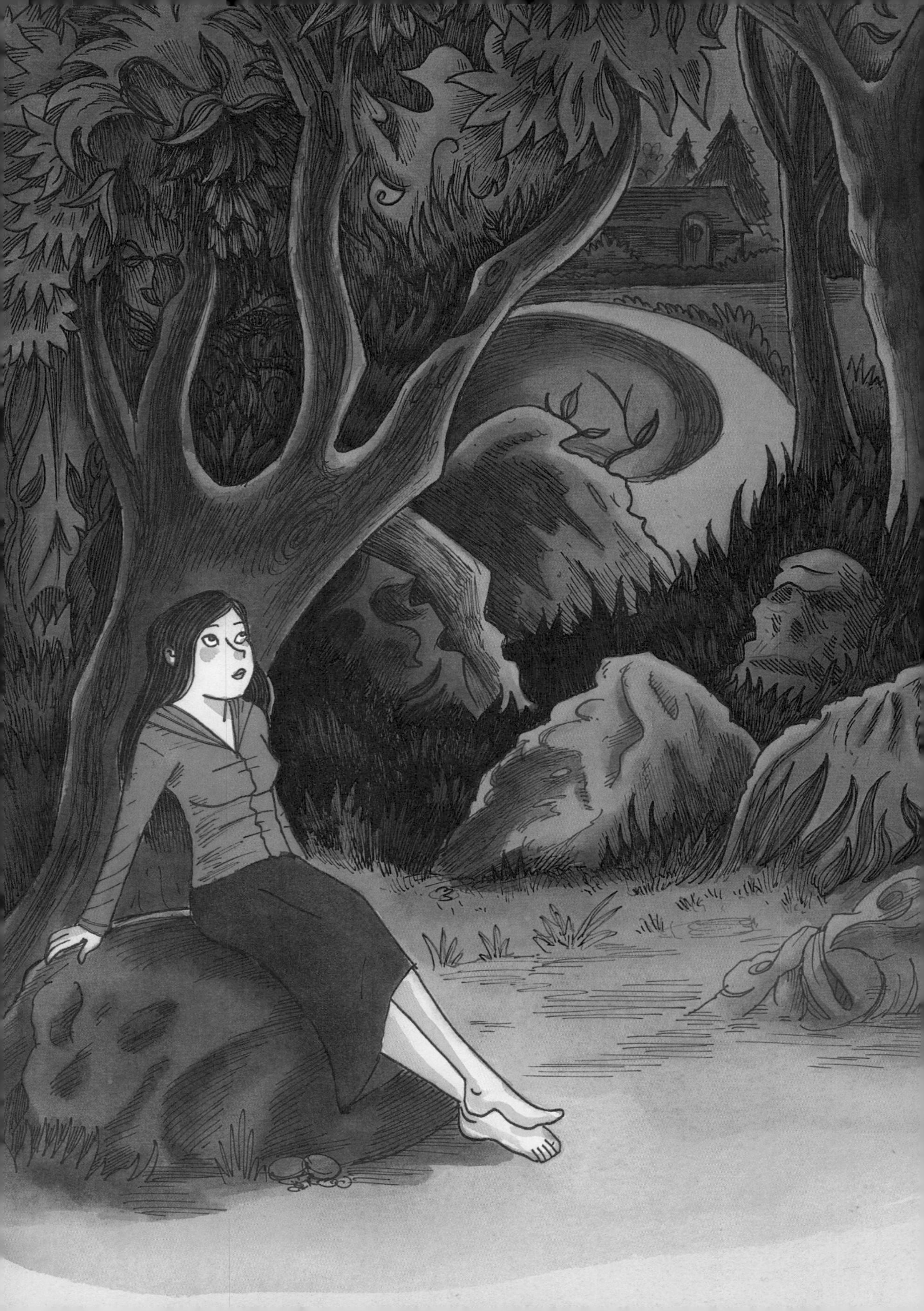

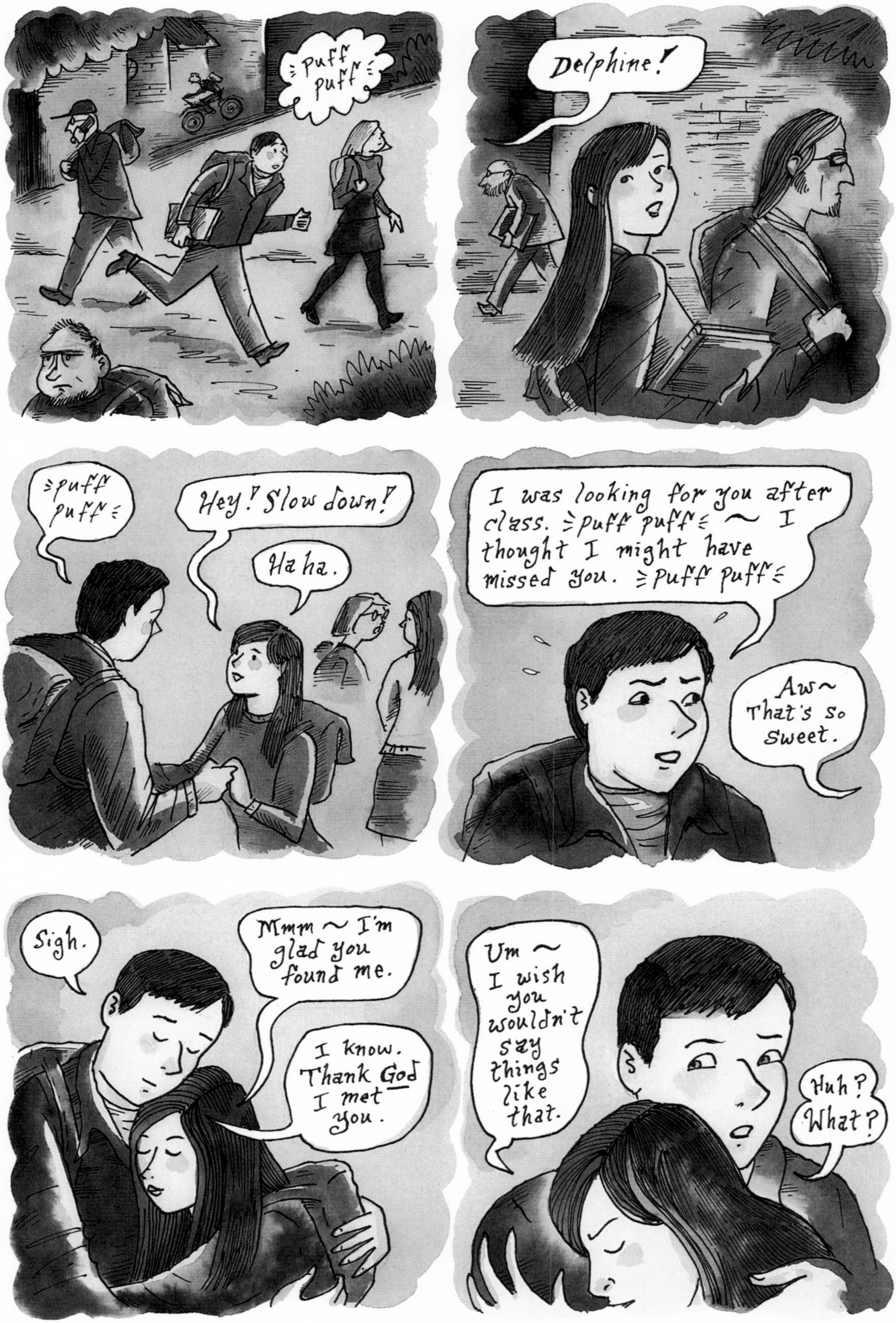

puff puff
Delphine!
puff puff
Hey! Slow down!
Ha ha.
I was looking for you after class. puff puff ~ I thought I might have missed you. puff puff
Aw~ That's so sweet.
Sigh.
Mmm ~ I'm glad you found me.
I know. Thank God I met you.
Um ~ I wish you wouldn't say things like that.
Huh? What?

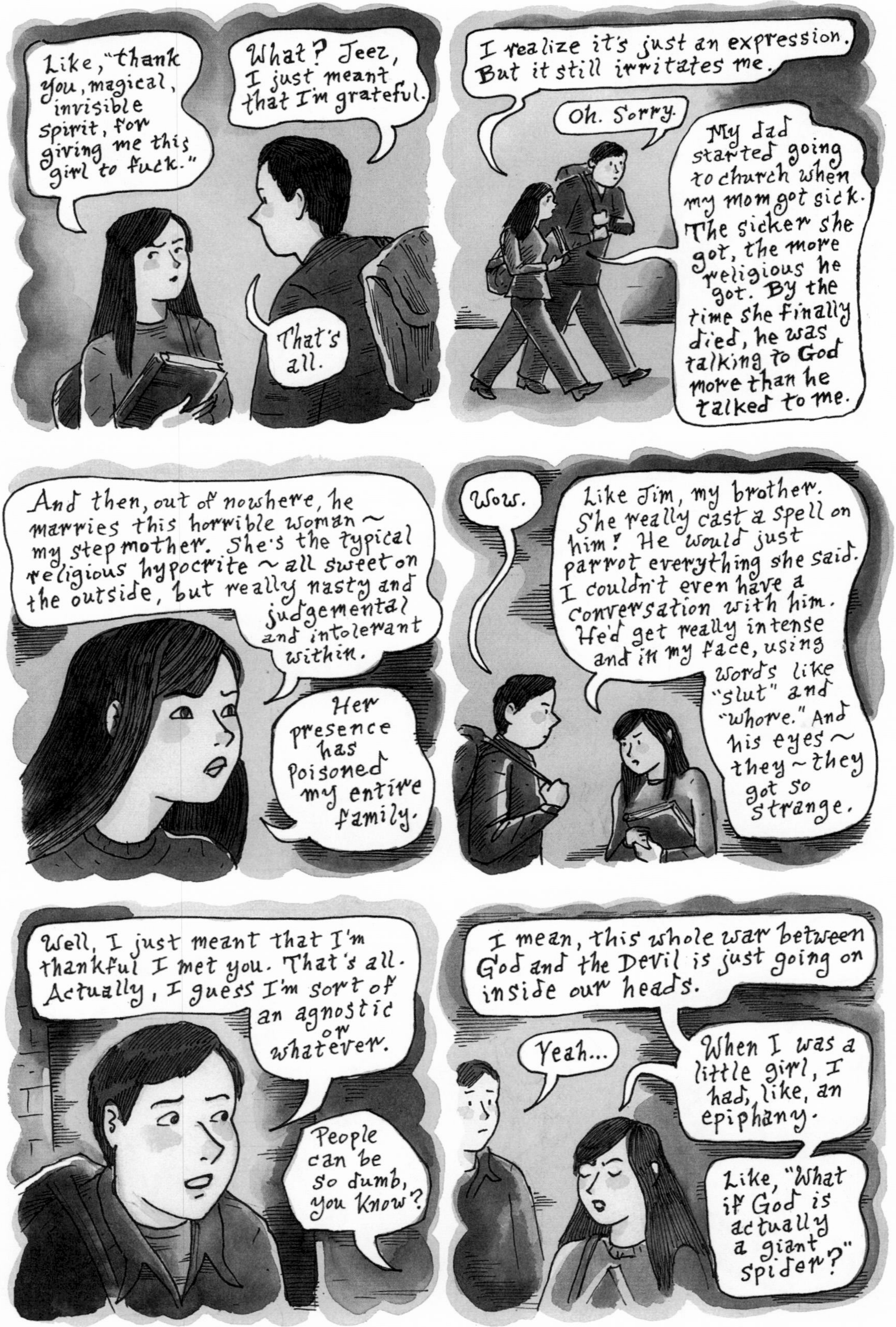

Like, "thank you, magical, invisible spirit, for giving me this girl to fuck."
What? Jeez, I just meant that I'm grateful.
That's all.
I realize it's just an expression. But it still irritates me.
Oh. Sorry.
My dad started going to church when my mom got sick. The sicker she got, the more religious he got. By the time she finally died, he was talking to God more than he talked to me.
And then, out of nowhere, he marries this horrible woman ~ my stepmother. She's the typical religious hypocrite ~ all sweet on the outside, but really nasty and judgemental and intolerant within.
Her presence has poisoned my entire family.
Wow.
Like Jim, my brother. She really cast a spell on him! He would just parrot everything she said. I couldn't even have a conversation with him. He'd get really intense and in my face, using words like "slut" and "whore." And his eyes ~ they ~ they got so strange.
Well, I just meant that I'm thankful I met you. That's all. Actually, I guess I'm sort of an agnostic or whatever.
People can be so dumb, you know?
I mean, this whole war between God and the Devil is just going on inside our heads.
Yeah...
When I was a little girl, I had, like, an epiphany.
Like, "What if God is actually a giant spider?"

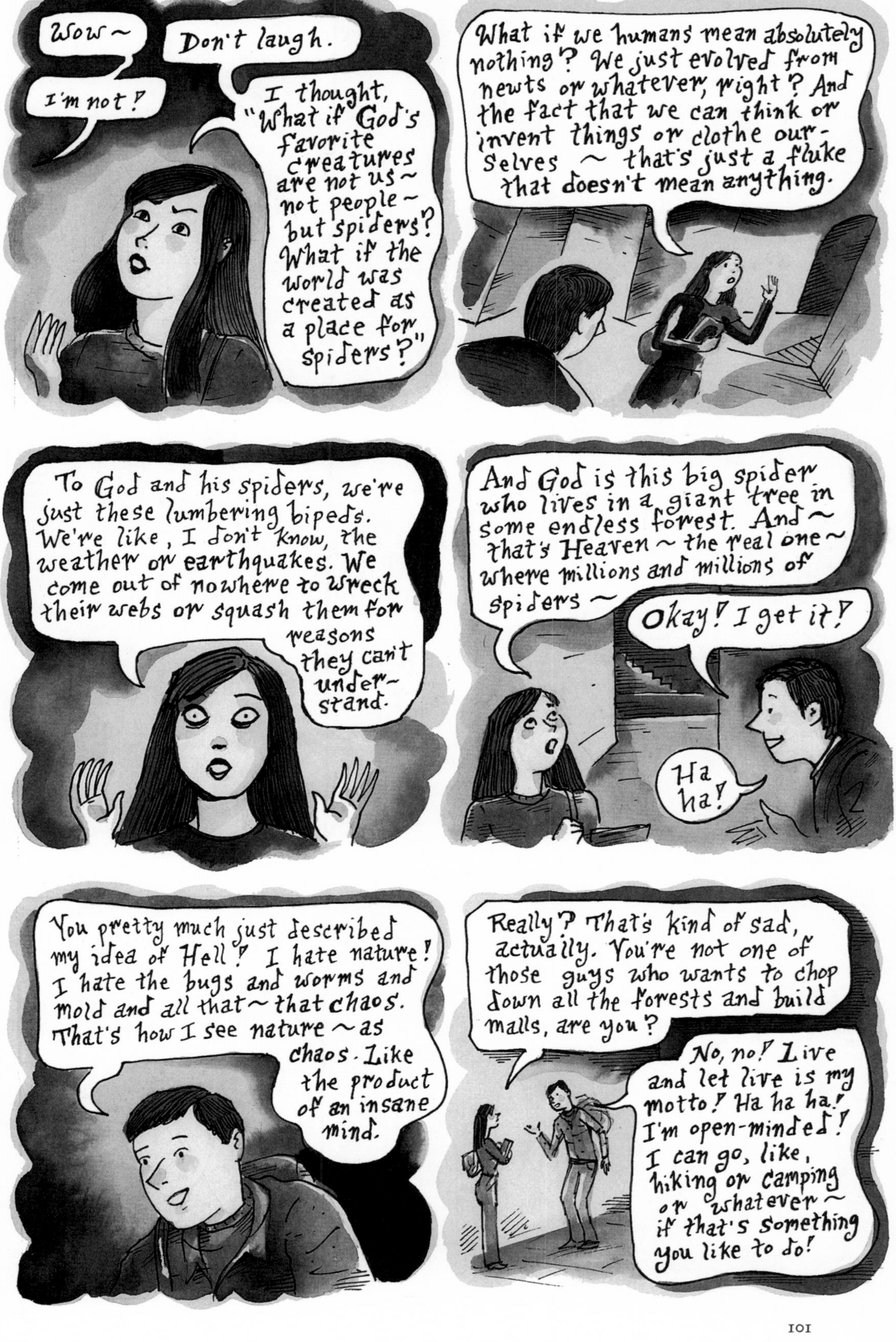

Wow~
Don't laugh.
I'm not!
I thought, "What if God's favorite creatures are not us~ not people~ but spiders? What if the world was created as a place for spiders?"
What if we humans mean absolutely nothing? We just evolved from newts or whatever, right? And the fact that we can think or invent things or clothe ourselves ~ that's just a fluke that doesn't mean anything.
To God and his spiders, we're just these lumbering bipeds. We're like, I don't know, the weather or earthquakes. We come out of nowhere to wreck their webs or squash them for reasons they can't understand.
And God is this big spider who lives in a giant tree in some endless forest. And~ that's Heaven ~ the real one~ where millions and millions of spiders ~
Okay! I get it!
Ha ha!
You pretty much just described my idea of Hell! I hate nature! I hate the bugs and worms and mold and all that~ that chaos. That's how I see nature ~ as chaos. Like the product of an insane mind.
Really? That's kind of sad, actually. You're not one of those guys who wants to chop down all the forests and build malls, are you?
No, no! Live and let live is my motto! Ha ha ha! I'm open-minded! I can go, like, hiking or camping or whatever ~ if that's something you like to do!

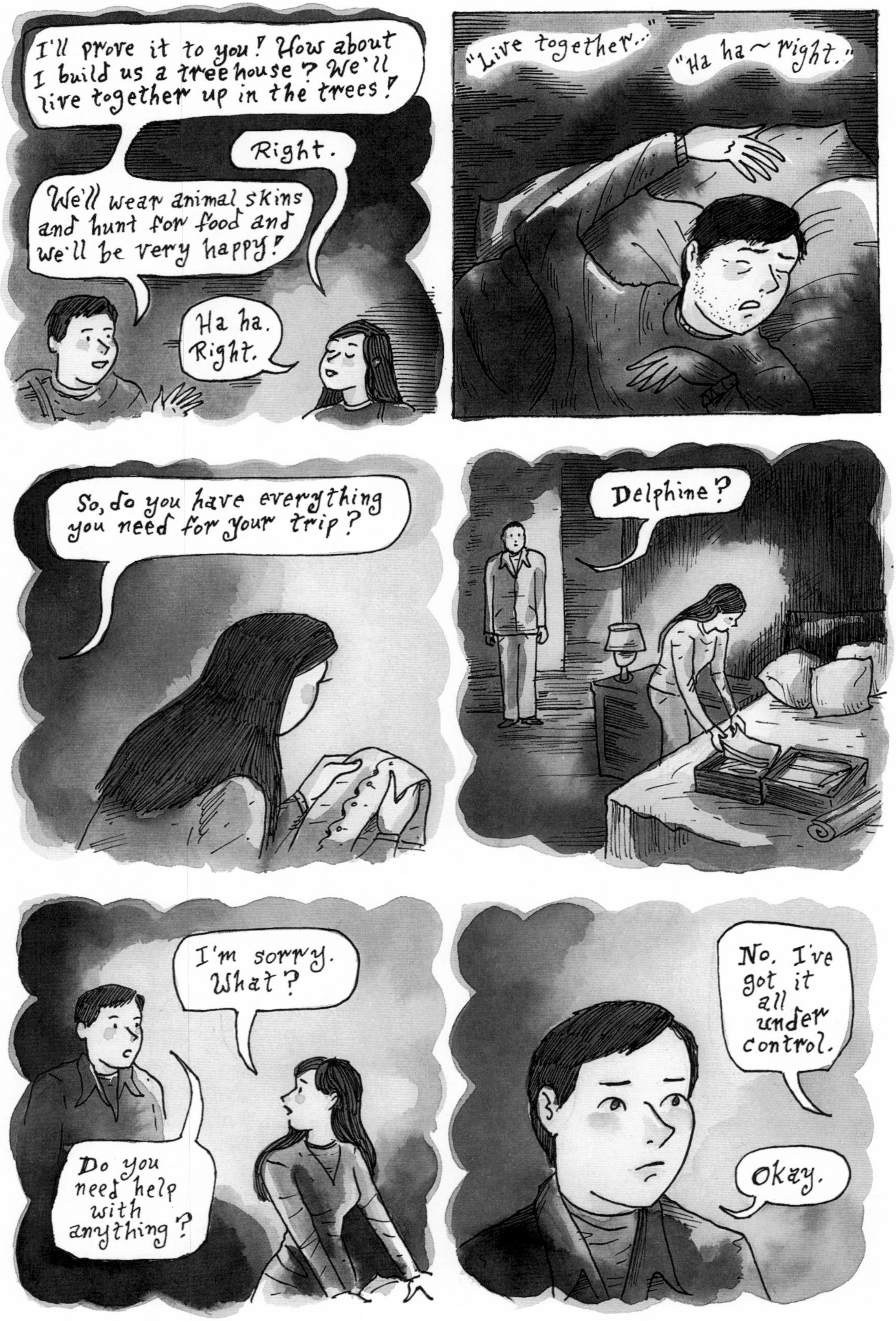
I'll prove it to you! How about I build us a treehouse? We'll live together up in the trees!
Right.
We'll wear animal skins and hunt for food and we'll be very happy!
Ha ha. Right.
"Live together..."
"Ha ha ~ right."
So, do you have everything you need for your trip?
Delphine?
I'm sorry. What?
Do you need help with anything?
No. I've got it all under control.
Okay.

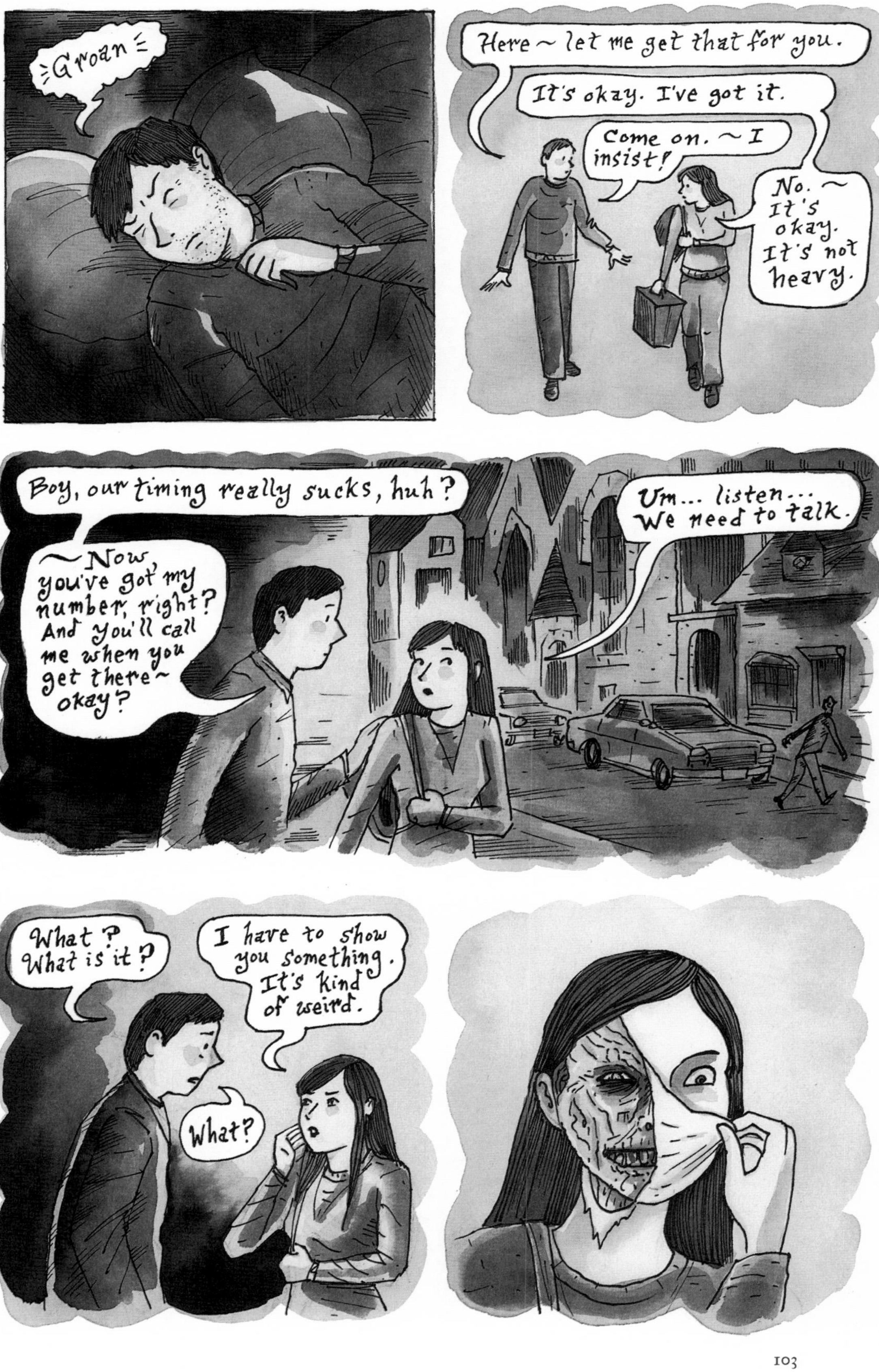
Groan
Here ~ let me get that for you.
It's okay. I've got it.
Come on. ~ I insist!
No. ~ It's okay. It's not heavy.
Boy, our timing really sucks, huh?
~ Now you've got my number, right? And you'll call me when you get there ~ okay?
Um... listen... We need to talk.
What? What is it?
I have to show you something. It's kind of weird.
What?

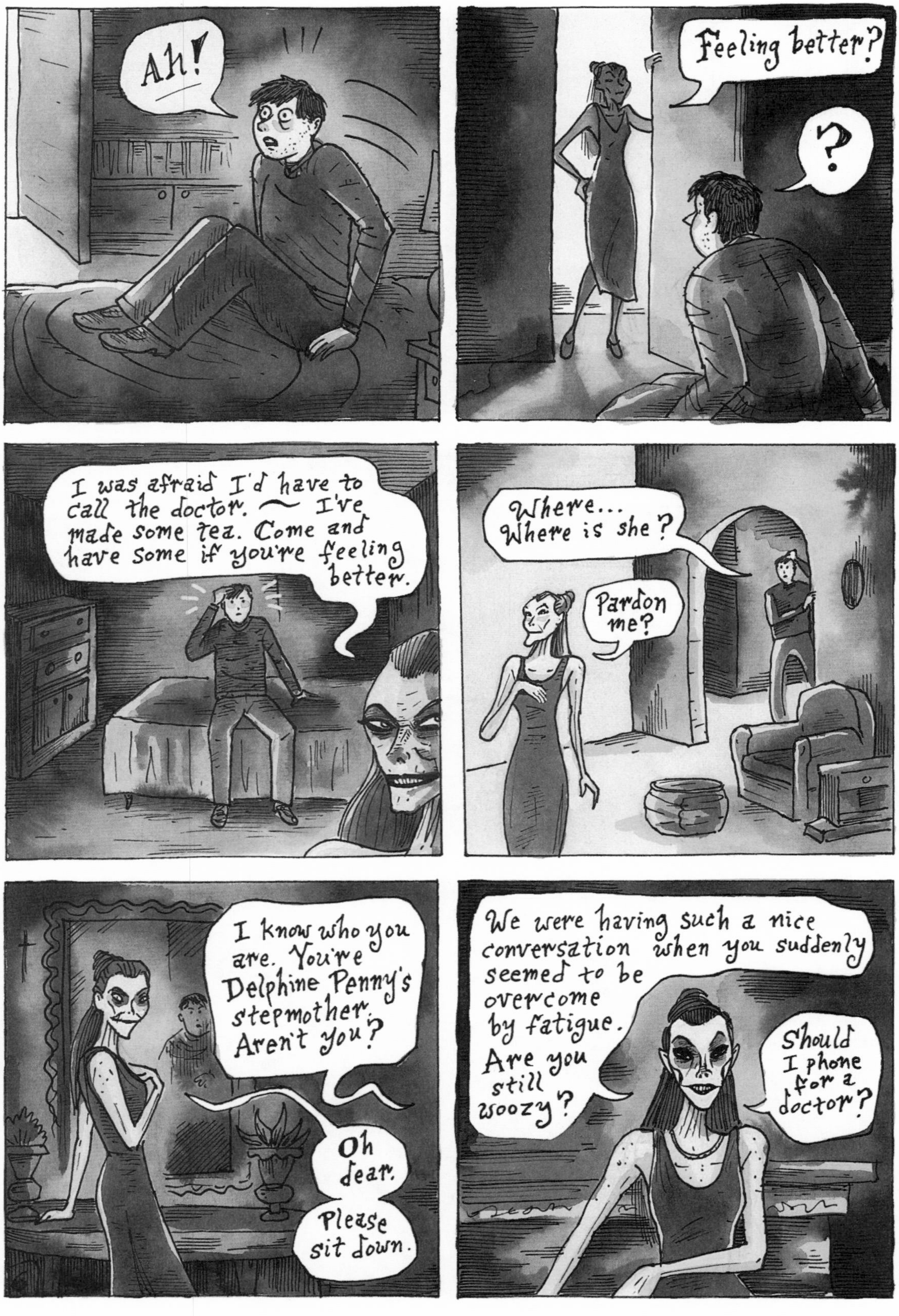
Ah!
Feeling better?
?
I was afraid I'd have to call the doctor. ~ I've made some tea. Come and have some if you're feeling better.
Where... Where is she?
Pardon me?
I know who you are. You're Delphine Penny's stepmother. Aren't you?
Oh dear.
Please sit down.
We were having such a nice conversation when you suddenly seemed to be overcome by fatigue.
Are you still woozy?
Should I phone for a doctor?

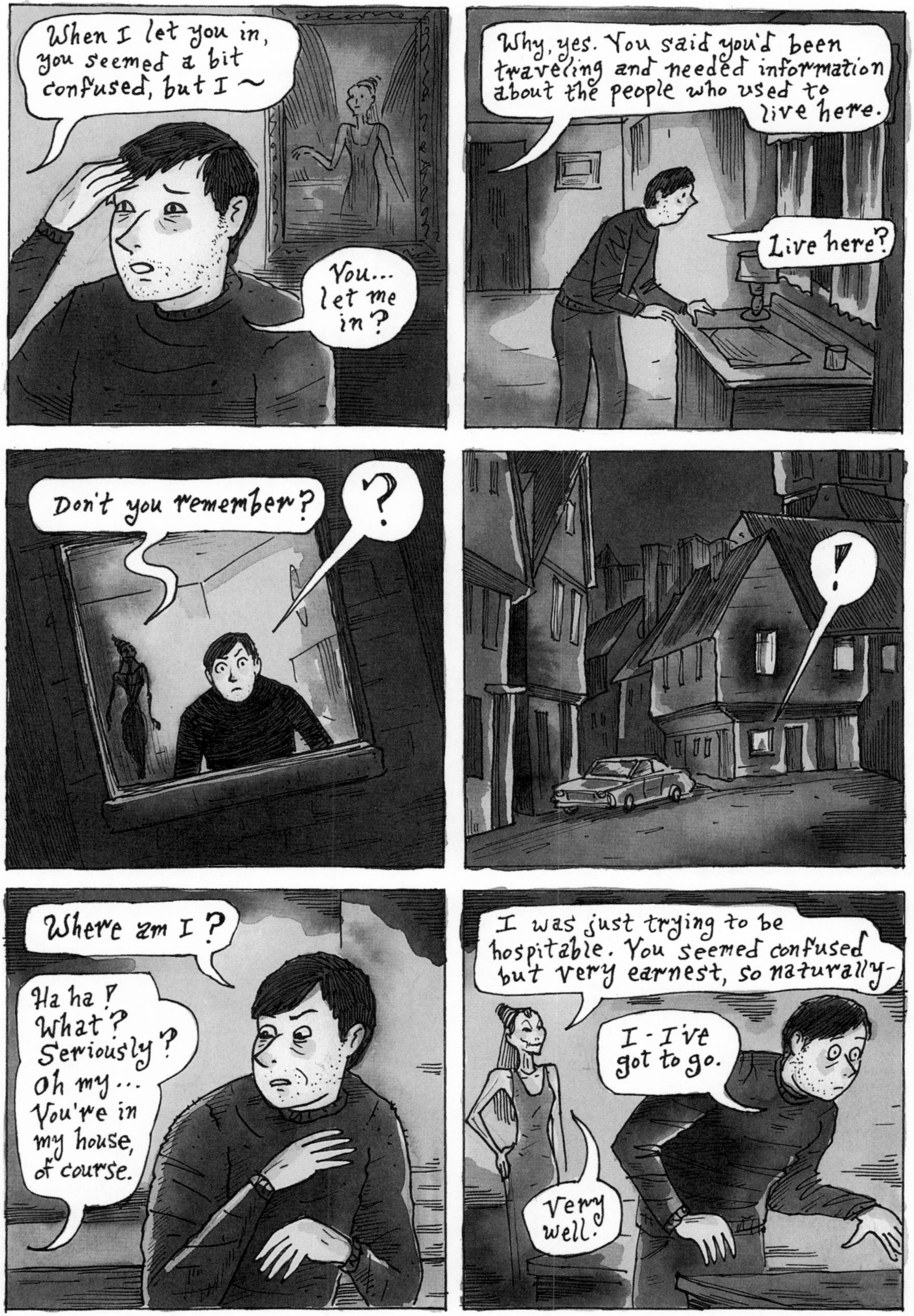
When I let you in, you seemed a bit confused, but I ~
You... let me in?
Why, yes. You said you'd been traveling and needed information about the people who used to live here.
Live here?
Don't you remember?
?
!
Where am I?
Ha ha! What? Seriously? Oh my... You're in my house, of course.
I was just trying to be hospitable. You seemed confused but very earnest, so naturally-
I-I've got to go.
Very well.

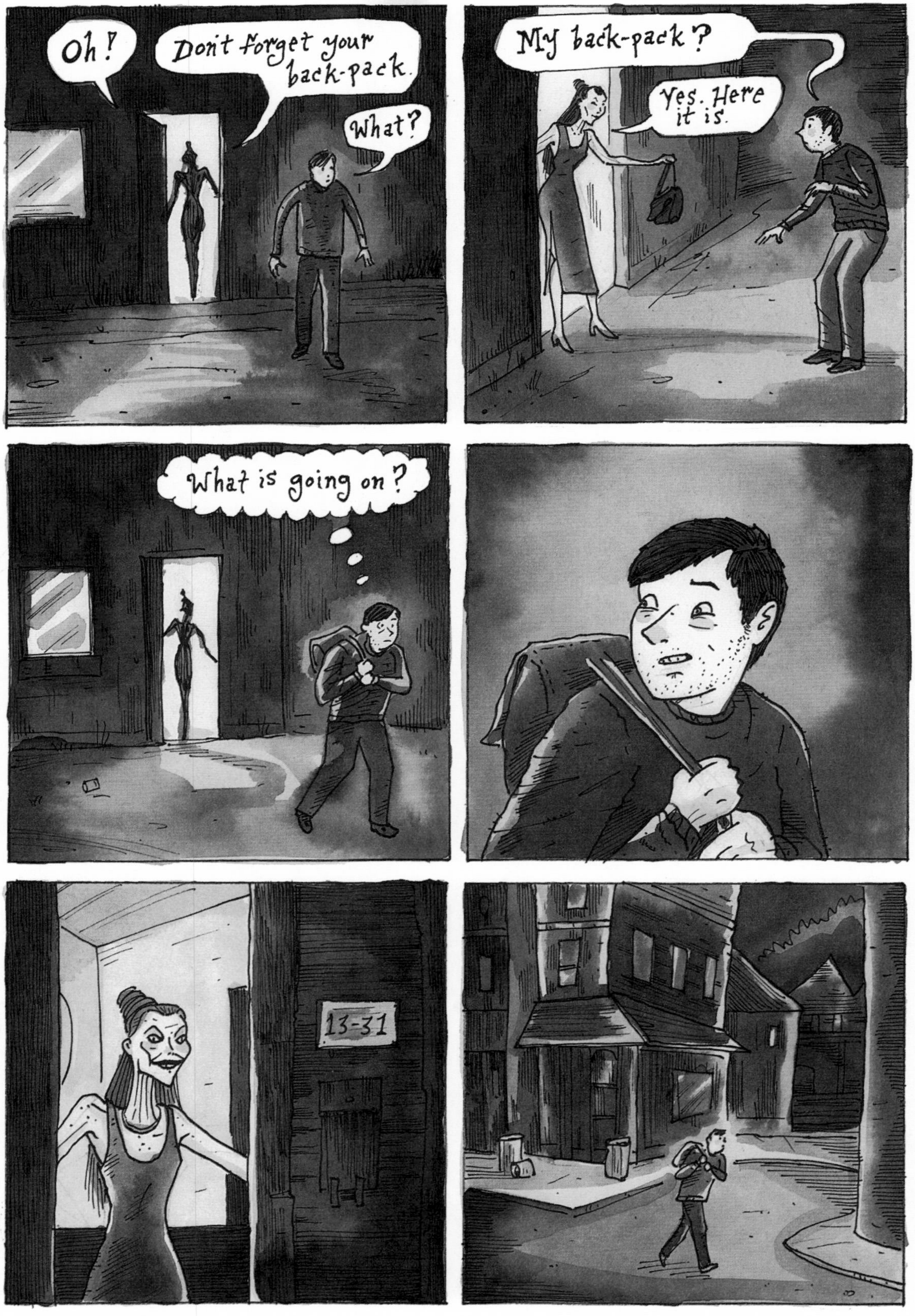
Oh!
Don't forget your back-pack.
What?
My back-pack?
Yes. Here it is.
What is going on?
13-31

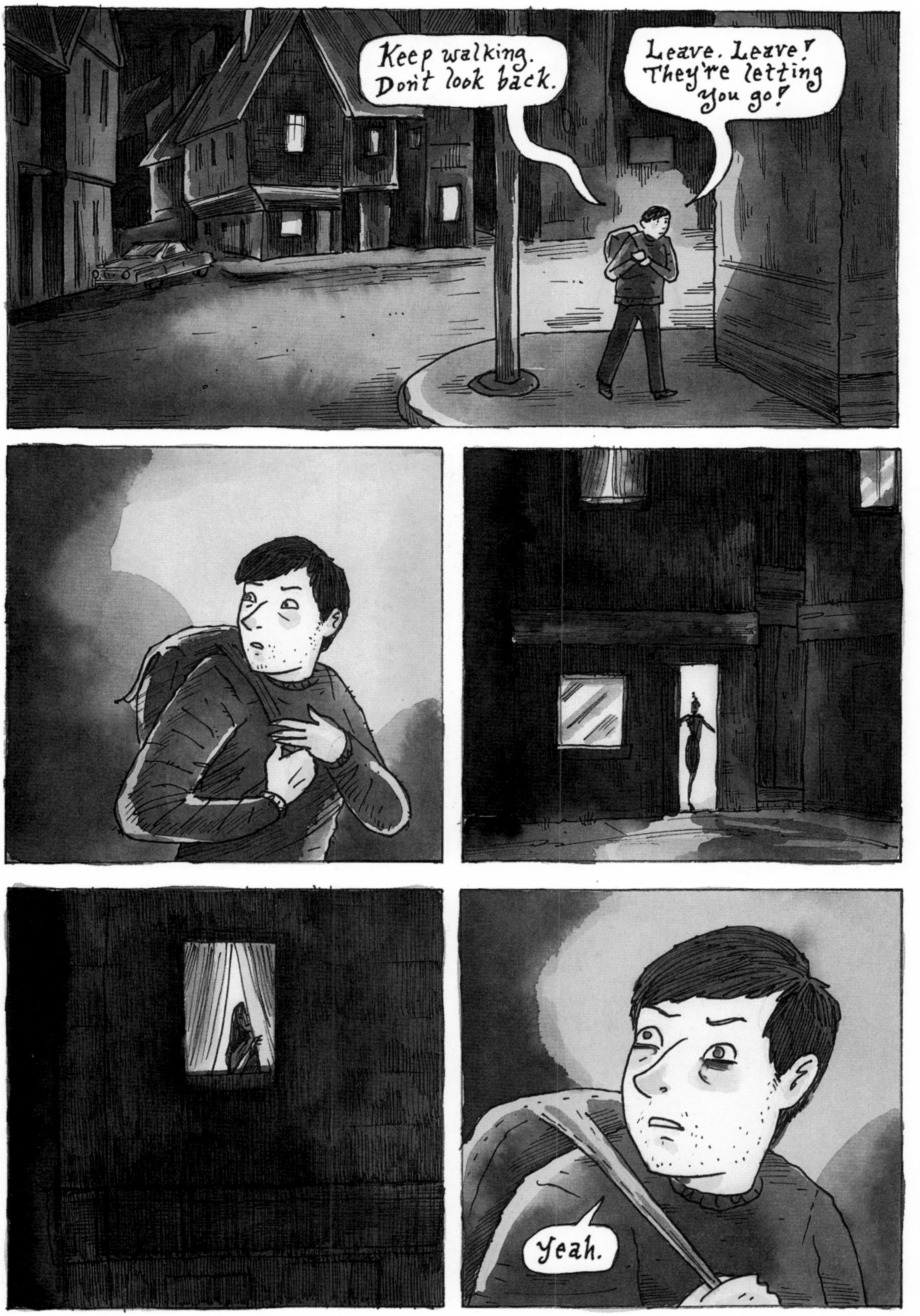
Keep walking. Don't look back.
Leave. Leave! They're letting you go!
Yeah.

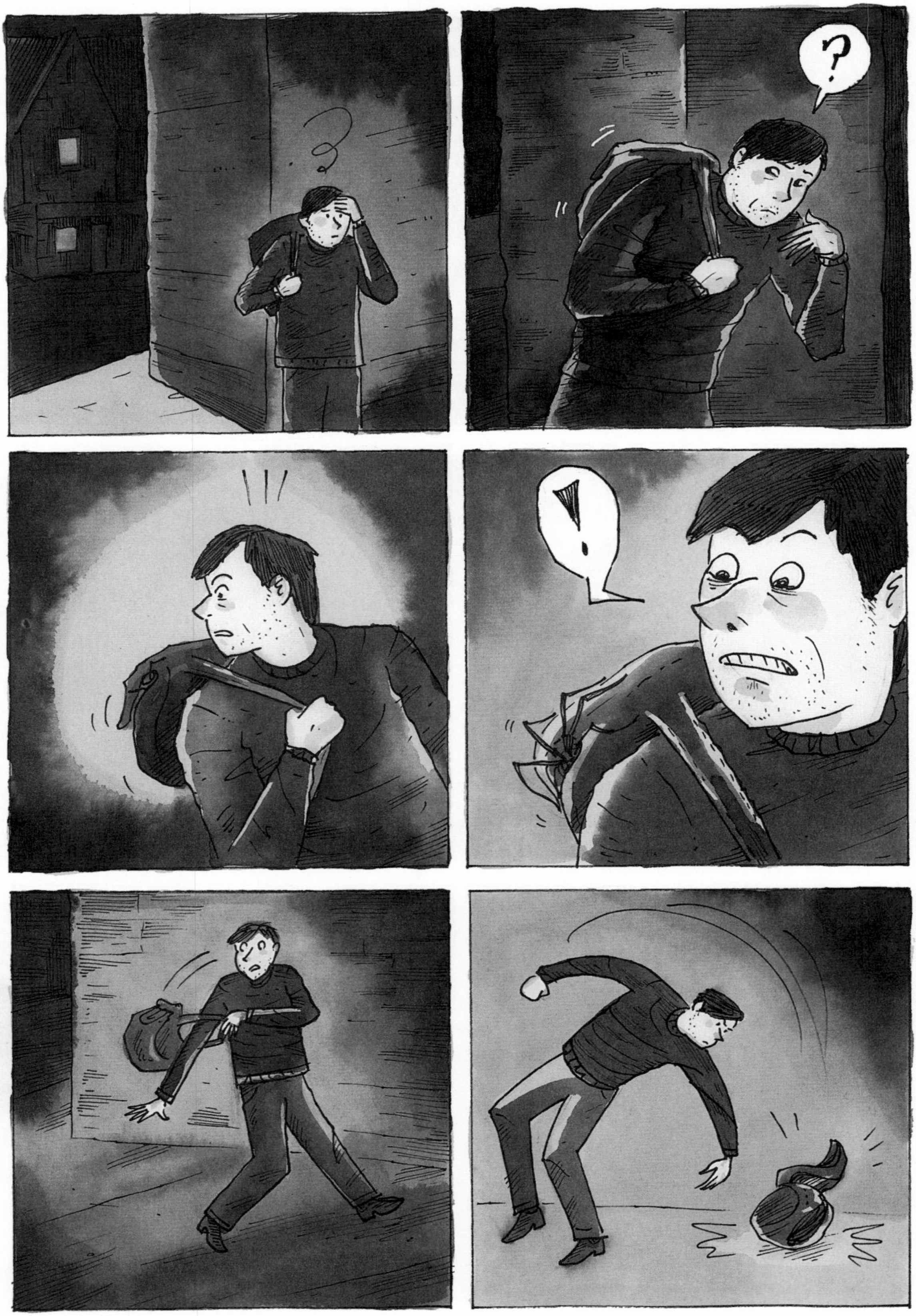
?
!

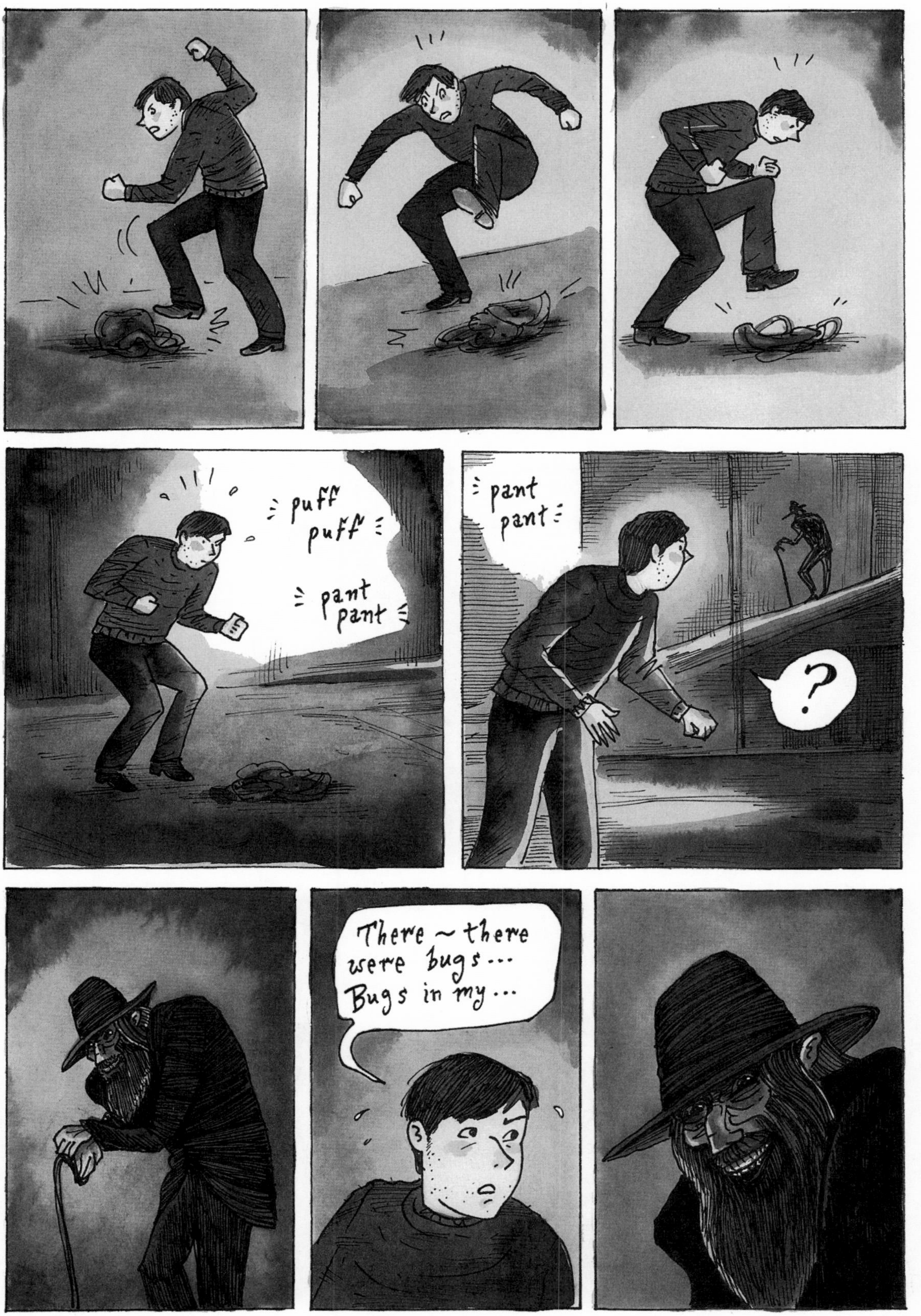
puff
puff
pant
pant
pant
pant
?
There ~ there
were bugs...
Bugs in my...

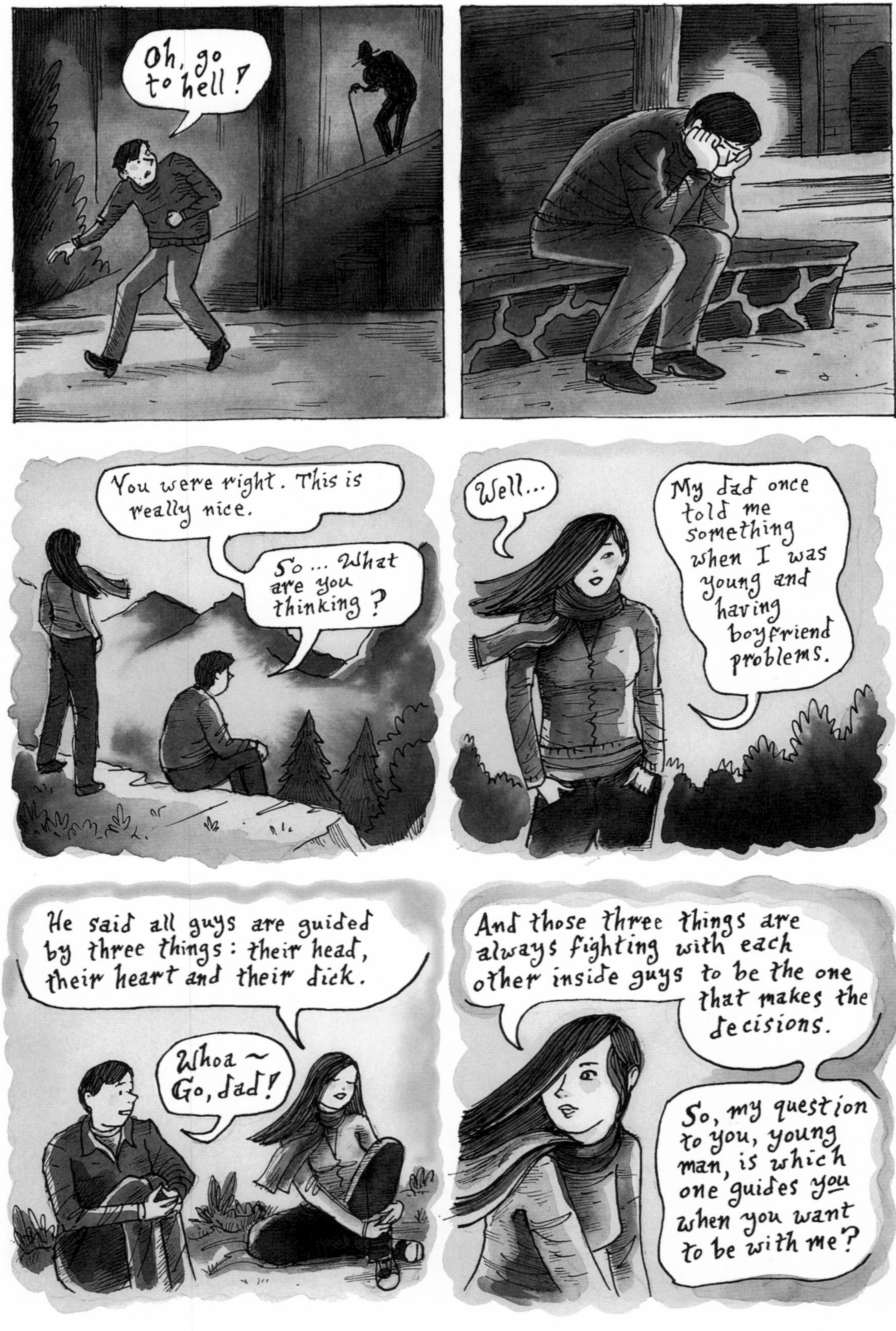
Oh, go to hell!
You were right. This is really nice.
So... What are you thinking?
Well...
My dad once told me something when I was young and having boyfriend problems.
He said all guys are guided by three things: their head, their heart and their dick.
Whoa ~ Go, dad!
And those three things are always fighting with each other inside guys to be the one that makes the decisions.
So, my question to you, young man, is which one guides you when you want to be with me?

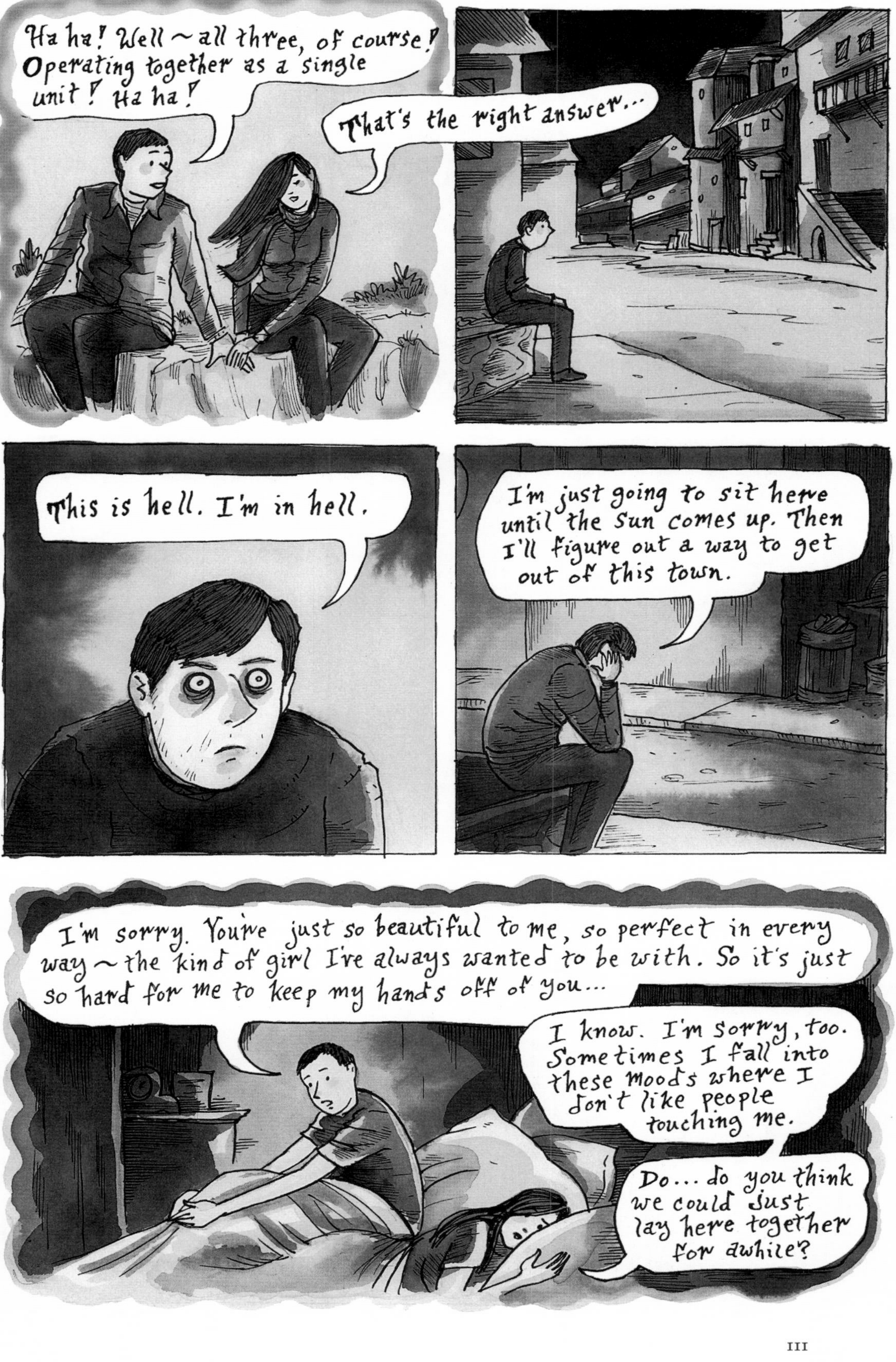
Ha ha! Well ~ all three, of course! Operating together as a single unit! Ha ha!
That's the right answer...
This is hell. I'm in hell.
I'm just going to sit here until the sun comes up. Then I'll figure out a way to get out of this town.
I'm sorry. You're just so beautiful to me, so perfect in every way ~ the kind of girl I've always wanted to be with. So it's just so hard for me to keep my hands off of you...
I know. I'm sorry, too. Sometimes I fall into these moods where I don't like people touching me.
Do... do you think we could just lay here together for awhile?

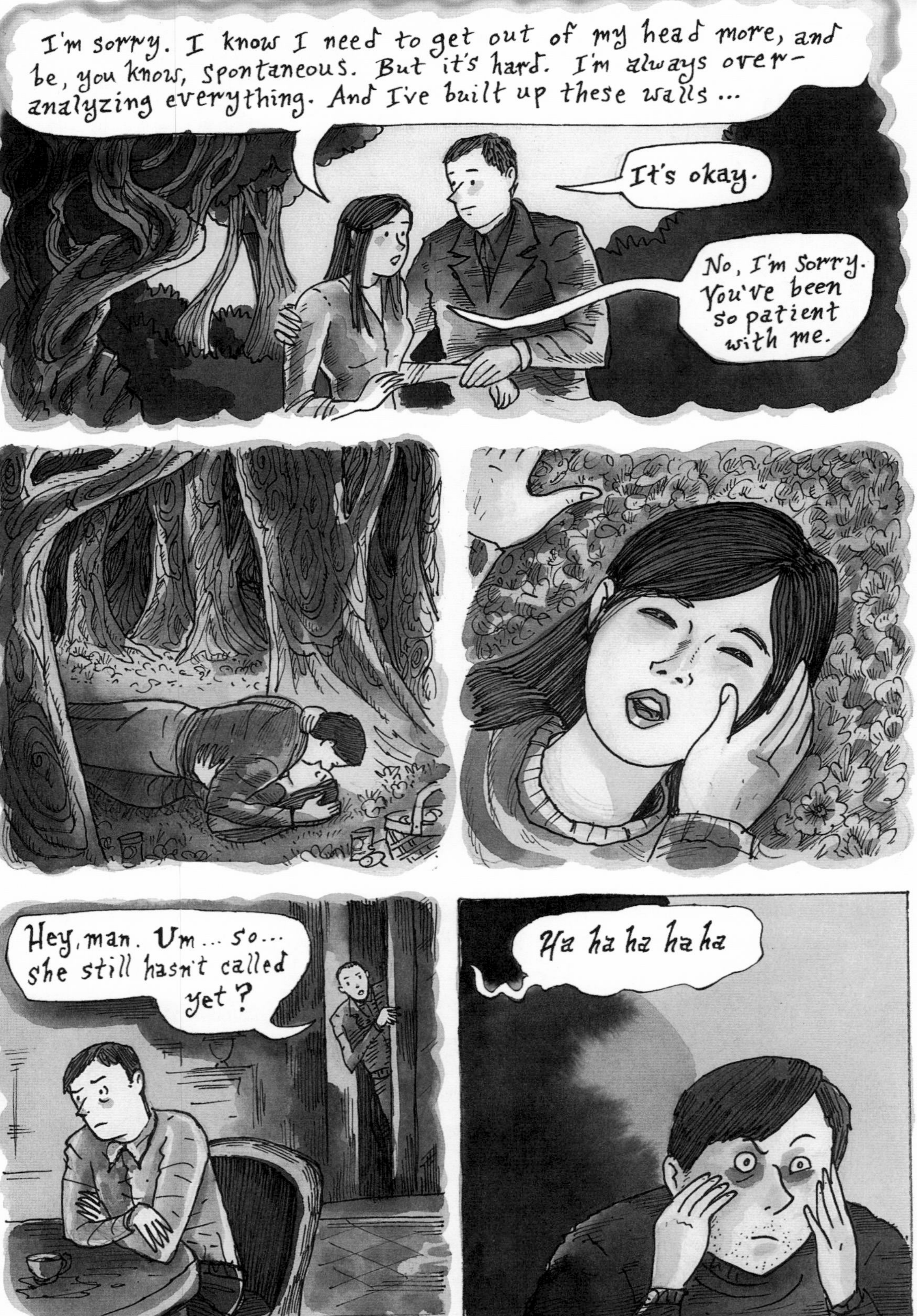
I'm sorry. I know I need to get out of my head more, and be, you know, spontaneous. But it's hard. I'm always over-analyzing everything. And I've built up these walls ...
It's okay.
No, I'm sorry. You've been so patient with me.
Hey, man. Um... so... she still hasn't called yet?
Ha ha ha ha ha

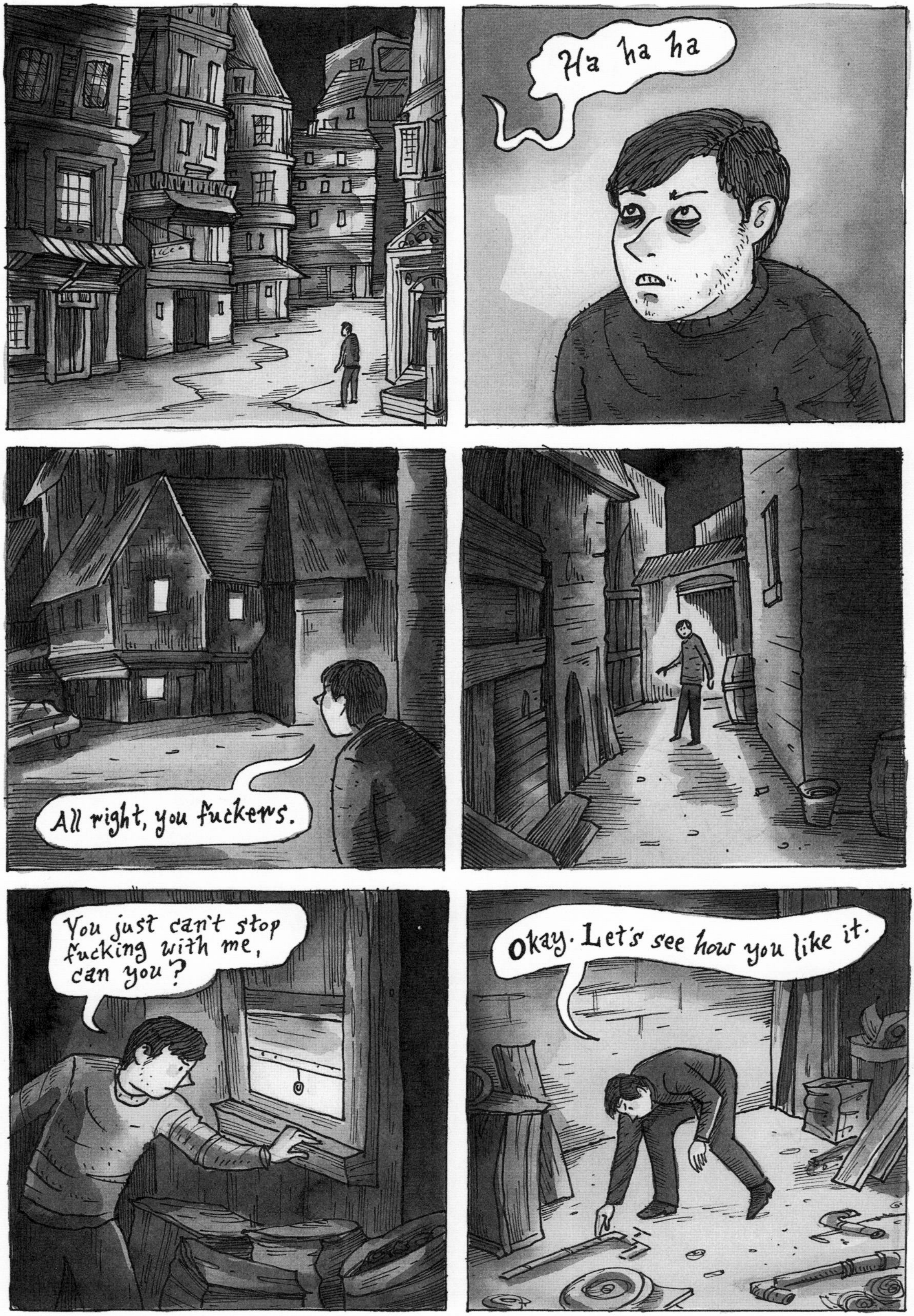
Ha ha ha
All right, you fuckers.
You just can't stop fucking with me, can you?
Okay. Let's see how you like it.

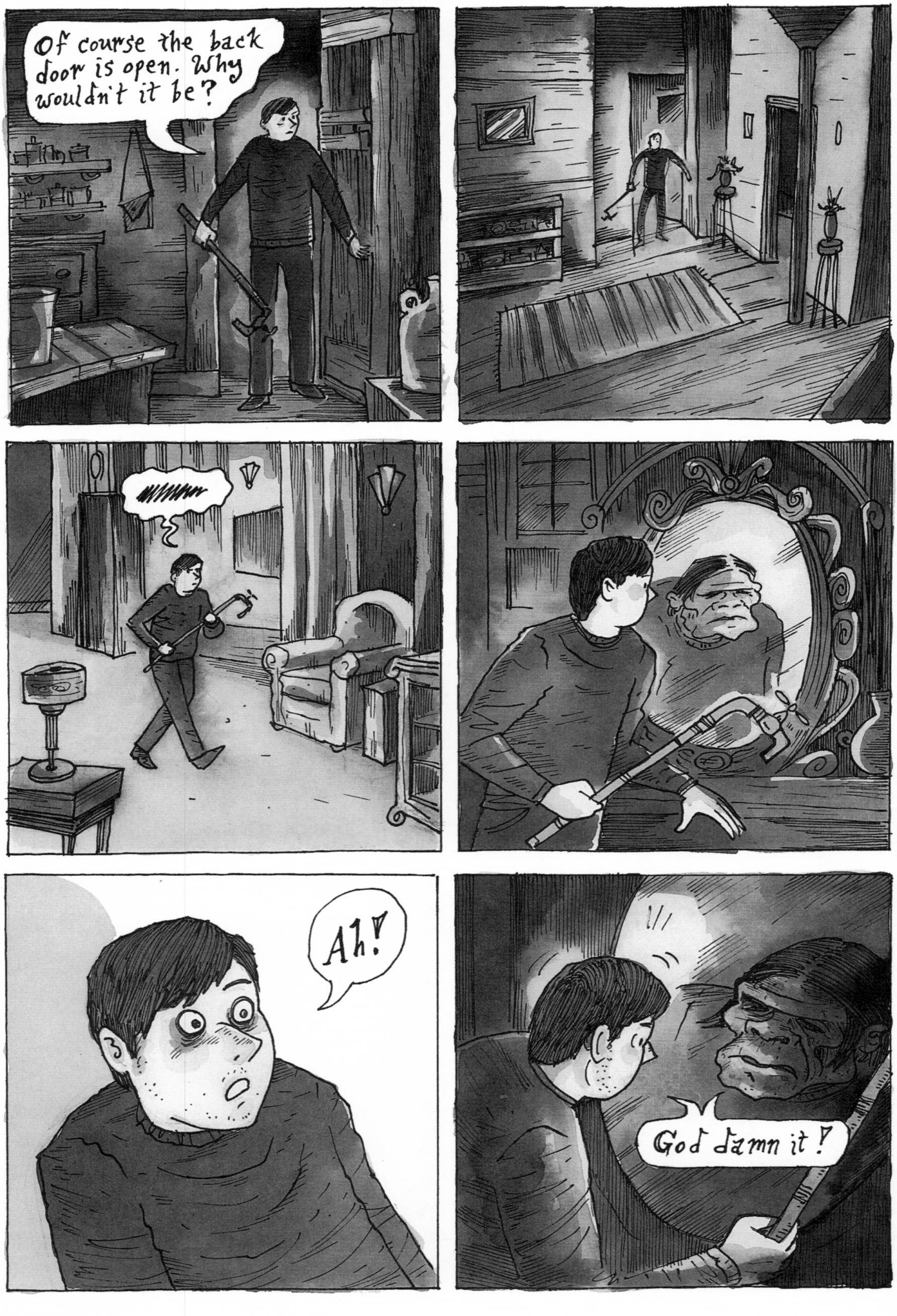
Of course the back door is open. Why wouldn't it be?
Ah!
God damn it!

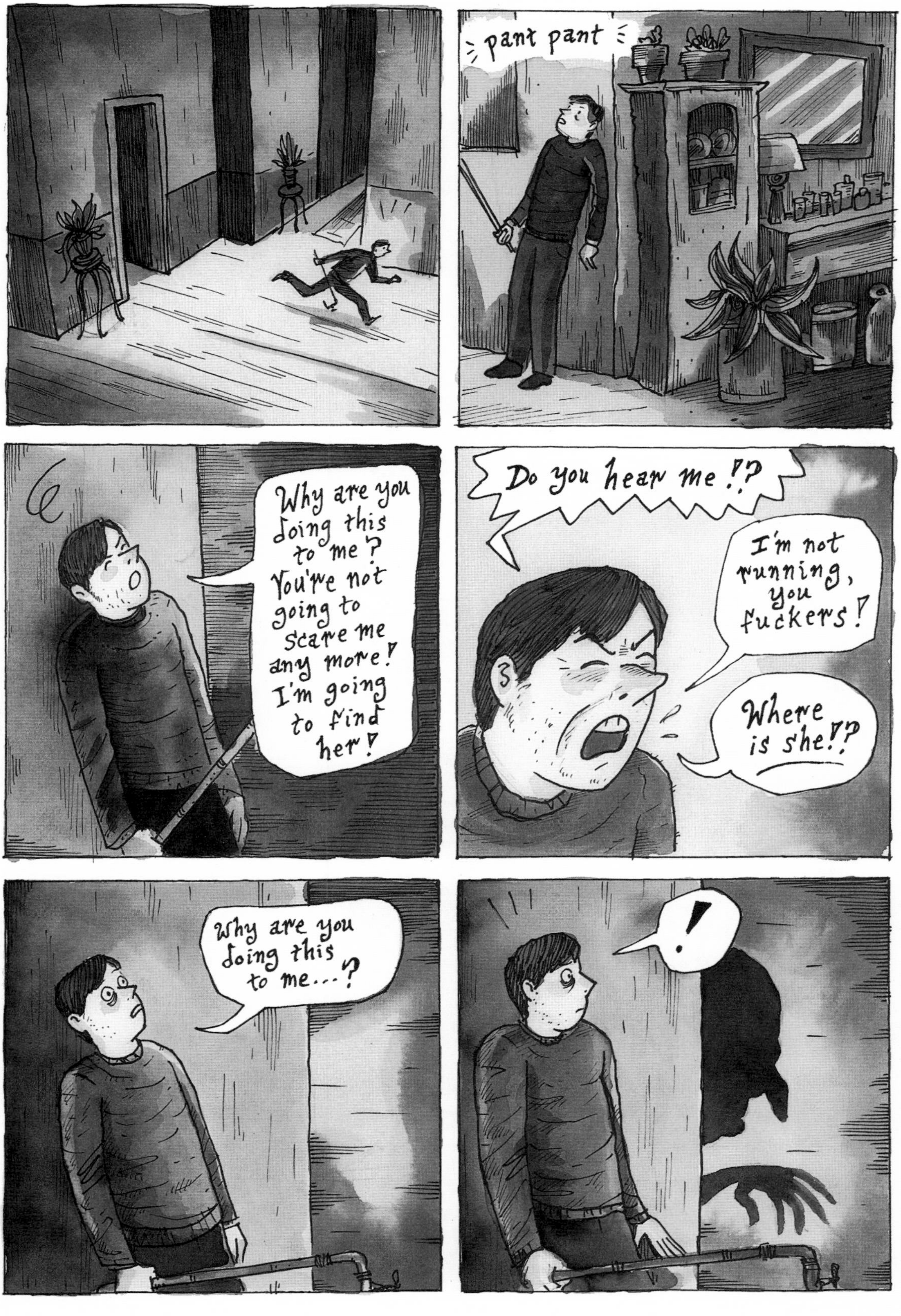
pant pant
Why are you doing this to me? You're not going to scare me any more! I'm going to find her!
Do you hear me!?
I'm not running, you fuckers!
Where is she!?
Why are you doing this to me...?
!

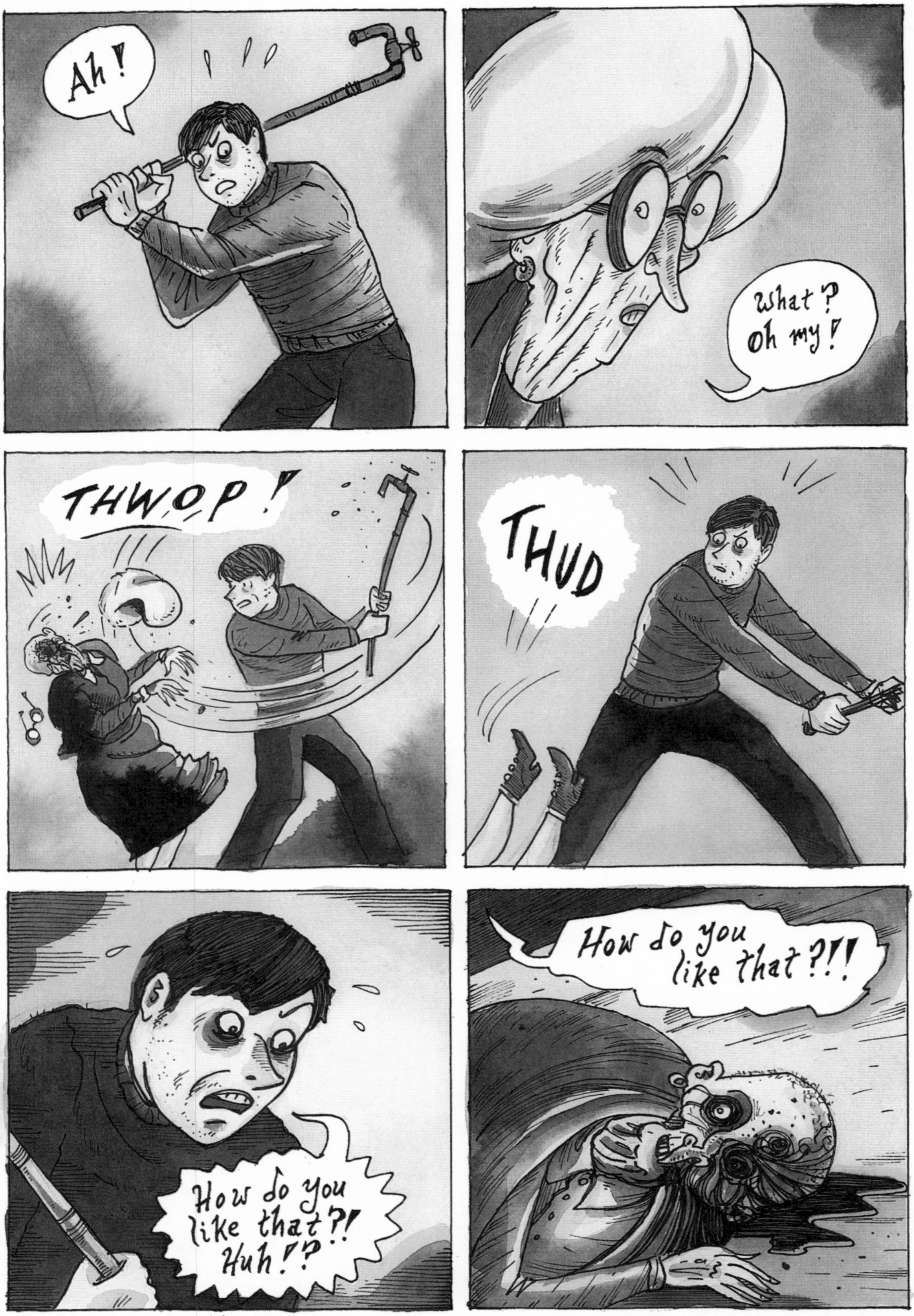
Ah!
What? Oh my!
THWOP!
THUD
How do you like that?! Huh!?
How do you like that?!!

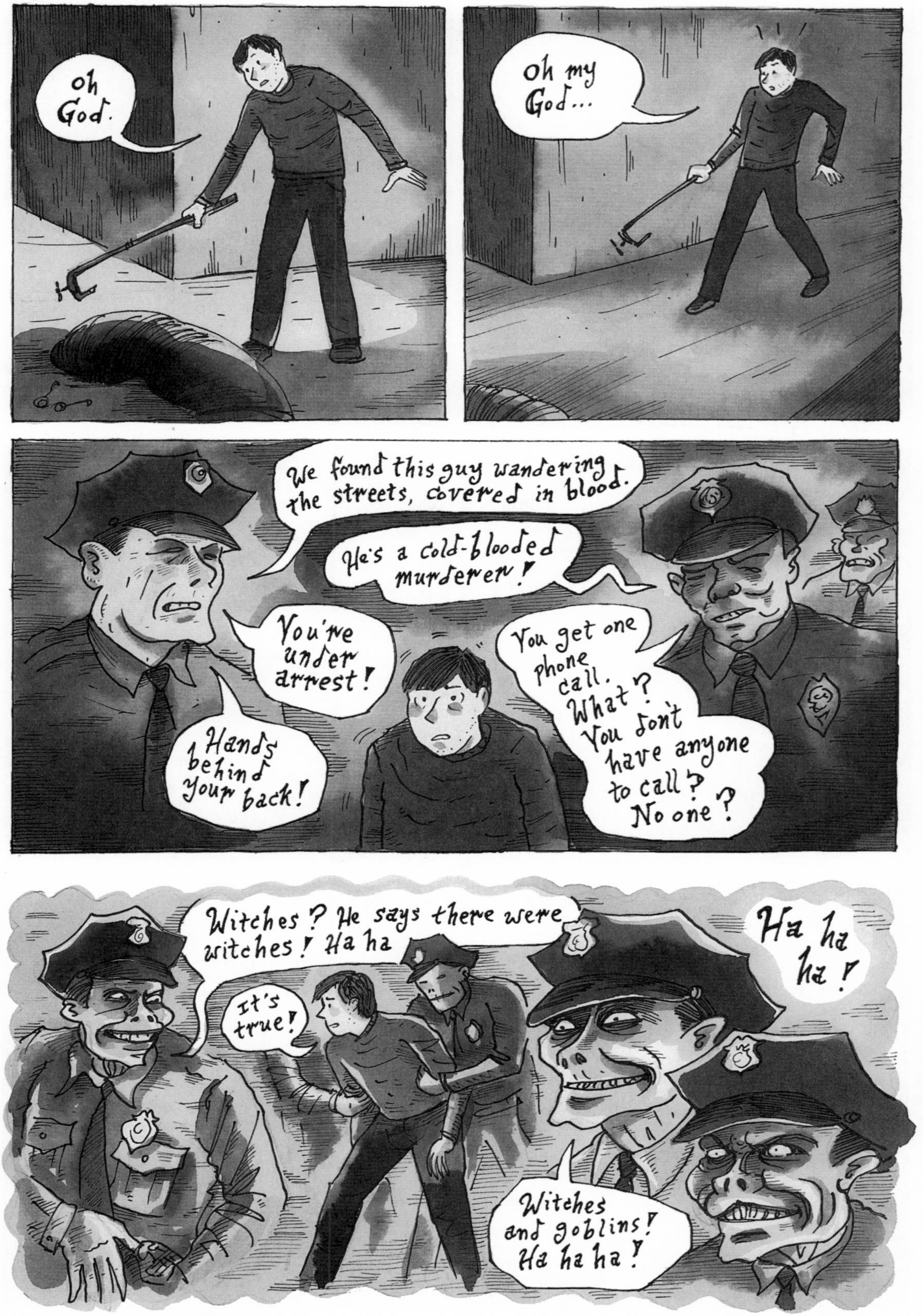
oh God.
Oh my God...
We found this guy wandering the streets, covered in blood.
He's a cold-blooded murderer!
You're under arrest!
Hands behind your back!
You get one phone call. What? You don't have anyone to call? No one?
Witches? He says there were witches! Ha ha
It's true!
Ha ha ha!
Witches and goblins! Ha ha ha!

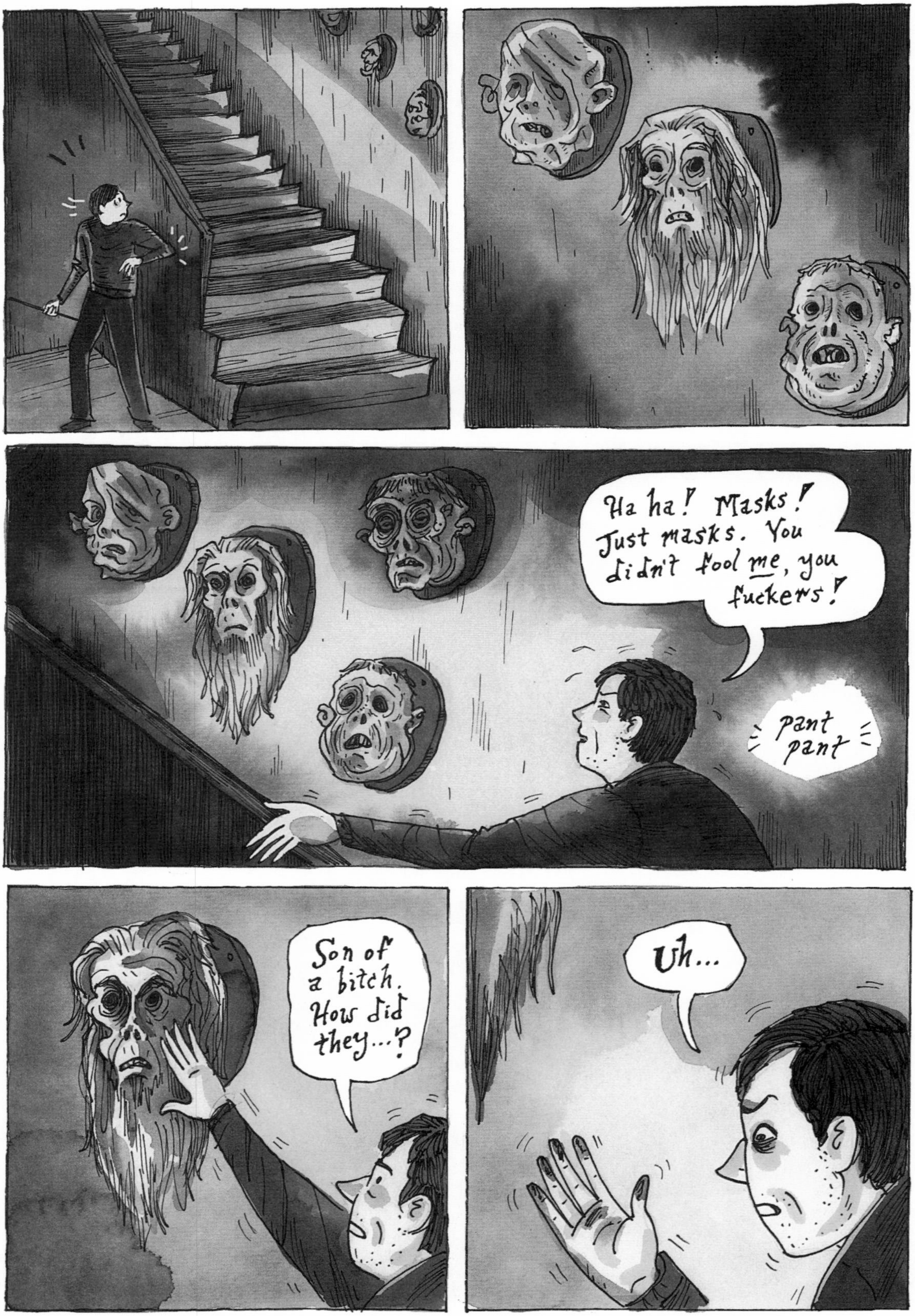
Ha ha! Masks! Just masks. You didn't fool me, you fuckers!
pant pant
Son of a bitch. How did they...?
Uh...

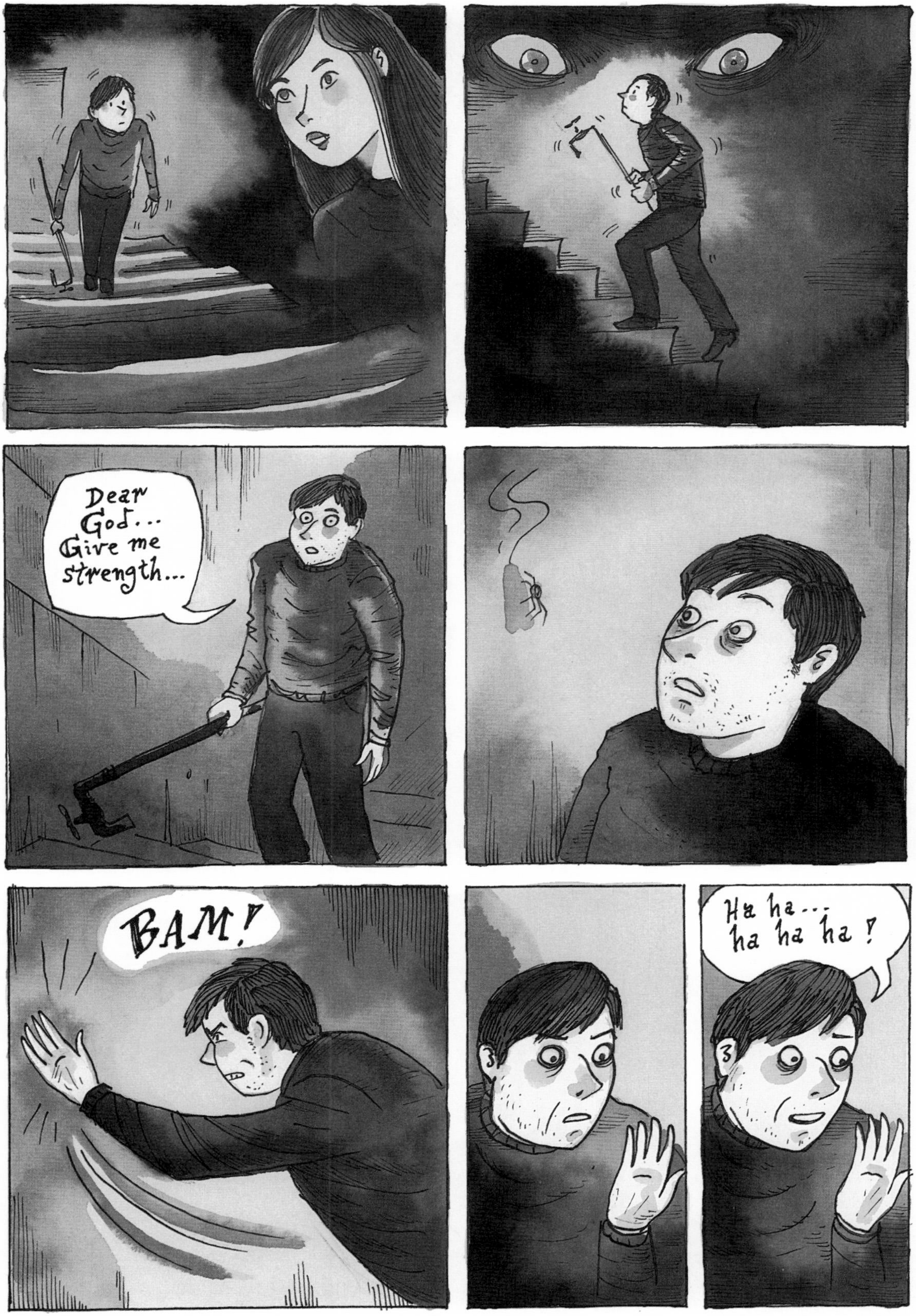
Dear God... Give me strength...
BAM!
Ha ha... ha ha ha!

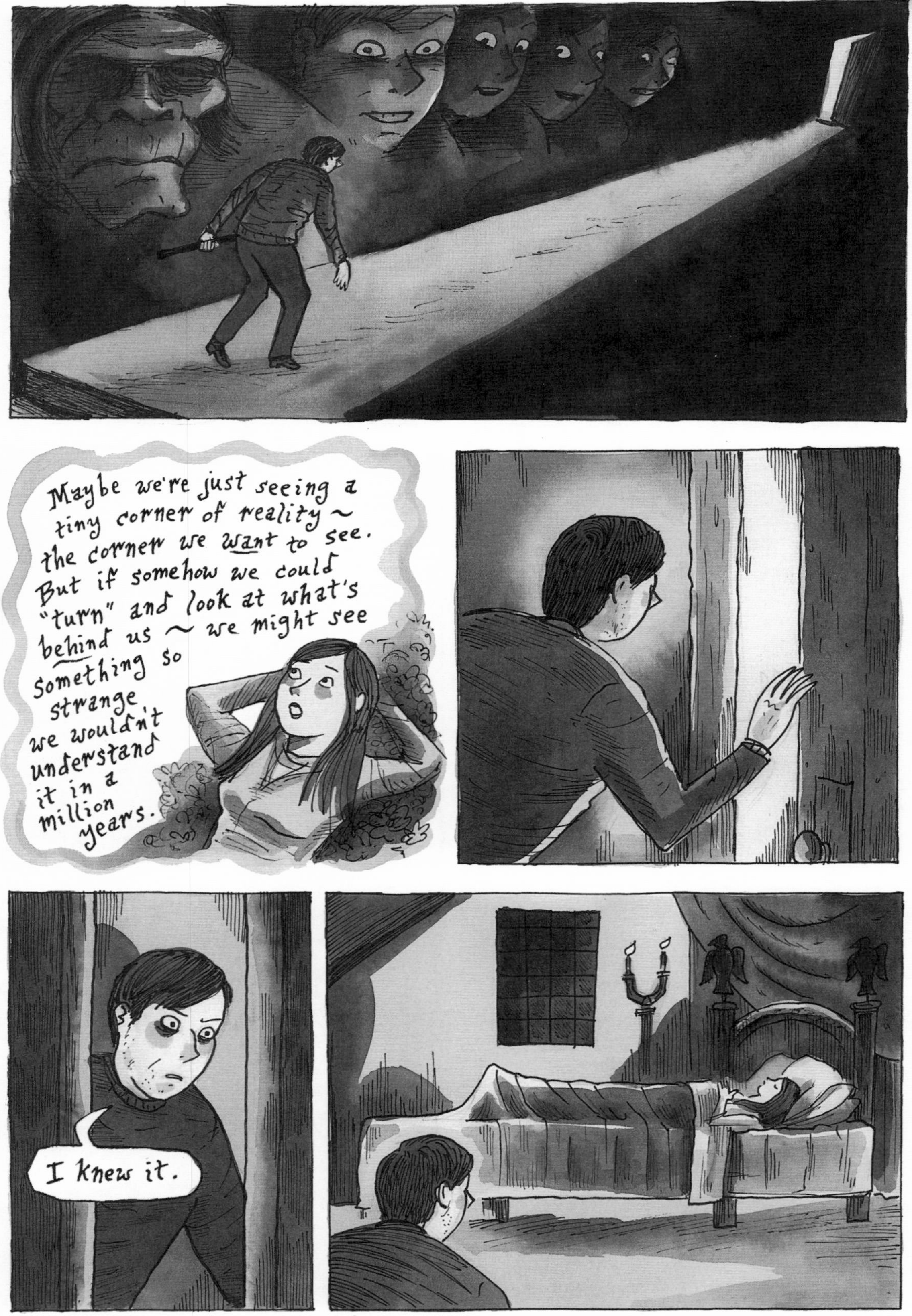

Maybe we're just seeing a tiny corner of reality ~ the corner we want to see. But if somehow we could "turn" and look at what's behind us ~ we might see something so strange we wouldn't understand it in a million years.
I knew it.

Delphine...?
Delphine!
Wake up!
Delphine.
What have they done to you?
Delphine.
Oh God. Wake up!

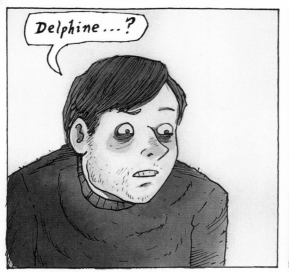

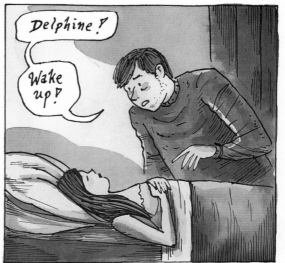

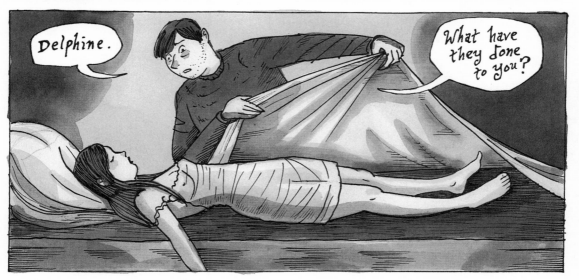

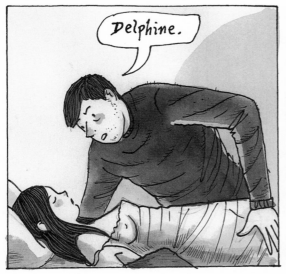

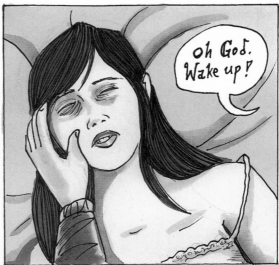

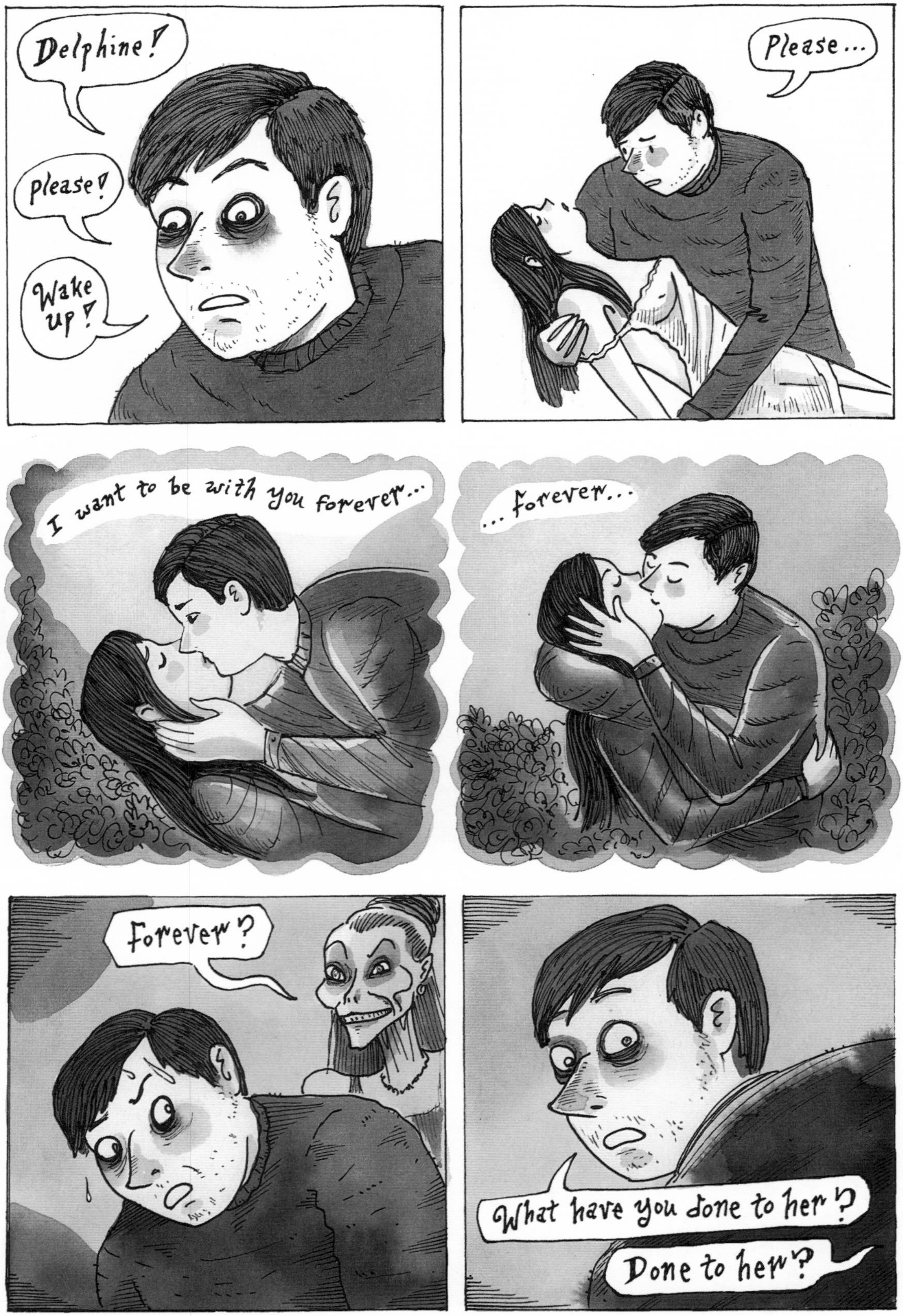
Delphine!
please!
Wake up!
Please...
I want to be with you forever...
... forever...
Forever?
What have you done to her?
Done to her?

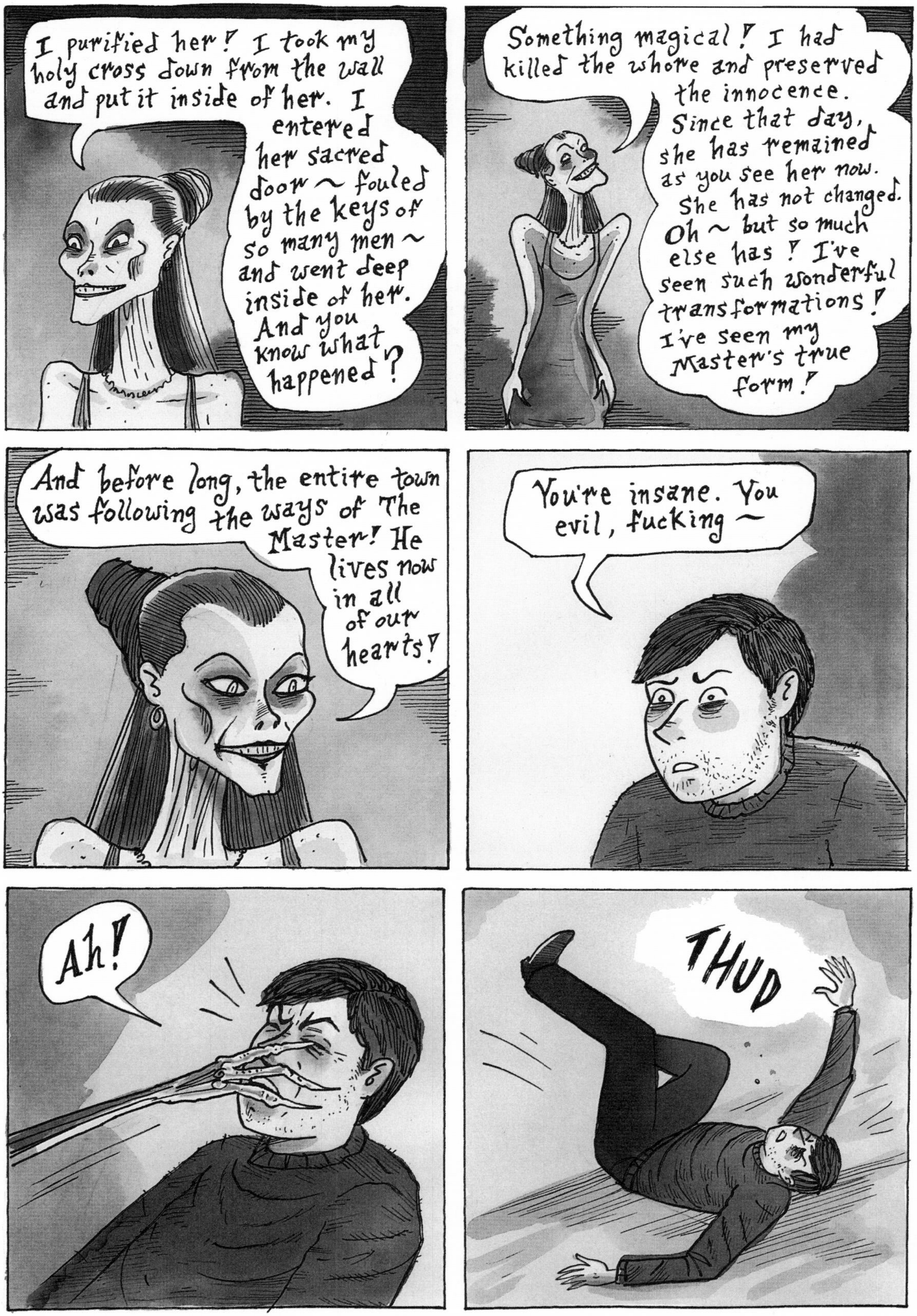
I purified her! I took my holy cross down from the wall and put it inside of her. I entered her sacred door ~ fouled by the keys of so many men ~ and went deep inside of her. And you know what happened?
Something magical! I had killed the whore and preserved the innocence. Since that day, she has remained as you see her now. She has not changed. Oh ~ but so much else has! I've seen such wonderful transformations! I've seen my Master's true form!
And before long, the entire town was following the ways of The Master! He lives now in all of our hearts!
You're insane. You evil, fucking ~
Ah!
THUD

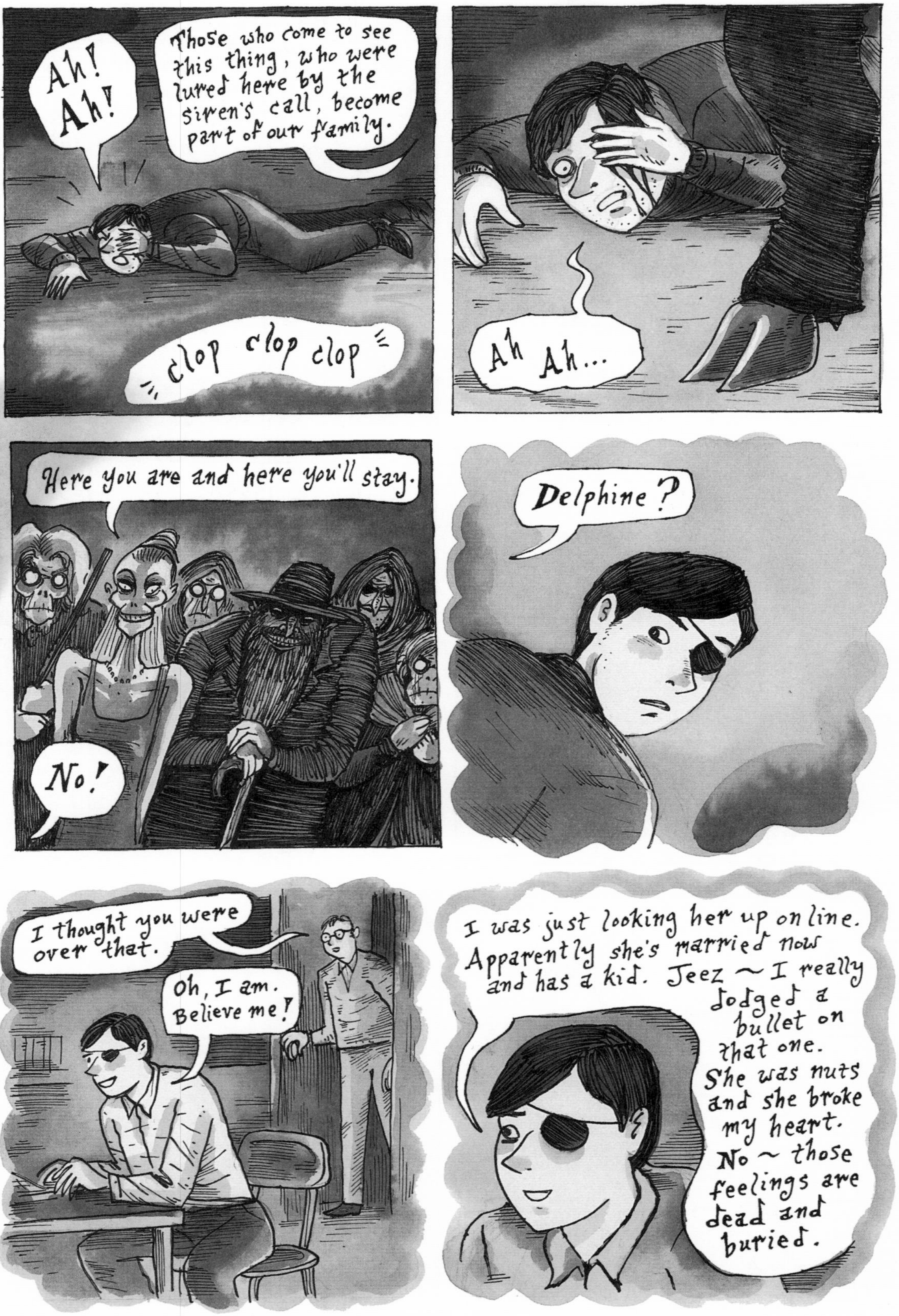

Ah! Ah!
Those who come to see this thing, who were lured here by the siren's call, become part of our family.
clop clop clop
Ah Ah...
Here you are and here you'll stay.
No!
Delphine?
I thought you were over that.
Oh, I am. Believe me!
I was just looking her up on line. Apparently she's married now and has a kid. Jeez ~ I really dodged a bullet on that one. She was nuts and she broke my heart. No ~ those feelings are dead and buried.

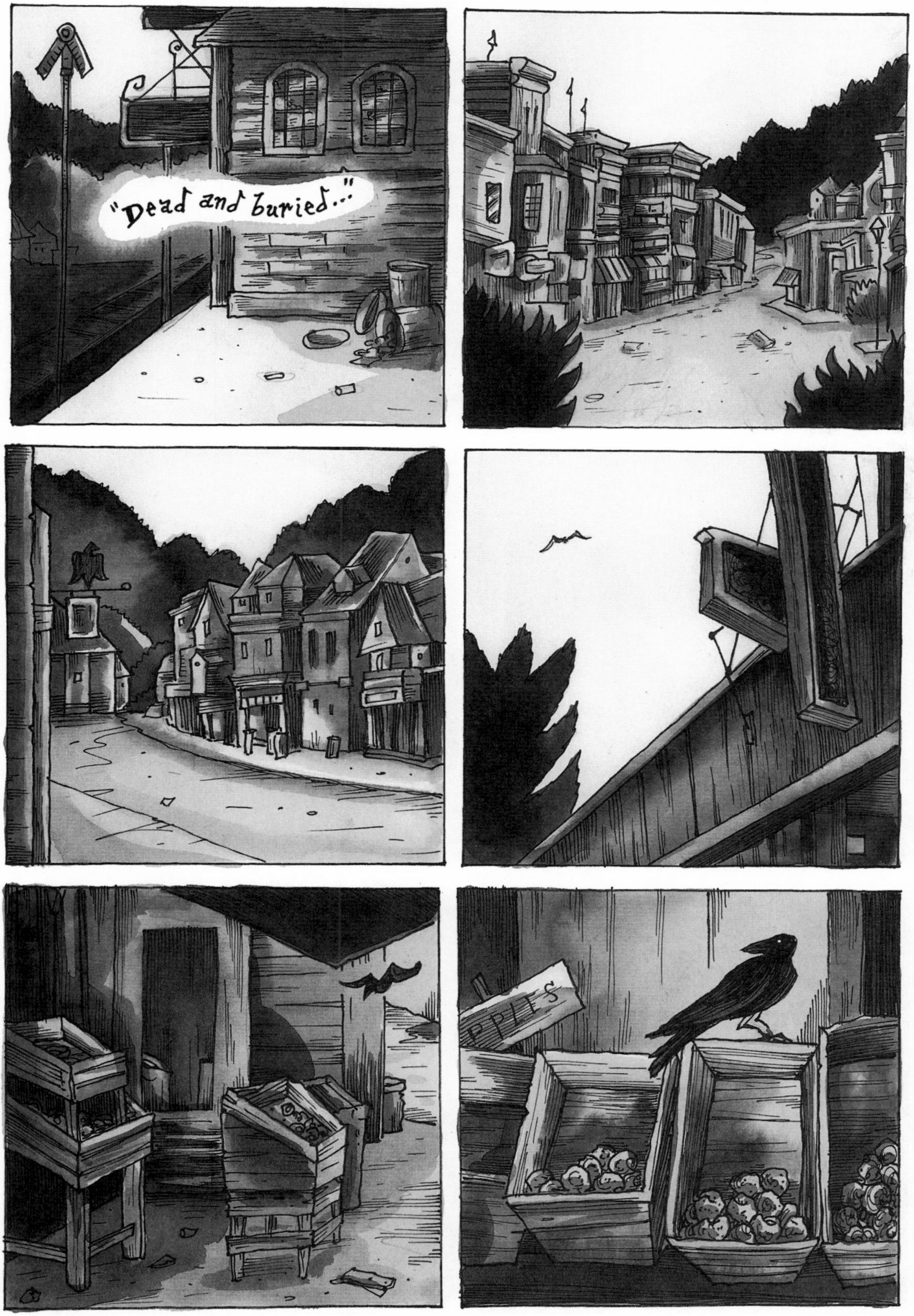
"Dead and buried..."
PPLES

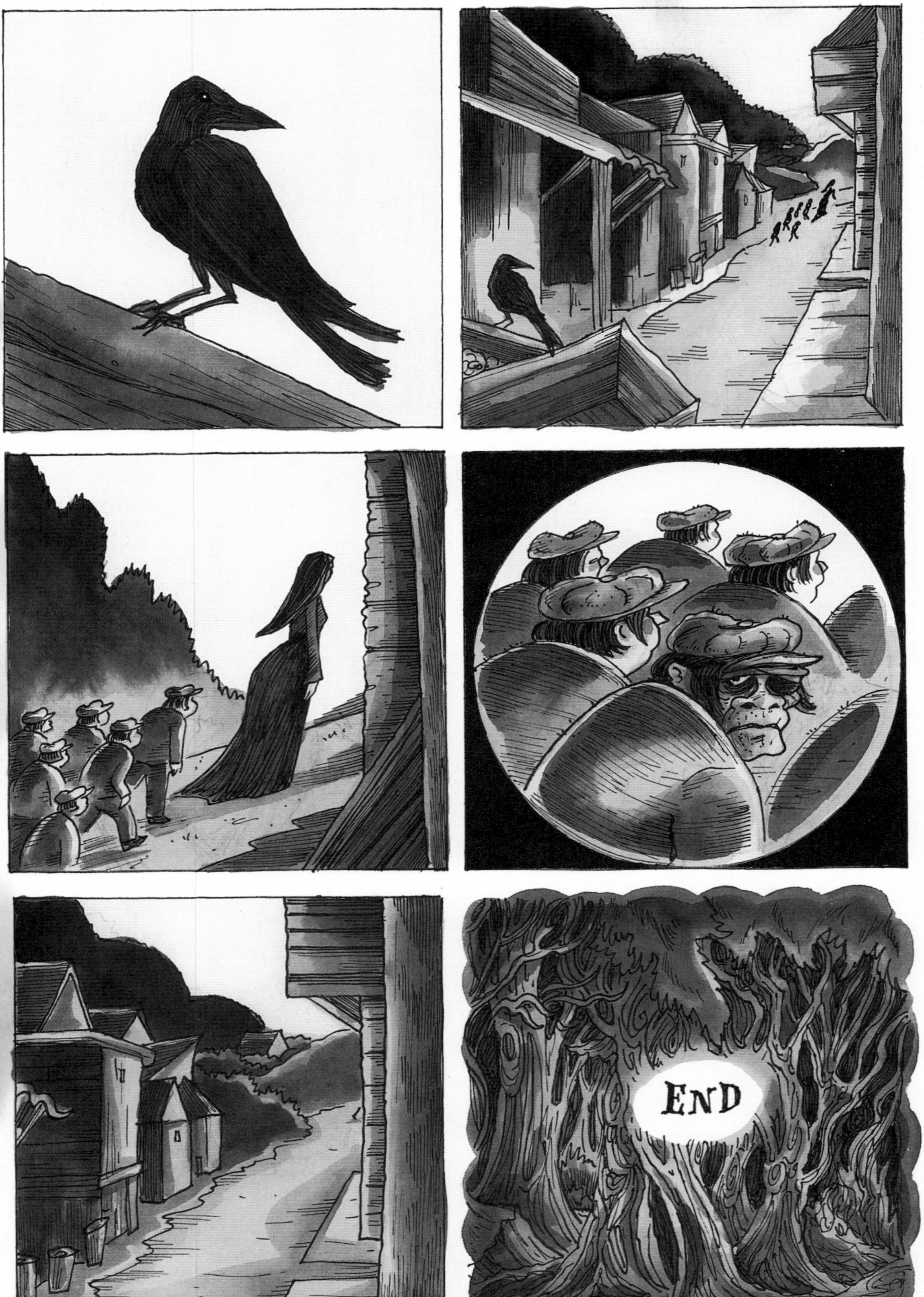
END

Other books by Richard Sala:

The Hidden (FANTAGRAPHICS, 2011)
Cat Burglar Black (FIRST SECOND, 2009)
The Grave Robber's Daughter (FANTAGRAPHICS, 2006)
Mad Night (FANTAGRAPHICS, 2005)
Peculia and the Groon Grove Vampires (FANTAGRAPHICS, 2005)
Maniac Killer Strikes Again! (FANTAGRAPHICS, 2004)
Peculia (FANTAGRAPHICS, 2002)
The Chuckling Whatsit (FANTAGRAPHICS, 1997)
The Ghastly Ones and Other Fiendish Frolics (MANIC D PRESS, 1995)

ICHARD SALA grew up with a fascination for musty old museums, dusty old libraries, cluttered antique shops, narrow alleyways, hidden truths, double meanings, sinister secrets and spooky old houses. He has written and drawn a number of unusual graphic novels which often combine elements of classic mystery and horror stories and which have been known to cause readers to emit chuckles as well as gasps. Although most of his books are written with teens and older readers in mind, his recent book, *Cat Burglar Black*, can be enjoyed by younger readers as well. He has also collaborated with Lemony Snicket and Art Spiegelman, and his illustrations and artwork have won awards and been published all over the world.

Fantagraphics Books, 7563 Lake City Way NE, Seattle, WA 98115. Designed by Jacob Covey with additional production by Paul Baresh. Edited by Kim Thompson. Associate Publisher: Eric Reynolds. Published by Gary Groth and Kim Thompson. This graphic novel originally appeared as four serialized comics magazines in the "Ignatz" series from Coconino Press; special thanks to "Ignatz" maestro Igort. All contents copyright © 2012 Richard Sala. This edition copyright © 2012 Fantagraphics Books. All rights reserved. Permission to quote or reproduce material for reviews or notices must by obtained from the author or publisher. • First Fantagraphics Books edition: November, 2012. ISBN: 978-1-60699-590-7. Visit the Fantagraphics Books website at www.fantagraphics.com; visit Richard Sala's website at www.richardsala.com; visit the Fantagraphics bookstore in the historic Georgetown neighborhood of Seattle, WA. Printed in Singapore.